Immanuel, God with Us

Immanuel, God with Us
150 Years

*"Immanuel is a community
growing in Christ,
living in grace, and
serving in love."*

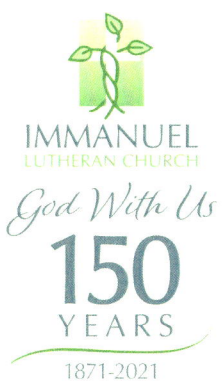

Ann Derr and Peggy Johnson

Immanuel Lutheran Church
Saint Paul, Minnesota

Copyright 2022 by Immanuel Lutheran Church, Saint Paul, Minnesota

Publisher: Immanuel Lutheran Church, 104 Snelling Avenue South, Saint Paul, Minnesota 55105; ilcsp.org; 651-699-5560

Anniversary logo by Nikola Kratky, graphic designer and illustrator, kratkynikola@gmail.com

Book design and production by Dorie McClelland, springbookdesign.com

Printed in the United States of America by Bookmobile

ISBN: 979-8-218-08241-3

Dedication

This book is dedicated to the nine immigrants who established our church in 1871 and to the many members (past and present) who have given and continue to give so much to keep Immanuel strong in faith and service.

> "Lord God, you have called your servants to ventures of which we cannot see the ending, by paths as yet untrodden, through perils unknown. Give us faith to go out with good courage, not knowing where we go, but only that your hand is leading us and your love supporting us; through Jesus Christ our Lord."
>
> —Morning Prayer from *Lutheran Book of Worship*.
> Augsburg Publishing House: Minneapolis, 1978, page 138

Contents

Preface   *ix*
Letter from Saint Paul Area Synod Bishop Patricia Lull   *xi*
Letter from Pastor Cindy Bullock   *xii*

Chapter 1   Immanuel's History   *3*
Chapter 2   Immanuel Facilities   *31*
Chapter 3   Worship, Music, and Art   *63*
Chapter 4   Christian Education and Programming   *95*
Chapter 5   Building Community   *121*
Chapter 6   Benevolence and Social Action   *165*
Chapter 7   Governance and Organizational Structure   *195*
Epilogue   *217*

Appendix A: Pastors of Immanuel, Macalester Park, and Highland Park Lutheran Churches   *221*

Appendix B: Sons and Daughters of Immanuel, Macalester Park, and Highland Park Lutheran Churches Who Became Pastors, Missionaries, and Served the Church in Leadership Positions   *250*

Appendix C: Church Secretaries, Parish Administrators, Church Administrator   *262*

Appendix D: Immanuel Members for 25 years or More   *263*

Appendix E: Sunday School Superintendents, Directors of Christian Education; and Director of Children and Family Ministry, Sunday School Secretaries, and Treasurers   *265*

Appendix F: Choir Directors, Ministers of Worship and Music, and Directors of Worship and Music   *266*

Appendix G: Organists   *268*

Appendix H: Youth Directors, Youth Ministers, and Directors of Youth and Family Ministry   *269*

Appendix I: Learning and Advocacy Activities Sponsored by the Social Action Team, 1997–2021   *271*

Appendix J: Boy Scout Troop 90 Scoutmasters   *274*

Appendix K: Immanuel Lutheran Church Presidents   *275*

Appendix I: 2022 Immanuel Lutheran Church Council, Officers, and Program Team Chairs   *276*

Bibliography   *278*

Preface

This book is written to document the first 150 years of Immanuel Lutheran Church in Saint Paul, Minnesota. Records, documents, files, and photos located at the church were a primary resource. Collections at the Luther Seminary archives were consulted as well as published materials. Of critical importance have been the members of Immanuel, who wrote sections, participated in interviews, and answered questions. Special thanks are due to former pastors, former youth directors, and their families. This history could not have been written without the help of countless people. Their contributions have been essential. We thank the following:

Deb Ahlquist, David and Stephanie Alstead, Mark and Sandy Anderson, Ba Lam, Luci J. Baker Johnson (daughter of Lyle and Eunice Baker), Gay Bartholic, Phyllis Bentley, Rev. Cindy Bullock, Russ Carlson (former Immanuel church administrator), Chris Cherwien (Director of Worship and Music), Heather Cordes, Paul Daniels (Luther Seminary Archivist), Christine Danielson, Zachary Danielson, Douglas Derr, James Duckstad (great grandson of Rev. Bennie Duckstad, former Immanuel pastor), Lori Dufresne, Russell and Bonnie Edhlund, Dale Fierke, Craig and Elsie Fohrenkamm, Roger Forman, Rev. Sylvan Hengesteg (former Immanuel assistant pastor), JoAnn Hogensen, June Husom, Harvey Jaeger, Rev. Rolfe Johnstad (former Immanuel youth director), Jan Johnshoy, Marlene Johnshoy, Vernon Jorgensen, Emily King (Director of Children and Family Ministry), Donald Kyser, David and Susan Klevan, Rev. John Lohre (former Immanuel assistant pastor), Kelsey Maniaci, Rev. John Marboe (former Immanuel pastor), Louise Meltvedt (daughter of Truus Ingebritson), Kari Moeller, Rev. Dana Nissen (former Immanuel pastor), Penny Nordquist, Per Mer Security, Raymond Peterson, Judie Prayfrock, Rev. David and Genevieve Quarberg (former Immanuel interim pastor), Rev. Larry Rehlander (former Immanuel pastor), Rev. Phillip Robert Ruud (son of Immanuel members), Rev. Charlie Ruud (grandson of Immanuel members), Jerald Sandahl, Jeffrey Schmidt, Rev. Susan Smith (former Immanuel pastor), David Stark, Ronald Struss, Deanna Thompson, Mark Thompson,

John Toso, Jane Tripple, Douglas and Peg Wangensteen, Rev. William White (former Immanuel youth director), Larry Wilson, Lynnette Zika.

The Immanuel Foundation has our deep appreciation for providing funding for the production and publication of this book. We also give special thanks to Dorie McClelland, Spring Book Design, for her invaluable design and technical skills, and her creativity in bringing this book to publication.

This book is enriched by countless photos, taken by Immanuel members and staff over the years. We are unable to give credit to those photographers, but are grateful for their work in documenting Immanuel's events and activities.

We apologize if we have omitted anyone. All errors are the responsibility of the authors.

SAINT PAUL AREA SYNOD
EVANGELICAL LUTHERAN CHURCH IN AMERICA

105 WEST UNIVERSITY AVENUE   ST. PAUL, MN 55103-2094
651.224.4313 | FAX 651.224.5646 | WWW.SPAS-ELCA.ORG

June 21, 2022

Immanuel Lutheran Church
104 Snelling Avenue S
St. Paul, MN 55105

Dear Sisters and Brothers in Christ,

I write to commend you as you are finally able to celebrate the 150th Anniversary of your congregation in person. A century and a half of faithful witness is a significant milestone. From your beginnings in the Norwegian immigrant community, you have moved and grown, taking on new challenges in every decade. I pray that your celebration is filled with deep joy and gratitude for all that has been and deep hope and wonder about the next steps in your journey with God.

I am grateful for the servant leadership you express within and beyond your congregation. Your love for one another and your desire to be present in the wider community as bearers of God's grace is well known throughout this synod. You are stepping forward to discover all over again the neighbors God has given you and the opportunities to be about God's work in the 21st century. I look forward to being with you later this year.

Thank you for trusting that God called you into being as a congregation and trusting that the Spirit of our Living God is even now leading you into your future. May you remember this season as a time of renewal in your life together.

Yours in Christ's service,

Patricia Lull, Bishop

Grace to you and peace, from God our creator, Christ our savior, and the Spirit who guides us.

I give thanks to God for the great cloud of witnesses at Immanuel, who have followed the Christ for the past 150 years. Men and women, children and elders, individuals, and groups who have dedicated time, wisdom, and hard work to proclaim the gospel through their lives of faith.

As I look through the documents and pictures preserved through the years, I see people with many different gifts. There have been teachers, executives, artists, wise elders, prophets, activists, poets, youth, and so many others, all forming a community together with a single goal—to follow Jesus. Together we have followed Christ through wars and peace, through two pandemics, through technological and theological changes. We may not always agree (okay, we don't usually agree), but we know we can only be a church together.

So, my brothers and sisters in Christ, I am grateful for our history together as Immanuel. You will see in these pages the work, devotion, and faith of both our forebearers and those who hold the faith in the present. Many thanks are due to those who researched, collected, and sorted through all the historical documents to bring you these pages. Ann and Peggy, you are a blessing to us!

As we move into the next 150 years, my hope is that Immanuel will always know that we are God's beloved, called to make a difference in the world. I pray that we will always listen and discern the calling of the Spirit, and that what we do together will be good news to this neighborhood, this city, and beyond.

A sister in Christ,
Pastor Cindy Bullock

Immanuel, God with Us

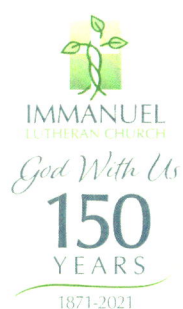

> **2**
> 1871. Fortegnelse over Kommunikanter.
>
> Tirsdagen den 19de December:
> 1. Snedker Joh. Nilsen og
> 2. Hustru Nelle Johanne Nilsen.
> 3. Snedker Hans Bergh Larsen og
> 4. Hustru Bergithe Kristine Olsen.
> 5. Stenhugger Nils Nikkolajsen og
> 6. Hustru Lovise Andersen.
> 7. Skrædder Anders Olsen Oppegaard og
> 8. Hustru Maren Johannesen.
> 9. Snek Hjulmager Nils Larsen Nordahl.

Immanuel's Founding Members

Fortegnelse over Kommunicanter
(List of Communicants)

Tirsdagen den 19th December, 1871
(Tuesday December 19, 1871)

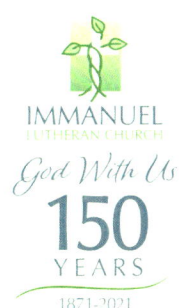

CHAPTER 1

Immanuel's History

Origins

On December 19, 1871, a group of nine Norwegian immigrants gathered together in Saint Paul for Holy Communion with a traveling Norwegian pastor, Rev. Osten Hanson. They probably met in one of the immigrant's homes. These founding members of what is now Immanuel Lutheran Church were:

1. Johan (John) Nilsen b. 11 Dec 1839 (carpenter)
2. Nelle Johanne Nilsen b. 26 Sep 1834 (housewife; married to Johan Nilsen)
3. Hans Bergh (aka Berg) Larsen, b. 1842 (carpenter)
4. Bergethe Kristine Olsen (aka Bergitte Christine Olesdatter) b. 1837 (married Hans Bergh Larsen; housewife)
5. Nils Nikkolaysen (aka Nels Nichols) b. 1832 (stonemason)
6. Lovise (aka Louise) Andersen b. Oct 1835 (married to Nils Nikkolaysen; housewife)
7. Anders Olsen Oppegaard (tailor; future pastor of Immanuel)
8. Maren Johanessen (aka Johanesdatter) (housewife; married Anders Olsen Oppegaard)
9. Nils Larsen Nordahl (wheelwright)

1-1. Pastor Osten Hanson, Immanuel's first pastor in 1871

During the early years (1871–1880), the first congregation was served by 13 different visiting pastors, seminary students, and teachers, many returning multiple times. All of these were affiliated with the Haugean movement. These early preachers are listed in Appendix A.

The evolution of Immanuel Lutheran Church is tied to the history of Lutheran church bodies in the United States, a history of separations and mergers. Immanuel is now a church of the Evangelical Lutheran Church of American (ELCA; established in 1988), and part of the Saint Paul Area Synod of the ELCA.

☙ *The **Haugean movement** or Haugeanism (Norwegian: haugianere) was a pietistic state church reform movement intended to bring new life and vitality into the Church of Norway, which had been often characterized by formalism and lethargy. The movement was named after Norwegian revivalist lay preacher Hans Nielsen Hauge and emphasized personal diligence, enterprise, and frugality. The Hauge Synod in American (Norwegian: Hauges norsk lutherske Synode i Amerika) was formed in 1876 and was "low church," de-emphasizing formal worship and stressing personal faith in the Haugean tradition. Red Wing Seminary was the Hauge Synod educational center located in Red Wing, Minnesota. The Hauge Synod opened the Red Wing Seminary in 1879, and it continued in operation as a seminary until 1917. The school continued as an academy and junior college until 1932, when St. Olaf College, Northfield, Minnesota, absorbed these programs. Many of Immanuel's pastors and seminary students attended the Red Wing Seminary, and five of them were either professors or presidents of Red Wing Seminary.*

Norwegian Heritage

Immanuel's Norwegian heritage can be traced to the nine Norwegian immigrants who first met to found a church in 1871. Connections with Norway were reinforced by the pastors who visited that early church. To a great extent, the Immanuel congregation was served by pastors from Norway in its first years. During Immanuel's first 50 years of existence, it had 34 different pastors—29 of whom were born in Norway (one was from Sweden and four were born in the U.S.)

Immanuel's Norwegian legacy remained strong for many years, with the Norwegian language predominant in worship, education, newsletters, and church records. The women's groups conducted meetings in Norwegian until 1907. The confirmation registers used the Norwegian language until the early 1920s. Sermons were regularly in Norwegian until 1924 when only one service in Norwegian was held per month, with the rest in English. By 1930, all services were English. Pastor Bennie L. Duckstad (1924–1945) discontinued the use of Norwegian for worship because he felt his Norwegian was not good enough for preaching.

Rosemaling (rose painting), a Scandinavian decorative folk painting, was added to the kitchen when it was repainted in the late 1970s by Addie Pittelkow. An Immanuel rosemaling group met regularly in 1992. Church groups attended the *Syttende Mai* (May 17th, Norwegian Constitution Day) celebrations at Minnehaha Park for many years. *Syttende Mai* trips visited Hanska, Minnesota, in the late 1970s and early 1980s. The church has a framed example of Hardanger lace, created by long-term Immanuel member Ragna "Rags" Lindgren. Annual lutefisk dinners, started by Immanuel church women in 1935, continue to this day. In December 1974, the Women of the Church celebrated the holidays with a Norwegian-themed party. The bake sale that accompanies the lutefisk dinner sells traditional Norwegian treats—lefse, krumkake, sandbakkels, and rosettes.

Immanuel, 150 Years: God with Us

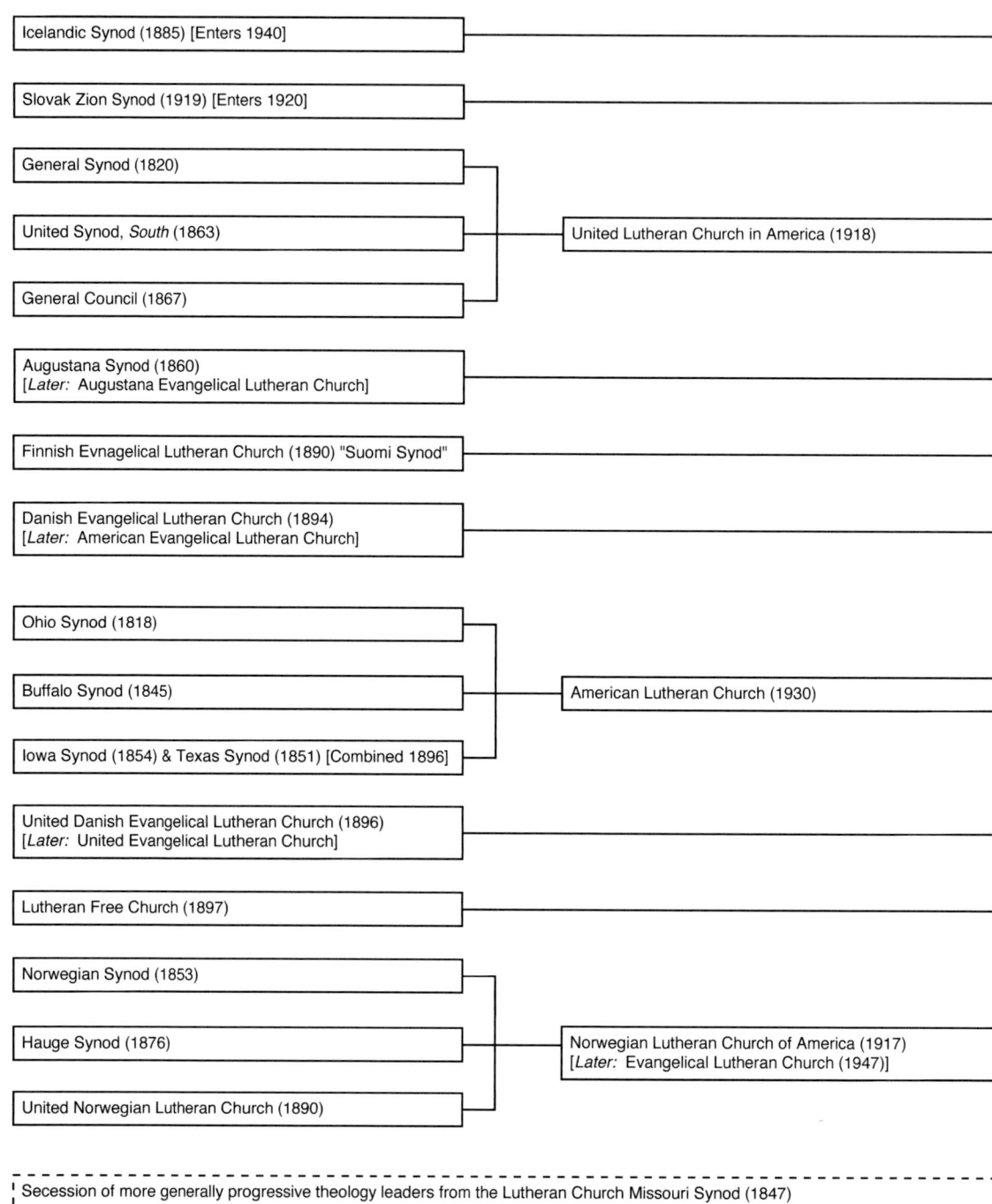

IMMANUEL'S HISTORY

ELCA Synod History

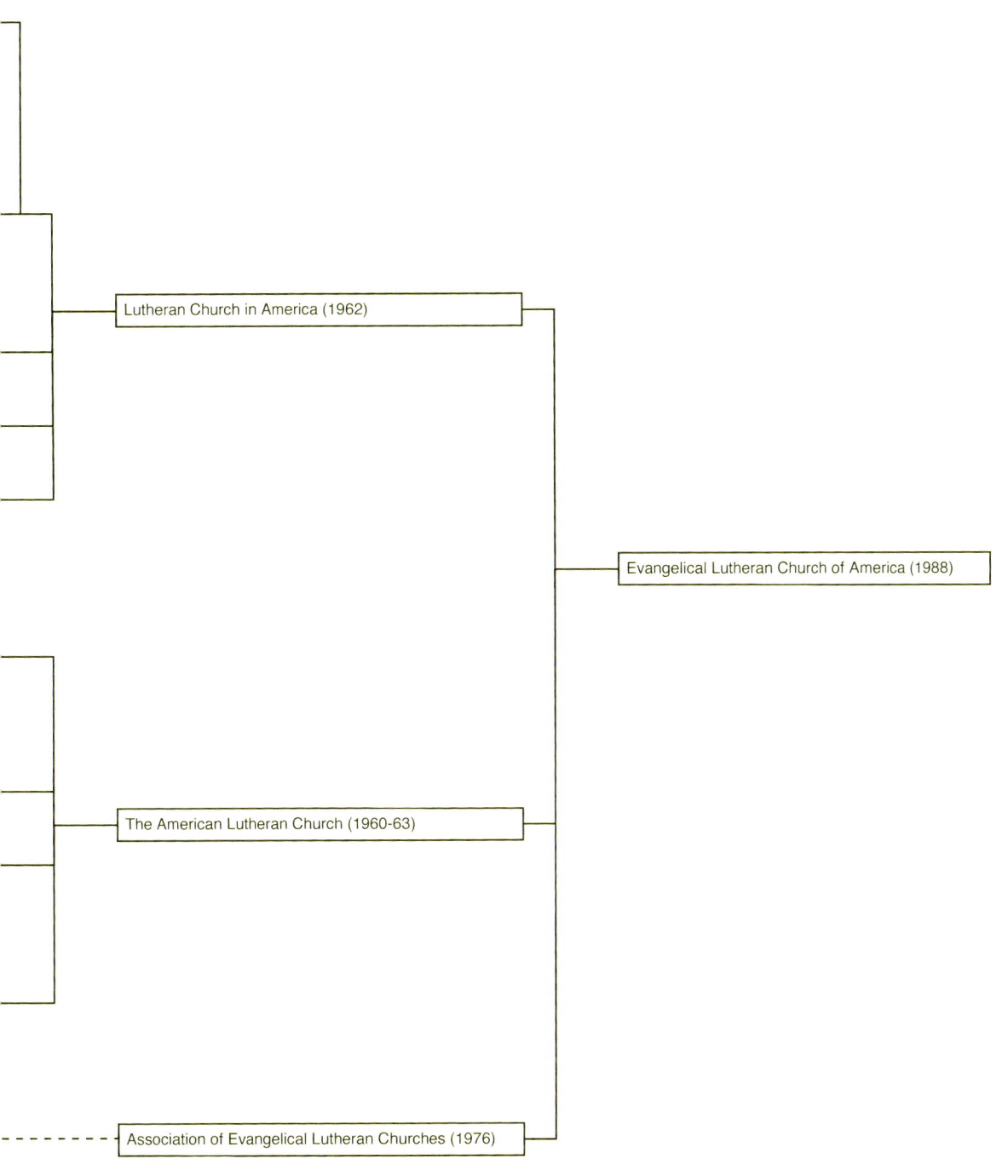

1–2. Evolution of Lutheran Synods (prepared by Stephanie Alstead)

1-3. Rosemaling on kitchen stools painted by women of the congregation

Pastors and Ministry

The Rev. Osten Hanson (1836–1898), Immanuel's first visiting pastor, was born in Norway, as were most of Immanuel's early pastors through the 1920s. He was president of the Hauge synod in 1876, its vice-president for some 20 years, president of the board of regents of the Red Wing Seminary for several years, and again president of the Hauge synod in 1887–1893. He was a founder of the Red Wing Seminary (a Hauge Synod seminary) and also of the mission society that established the Norwegian Lutheran Church mission in China.

Another early visiting pastor, Elling Eielsen (Sunve), was the first Norwegian Lutheran minister ordained in the United States in 1843. His followers organized a new synod, the Evangelical Lutheran Church in America (Eielsen Synod) in 1846 and Eielsen served as its first president 1846–1883. He traveled widely in the U.S. as a home missionary, always on foot. Eielson walked 1,000 miles each way between Chicago and New York to get Luther's Small Catechism published in English and bring it back to Chicago.

1-4. Pastor Elling Eielsen walking to Chicago with Luther's Small Catechism in a backpack (stained glass window in the Hauge Room, Rolvaag Memorial Library, St. Olaf College, attributed to St. Olaf Prof. Arnold Flaten)

In the early days, some deacons of the congregation preached in the absence of a pastor. The Hauge movement encouraged lay preachers. For example, Ole H. Oace, Immanuel elder, deacon, and president of the congregation, preached in 1919 when the pastor was not available.

Immanuel's first called pastor was Fredrick Herman Carlson, who split his time between Immanuel and a Lutheran congregation in Minneapolis, serving during 1880–1882 and riding the train between the two cities. Immanuel's first fulltime pastor from 1884–1892 was Martin Gustav Hanson, a graduate of Red Wing Seminary. He was the son of Osten Hanson, who was Immanuel's first visiting pastor. At that time, Immanuel, although one congregation, had two locations—East Immanuel and West Immanuel. Rev. Carlson served both East and West Immanuel, as did all the pastors who followed until January 20, 1913, when East Immanuel became a separate congregation. The two congregations continued to publish joint parish newsletters for several more years.

1-5. Pastor Fredrick Herman Carlson, Immanuel's first called pastor in 1880

> ◦ *We have had at least 25 different pastors since we started meeting to form our church in 1871. They were all born in Norway as far as I know, which makes it so nice for all of us in the congregation who speak Norwegian better than English. They were traveling preachers and they would come to us when they were in Saint Paul and preach, have communion, baptize our babies, marry couples, and conduct funerals. Now we have our very own Pastor Carlson. We share him with East Immanuel, which has its own church building about a mile away. He also serves a congregation in Minneapolis. He goes there by train.*
> —*Karen Christensen (Mrs. Ole Christensen), 1881*

In 1900, the U.S. Census of Religious Bodies counted 161 church organizations in Saint Paul. About 63 percent of the population were members of a church. There were more Lutheran churches in Saint Paul than any other denomination at this time. Roman Catholics had fewer churches, but more members.

Pastor Gustav Marius Bruce served as Interim Pastor for Immanuel and Macalester Park Churches during the time of their merger in 1920. He was a professor at the Red Wing Seminary until 1917 when he came to serve at Immanuel. His leadership was critical in guiding the two congregations through their merger. He and his wife, Minnie, maintained close ties with Immanuel for decades. Dr. Bruce baptized and married many Immanuel parishioners during the next decades and he spoke at Immanuel's 25th anniversary celebration in 1946. J. Walter Johnshoy and Martinus Casper Johnshoy, pastors at Macalester Park Lutheran Church, also assisted during the 1920 merger. They are ancestors of two current members of Immanuel's congregation: Jan Johnshoy and Marlene Johnshoy.

Until 1945, the pastor was the only paid position at Immanuel. When Pastor Conrad Mervin Thompson began his Immanuel call in 1945, he hired Hilma Lundby as the first professional assistant to the pastor. She served many roles, including office secretary, youth director, and parish visitor. For many years, positions such as choir director, organist, and Sunday School superintendent were unpaid or paid only a modest amount. For example, the organist was paid $15 a month in 1932—however, this was during the Great Depression and the pastor's annual salary was only $2,100 ($175/month).

1-6. Hilma Lundby, first hired staff person in 1945

The merger of Immanuel with Highland Park Lutheran Church in 1960 brought in a second pastor. Pastor Roald Carlson from Immanuel was lead pastor, and Pastor John Adrian Pfeiffer from Highland joined the staff as Associate Pastor. The two pastors alternated preaching every other Sunday. There were certainly challenges in blending the styles of two congregations, both for the pastors and for the congregation. Highland Park Luther Church was part of the German Lutheran tradition and Immanuel had a Norwegian background, and the two churches had their own practices and organizational structure. One parishioner who joined Immanuel coming from Highland Park recalls that it was not a difficult transition for the children, but the adults had a harder time and tended to form cliques. Pastor Carlson led the Confirmation classes and was the more progressive pastor. The students loved him.

Pastor Elder Kenneth Bentley served Immanuel from 1964 to 1992. His 28-year term is the longest tenure of Immanuel's pastors. He is known for creating "Bentley's Bundle," a ready cash fund that was used to provide immediate financial support for those in need. He enjoyed acting in plays at Immanuel. Pastor Bentley was instrumental in establishing the Southeast Asian Ministry, which supported the resettlement of refugees from Vietnam, Laos, and Cambodia. He served as its first president in 1982.

In 1966, Immanuel voted to call an assistant pastor instead of having a seminary intern assist the pastor. Rev. James Tangen was the first assistant pastor—he started July 1, 1966. His primary responsibilities focused on the youth, which had been the case for seminary interns before him and for assistant pastors who followed him.

Rev. Susan Smith, who served from 1995–1997 as associate pastor, was the first woman called by Immanuel. Rev. Joy Bussert was the second woman pastor at Immanuel (2002–2009), also serving as associate pastor. Rev. Cindy Bullock was the third female pastor and was called in 2011 to serve as Immanuel's sole pastor.

1-7. Pastor Elder Bentley as Jesus in an Easter play (ca. 1970)

Immanuel has had several models of ministry over the years, from visiting pastors to shared pastors, two or three pastors, interns from Luther seminary, interim pastors, and both paid and unpaid staff. Leif Ingvar Monson (1979–1980), Melvin P. Kaatrud (1965–1971), Paulus William Pilgrim, Sr. (1972–1980), and Ralph Wilbur Glenn (1980–1999) were part-time outreach and visitation pastors, calling on home-bound parishioners and seniors. Pastor Glenn was tireless. In 1991, he made 1,145 calls on individuals in their homes or care facilities and called on 145 people in hospitals. Immanuel has had both assistant and associate pastors, who served with a senior pastor.

In 2001, Immanuel added the role of "worship assistant" or assisting minister, a lay member in the congregation who assists with the Sunday service. Immanuel member Stephanie Alstead remembered being asked to become an assisting minister and thinking, "That will be so hard. I should do it"—and she accepted the invitation. Ray Peterson, another assisting minister, saved the church from catching fire one Christmas Eve candlelight service. Candles were brought to the front of the church and inserted in a bowl of sand. The dripping wax formed a large pool and one candle started the pool of wax on fire. The assisting minister rejected the proposal to pour water on it, ran down to the kitchen, and came back with a large metal platter that he used to smother the fire.

1-8. Stephanie Alstead, assisting Pastor Cindy Bullock (2015)

Immanuel's pastors have had other jobs and talents before their time as pastor, while serving as pastor, or after leaving Immanuel. These include farmer, carpenter, coal mine engineer, writer, semi-professional basketball player, garbage collector, medical doctor, professor, janitor, sailor, composer, police crisis intervention counselor, journalist, inventor, and translator. These talents and experiences have served to enrich their understanding and connection to the congregation.

1-9. JeMae Gulliksen, parish nurse (ca. 1997)

Others have supported Immanuel's ministry. In 1994, Christy Frazier, RN, was hired as a part-time parish nurse, working five hours a week. Her work was coordinated through and partially funded by the Lyngblomsten Parish Nurse program. She did home visits; provided health counseling, education, referrals, and prayers for the sick and grieving; wrote articles for *The Messenger;* did monthly blood pressure screening; and answered health questions. JeMae Gulliksen followed Christy Frazier and served as parish nurse until 1998. In 1994, Immanuel member, Kim Thompson, was hired as a part-time volunteer coordinator, a position she held for two years.

Mergers with other Lutheran congregations (Macalester Park Lutheran in 1921 and Highland Park Lutheran in 1960) added to the list of pastors who served the congregations that became Immanuel Lutheran. A complete list of all 76 pastors from Immanuel, Macalester Park, and Highland Park Lutheran Churches with brief biographies can be found in Appendix A.

Immanuel has a rich history of sons and daughters of former pastors and congregation members who joined the ministry, were missionaries, and served the church in many ways. Two sons, a granddaughter, and a nephew of early members Solfest and Clara Aalbue became Lutheran pastors. Four sons of Macalester Park Lutheran pastor Joseph Walter Johnshoy became Lutheran pastors. Three sons and three grandchildren of Pastor Conrad Mervin Thompson became␣Lutheran pastors or served the church in other ways. See Appendix B for a complete list of known "Sons and Daughters of Immanuel, Macalester Park, and Highland Park Lutheran Churches Who Became Pastors, Missionaries, and Served the Church."

Challenges and Difficult Times

Challenges make us stronger and better prepared to face the future. Immanuel has faced many challenges (some internal and some external) over the years, and has grown stronger and more compassionate because of them. Mergers with other congregations were not as smooth as one would hope. Combining congregations, each with its own history and culture, brings conflict. For example, discussions leading up to the 1921 merger with Macalester Park Lutheran Church and calling the first pastor were dominated by whether the merged congregation should be part of the Hauge Synod or the Norwegian Lutheran Church of America. After the merger, the women's groups resisted combining and the two congregations' women's groups continued to operate separately for four years.

The 1930s were a transitional and often difficult period for the Norwegian immigrants. Lars W. Boe (president of St. Olaf College), observed, "Ours is a mediating generation. By training and tradition we live in the spiritual and cultural land of the fathers. With our children we are steadily marching into the land of tomorrow. Ours is the riches of two cultures and often the poverty of the desert wanderer. We live between memory and reality. Ours is the agony of a divided loyalty and joy in the discovery of a new unity. Like Moses of old we see the new but cannot fully enter in. To us has been given the task of mediating a culture, of preserving and transferring to our children in a new land the cultural and spiritual values bound up in the character, art, music, literature, and Christian faith

of a generation no longer found even in the land from which the fathers came."
—quoted in Eugene L. Fevold, "The Norwegian Immigrant and His Church," Norwegian-American Studies, *23 (1967):16.*

World War I, World War II, the Korean War, the Vietnam War, the Gulf War, and the war in Afghanistan have taken a toll on members and their families. While all of Immanuel's servicemen returned safely from World War I, three of the 101 service personnel who served in World War II did not return. Immanuel members supported the war efforts in many ways—from rolling bandages to baking cookies to writing letters to service personnel. Immanuel has sought to provide a safe and caring place to discuss conflict and war. In 2003, Immanuel members Richard Pemberton and Deanna Thompson provided leadership for a special series on Iraq that began with a retreat around the theme of "How to Talk to Children about War." An Adult Forum explored various Christian approaches to war and peace, including the Pacifist Tradition and the Holy War Tradition as well as the Just War Theory.

The 1918/19 Spanish flu pandemic and, more recently, the COVID pandemic have challenged and stressed the congregation. Church records indicate that at least two members of Immanuel died of influenza in 1918 and 1919. During the COVID pandemic, Immanuel moved to offering remote services beginning in April 2019, first by Zoom and then through Facebook and YouTube live stream. All gatherings in the building were suspended for 15 months. Refer to Chapter 2 for more details. A special committee was formed to guide reopening of the sanctuary and church facilities, aiming to ensure the safety of all. Several members worked together to provide remote delivery of services.

Some conflicts have been internal. The staunch Haugeans were not pleased to merge with a church in the Norwegian Lutheran Church of America. Not all congregation members agreed with and supported certain pastors. The Evangelical Lutheran Church in America decisions about ordaining women and LGBTQ Lutherans were not universally welcomed. Even decisions about remodeling projects, the format of worship services, music, and managing finances have created tension and stress. Some congregation members left Immanuel as a result of disagreements within the congregation, with pastors, and with doctrine.

Immanuel has grown in its ability to engage in civil discourse and address issues that cause conflict and misunderstanding. In 2013, when the Minnesota legislature approved same gender marriages, Immanuel held a "Respectful Conversation" to discuss the matter among members. This resulted in the Council welcoming same gender couples for marriage at

Immanuel. In 2020, Immanuel together with Pilgrim Lutheran, Fairmount Avenue United Methodist, and Macalester Plymouth United formed the Joint Church Antiracism Team (JCART), which offers speakers, study groups, tours of scared Native American sites in the Twin Cities, and other ways to learn about the experiences and current needs of Native Americans who lived on the land where Immanuel stands today. Opportunities were provided to learn about Indian boarding schools. Immanuel investigated its own participation in this controversial assimilation program of the early 20th century.

Immanuel's Moves and Buildings

In 1871, Immanuel Lutheran Church was called *Den Evangelisk Lutherske Emmanuel*. Members probably met in private homes and later in the rented upstairs of a house on 13th Street until 1881, when Immanuel's first sanctuary was purchased from the Norwegian Evangelical Lutheran Church at 233 15th Street for $60.00. It was moved to 14th and Canada Streets (269 14th Street). The pastors serving the congregation in the early years lived in a parsonage behind the church at 277 14th Street.

1-10. Immanuel's first church (Canada and 14th Streets; 1880–1889)

In 1886, Immanuel members who lived on the East Side of Saint Paul decided they needed a church closer to where they lived. This resulted in the creation of East Immanuel, which was still part of Immanuel and shared pastors with "West" Immanuel until 1913. The East Immanuel congregation built a sanctuary at 1019 Jessie Street in 1886, and called it East Emmanuel Norwegian Evangelical Lutheran Church of the Hauge Synod. Their first church was a frame church at Jessie and Lawson. It was used by the congregation for 45 years. The church is now a private home. A bigger church was built at Payne and Rose Avenues in Saint Paul. The church basement was dug in 1926 and the building was erected in 1931. They were called East Immanuel Norwegian Evangelical Lutheran Church of the Hauge Synod. The congregation folded sometime after 2013 and the building continues to serve another Lutheran congregation.

1-11. East Immanuel's first church (Jessie and Lawson Streets; built in 1886)

The original Immanuel church on 14th and Canada Streets was torn down in 1890 and a new brick church built at the same location at the cost of $6,000. It was dedicated in 1891. The congregation was called *Emanuels norsk evangelisk lutherske Menighet af Hauges synode i Saint Paul*. By 1900 the congregation was called Emmanuel Norwegian Evangelical Lutheran Church. (It is not clear when the spelling of Emmanuel was officially changed to Immanuel.) The building at 14th and Canada was Immanuel's church home for nearly 25 years until it was sold in 1914 to a Jewish congregation for use as a synagogue. Eventually, this building was torn down, and the location is now an onramp for Regions Hospital.

1-12. East Immanuel's second church (Payne and Rose Avenues; completed in 1931)

1-13. Immanuel's second church (Canada and 14th Streets; 1890–1914)

A new church for "West" Immanuel was built at Aurora and Saint Albans (678 Aurora Avenue) in 1915. The congregation was called Immanuel Norwegian Evangelical Lutheran Church. It was nearly debt free by the time construction was completed. Services were held on Sundays at 10:45 AM and 7:30 PM in Norwegian. English services were held on the first Sunday of the month and every Sunday evening. Sunday school was at 9:30 AM in both Norwegian and English. This church is, at the time of this writing, the home of the Saint Albans Church of God in Christ.

1-14. Immanuel's third church (Aurora and Saint Albans Streets; 1915–1922)

Merger with Macalester Park Lutheran Church

Also in 1915, a few families from the Trinity Norwegian Evangelical Lutheran Church (515 N. Farrington Street) who lived in the Macalester neighborhood started a Sunday School in Bucka's Hall, above Bucka's grocery store (1676 Grand Avenue; now Frattallone's Hardware Store). They wanted a location that was in convenient walking distance for their children to go to Sunday School. The people involved were:

Mr. & Mrs. Solfest J. Aalbue and 3 children (her name was Clara/Klara)
Mr. & Mrs. John H. Abbe and two children
Mr. & Mrs. A.M. Anderson
Mr. & Mrs. Oscar Anderson and 5 children
Mr. & Mrs. Arnold Aune and 2 children
Mr. and Mrs. A.W. Brissman and 5 children
Mr. & Mrs. M.A. Deck and 2 children
Mr. & Mrs. Ole R. Eide and 3 children
Mr. & Mrs. John Hoitorant
Mr. & Mrs. M. Merrick and 5 children
Mr. Arthur M. Morgan
Mr. & Mrs. Peter O. Nasvik and 8 children
Miss Lillie S. Olson
Mr. & Mrs. P.A. Peterson and 5 children
Mr. & Mrs. Hans Sevlie and 4 children
Mr. & Mrs. Charles H. Tente and one child
Mr. & Mrs. Martin Wangensteen and 2 children (grandparemts of current member Doug Wangensteen)

In 1917, those families formed a new congregation, Macalester Park Lutheran Church. The people listed above, along with Arthur Anderson, Mabel Anderson, and R.A. Tanner, are listed as Macalester Park founding members. They built a chapel at 1567 Goodrich Avenue. Arthur Anderson drew the plans for the building. Member Peter O. Nasvik was the contractor. This building sat where the current Immanuel Lutheran Church's chancel is today.

1-15. Macalester Park Lutheran Church's chapel used between 1918 and 1922 (1567 Goodrich Avenue)

In 1921, the the national Norwegian Lutheran Church of America asked Immanuel to move again because there were too many Lutheran churches from the same synod in the area around downtown Saint Paul, and more outreach into the Midway District was needed. Trinity Lutheran Church, Macalester Park Lutheran Church, and Immanuel Lutheran Church entered into negotiations to effect a merger that would have a strong congregation in the Midway area, and fewer Lutheran churches near downtown. A consideration in favor of the merger was the shortage of Lutheran pastors at that time. One point of discussion was that Trinity belonged to the United Norwegian Lutheran Church Synod, Macalester Park was part of the newly formed Norwegian Lutheran Church of America Synod, and Immanuel had a long-standing connection to the Hauge Synod.

The three congregations agreed to merge and called Rev. Olin Spencer J. Reigstad of Stoughton, Wisconsin, to serve as pastor. Pastor Gustav Marius Bruce (interim Immanuel pastor 1917–1921) steered the negotiations. He reported that some members of Immanuel wanted a pastor from the Hauge Synod but their nominee received only a few votes, so Reigstad was selected. Reigstad declined the call and Trinity Lutheran Church opted out of the merger, which nearly derailed the merger plans. (Note: When Trinity folded in the 1980s, several members of that church came to Immanuel, enriching the congregation.)

The merger of Immanuel and Macalester Park Lutheran Church went forward, and Macalester Park's chapel on Goodrich Avenue was torn down in preparation for new construction. Immanuel sold the church on St. Albans in 1922 to a Methodist congregation for $8,000. Using this money, a basement was built at Goodrich and South Snelling Avenues on the site of Macalester Park Lutheran's chapel. Edward N. Mohn was the architect and Peterson and Company built the structure. The corner stone was laid in 1923 by the Reverend Carl John Eastvold, Immanuel's pastor. The basement was 40 feet by 60 feet with an assembly hall, two classrooms, kitchen, toilets, and heating room. The main auditorium had an office, altar, pulpit, pipe organ, gymnasium, and seating capacity of 150. The name of the new merged congregation was Immanuel Evangelical Lutheran Church of Saint Paul.

Dr. Gustav Marius Bruce, the interim pastor who oversaw the merger, wrote in his 1922 annual report that it was a time of joy at what was accomplished and sadness because of the hatred and hostility that was directed toward him during this period. He noted,

> Though tinged with sadness, my joy is nevertheless great and sincere, for under God, I feel that we have accomplished great things, the importance and significance of which shall become

more and more evident as the years roll by . . . God grant that as the fruitage of the experiences of the past, the spirit of true spiritual democracy, loyalty, and cooperation may reign in our united congregation in the future.

Leading up to the merger, Pastor Bruce alternated services between Immanuel and Macalester Park. He noted that attendance suffered because the alternate use of the two churches proved confusing to many.

Merger with Highland Park Lutheran Church

Highland Park Lutheran Church was started as a mission congregation of the Minnesota District of the Ohio Synod. The Ohio Synod was the "Evangelical Lutheran Joint Synod of Ohio and Other States." It was a German-language Lutheran denomination whose congregations were originally located primarily in Ohio. The charter members of Highland Park were:

Mrs. J. Albert
Mr. and Mrs. F.W. Angerhofer
Mr. Victor Angerhofer
Mr. and Mrs. C.C. Clark
Miss Ruth Cox
Mr. Karl Cox
Mr. and Mrs. J.C. Daeffler
Mrs. F. Faehnrich
Mrs. L. Hang
Mr. Jul. Kolberg
Mr. M.R. Kuehn
Mrs. L. LeMaitre
Mrs. Eugene H. Pfeiffer
Mr. and Mrs. J. Rybak, Jr.
Mrs. R. Thoele
Miss Mildred Wenzel
Mr. and Mrs. R. Wenzel

Highland Park Lutheran Church erected a combination chapel and parsonage at Niles and South Snelling with the first floor serving as a worship hall and the second floor as living quarters for the pastor. The Rev. Eugene H. Pfeiffer of South Haven, Michigan, was called to be the first pastor and began his duties April 18, 1926. Twelve communicants came forward for the first Communion service. The church was formally organized in 1928 with

74 communicant members and 23 voting members. In 1930, a new church building was dedicated in the same location. On May 20, 1951, the congregation dedicated an addition on the east side of the building. The addition cost $25,000. In 1958, Highland Park Lutheran Church purchased a new parsonage at 1652 Beechwood Avenue.

1-16. Highland Park Lutheran Church used between 1930 and 1960 (Niles and South Snelling Avenue)

On October 2, 1960, Highland Park Lutheran Church became the second congregation to merge with Immanuel. A "Union Service" was held at the Macalester College gymnasium with Dr. Fredric Schoitz, president of the American Lutheran Church, preaching and officiating in the ceremony of union. Each congregation presented a pulpit Bible, a baptismal bowl, and a Communion tray at the worship service to symbolize a willingness to share the best they had with each other. The merger brought Marjorie O'Neil and Nellie Berry, two beloved Sunday School teachers, to Immanuel. The resulting growth in membership made it necessary to hold three Sunday services and two Sunday School sessions.

1-17. Union service, Macalester College gymnasium—(left to right) Rev. Roald Carlson, Dr. Fredrick Scholtz, Rev. John A. Pfeiffer (1960)

1-18. Congregation crossing South Snelling Avenue to attend union service (1960)

Parsonages and Parish Houses

Immanuel's first parsonage (housing provided by the church for the pastor) in the 1880s was at 277 14th St., located behind the church at 269 14th Street. Information about parsonages after this date is sketchy. When Pastor John Sevrin Sunde was called to be the first pastor following the merger of Immanuel with Macalester Park Lutheran Church in 1921, there was no parsonage for him. Records indicate that the church provided a housing allowance. Pastor Bennie Duckstad continued to rent a home in the 1930s.

In 1940, Immanuel purchased the house just west of the church on the corner of Goodrich and Snelling (1507 Goodrich) as a parsonage. Arrangements were made with Pastor Duckstad to redirect the amounts he had been receiving for rent toward payments for the new parsonage. Practically all details in arranging for this purchase were taken care of by Ralph H. Grove. The Ladies Aid and Loyal Worker's Societies met the payments on both the church mortgage and loan from the Synod's Extension fund—payments amounted to $240 every six months. Immanuel filed an application with the County Auditor for a grant exempting the church from future tax payments on the parsonage. This was granted by the County Commissioners. Volunteers reconditioned the parsonage lawn.

In 1947, Immanuel purchased a house at 104 South Snelling Avenue, just north of the church to use as a parish house (an auxiliary building used for business and social activities) and to provide additional rooms for Sunday School. During 1950, the congregation raised about $5,000 to clear the debt. In January 1951, Jack Ehlers, president of the congregation, A.R. Forman, chairman of the Board of Trustees, and Pastor Rueben Mostrom participated in a mortgage-burning ceremony. This parish house was demolished in 1951, and the parsonage at 1507 Goodrich was moved to 104 South Snelling. Moving the parsonage from Goodrich to South Snelling created space for the 1951–1953 church expansion on the west side (dedicated in 1953). At one time, plans were prepared for a tunnel to connect this parsonage to the church, but it was not built.

The annual report for 1957 indicates that approximately $1,700.00 was spent on the parsonage at 104 South Snelling—this included remodeling the kitchen by lowering the ceiling and building cupboards. In addition, baseboard radiators were installed, the dining room cabinets were changed, rooms were painted, and permanent awnings were installed over the front door and picture window. Much of the work was done by volunteers.

When the education wing was built (dedicated in 1961), the house then serving as the parsonage at 104 South Snelling was moved a second time.

The house and garage were sold for $2,250 and moved to a lot on Hague Ave., where they still stand. The house Immanuel owned at 90 South Snelling was used as a temporary home for Pastor Einar Roald Carlson and his family. Church women cleaned the temporary home and men moved everything out of 104 Snelling to 90 South Snelling. That house was later demolished for the parking lot.

1-19. Former parsonage being moved from South Snelling Ave. to a new location (1960)

Immanuel purchased a lot at 1489 Summit in 1960 for $6,000, and a new parsonage was built. A mortgage was signed with the First National Bank of Saint Paul to cover all new construction not covered by loan certificates. Immanuel member Stanley Uggen was appointed as special treasurer for the Loan Certificate Fund. The architect was Phillip Agnew and the contractor was Donald Kise. This parsonage was dedicated April 16, 1961, the same day the new education building was dedicated. Pastor Roald Carlson and his family moved into the new parsonage on Summit Ave. and lived there until 1964, when Pastor Elder Bentley was called to succeed Pastor Carlson. Pastor Bentley and his family moved into the parsonage at 1489 Summit and lived there for many years. Eventually the congregation agreed to sell the house to Pastor Bentley. He began to receive a housing allowance as part of his compensation package—as have all subsequent pastors.

For a few years following the merger with Highland Park Lutheran Church, Immanuel had two parsonages—the new parsonage at 1489 Summit, where Pastor Einar Roald Carlson and his family lived, and a parsonage at 1652 Beechwood, the home of Pastor John Pfeiffer (who was the pastor at Highland Park and who became Immanuel's Associate Pastor after the merger) and his family. This second parsonage was subsequently sold in 1964 when Pastor Pfeiffer took another call and left Immanuel.

Anniversary Celebrations

25th Anniversary

On November 5, 1946, the 25th anniversary of the merger of Macalester Park Lutheran and Immanuel Lutheran into one congregation was celebrated with a dinner served by the Women's Guild. Dr. Gustav Marius Bruce (former pastor of both Immanuel and Macalester Park) was the speaker. An anniversary worship service was held on Sunday, November 10, 1946. The offering of thanksgiving and appreciation was used to reduce property indebtedness. The theme of the sermon was "The Church with the Open Door."

50th Anniversary and 100th Anniversary

On September 26, of 1971, two events were commemorated: the 50th anniversary of the merger with Macalester Park Lutheran church in 1921 and 100 years as a congregation going back to 1871. A service of worship and thanksgiving was held at the Macalester College Field House with Pastors Elder Bentley and Sylvan Edward Hengesteg officiating. A coffee hour at church followed worship. Former pastors were invited to speak at an informal service later in the afternoon.

125th Anniversary

This year-long commemoration culminated with an anniversary celebration service and reception on September 29, 1996. Several milestones were celebrated: 125 years of existence as Immanuel Lutheran Church, 75 years since the merger with Macalester Park Lutheran church and building a church on the current site, and 36 years since the merger with Highland Park Lutheran Church. Immanuel member Dawn Hilbert wrote a special hymn, "This is the Day the Lord Has Made," for the anniversary. The sermon, given by Bishop Mark Hanson, was titled "The Bridge Between Memory and Hope." The service and reception were attended by nine current and former pastors: Pastors Larry Rehlander, Conrad Thompson, Philip Walen, Elder Bentley, Raymond Boyens, Einar Carlson, Milo Engelstad, Sylvan Hengesteg, and Susan Smith; Saint Paul Area Synod Bishop Mark Hanson; and Deaconess Diane Greve. A panoramic photo was taken of the entire congregation outside in front of the church. Bulletin inserts were provided throughout the year with stories and information about Immanuel's past. An anniversary history booklet was edited by Immanuel member Marcia Hanson with research done by members Bonnie Wilson, Adelaide Norgaard, Rachel Husom, Sue Browender, Kristofer Layon, and Nancy Reidell. An anniversary luncheon was held. For the 125th Anniversary celebration, five banners (for Lent, Easter, Pentecost, Reformation Sunday, and Advent) were created by Immanuel member Diane Schultz, and a hymnal bookmark was designed by member Tryg Anderson.

1-20. 125th Anniversary—Front row: Pastor Sylvan Hengesteg, Deaconess Diane Greve, Pastors Susan Smith and Larry Rehlander. Middle row: Pastors Phil Walen, Milo Engelstad, and Elder Bentley. Back row: Pastor Conrad Thomspon, Bishop Mark Hanson, Pastors Roald Carlson and Raymond Boyens (1996)

150th Anniversary

This anniversary of 150 years since the beginning of Immanuel Lutheran Church fell in the second year of the COVID pandemic. Many planned activities were cancelled, postponed, or modified. A banner was displayed from August to November 2021 on the front of the church facing Snelling Avenue proclaiming Immanuel's anniversary to the community. An Immanuel history trivia quiz was held as a Zoom event. PowerPoint shows highlighting various historical topics were presented after selected online Zoom worship services and later archived on the church website. Immanuel member Ray Peterson built a display case to showcase Immanuel artifacts, and celeratory bulletin boards were prepared.

A special worship service was held on October 10, 2021, with former Pastors Dana Nissen and John Lohre assisting Pastor Cindy Bullock. Bishop

Patricia Lull of the Saint Paul Area Synod of the ELCA preached. The congregation sang "God with Us, O Come, Immanuel," a new hymn commemorating the anniversary written by Immanuel member David Stark. Two booklets with text and photos were printed and distributed at the service: a *Self-Guided Tour of Immanuel Church Building Locations, Sister Churches, and Merger Partner Churches* and a brief illustrated church history, *Immanuel Lutheran Church God with Us 1871–2021*. The new banner made for the anniversary by member Sandy Anderson led the processional. Immanuel member Richard (Dick) Sundberg created attractive wood candleholders for the pastors and Bishop Lull. The day was warm and sunny, and the attendees enjoyed cake and coffee on the south lawn and received mugs commemorating the anniversary.

1-21. 150th Anniversary—Bishop Patricia Lull, Pastors Cindy Bullock, John Lohre, and Dana Nissen with anniversary banner (2021)

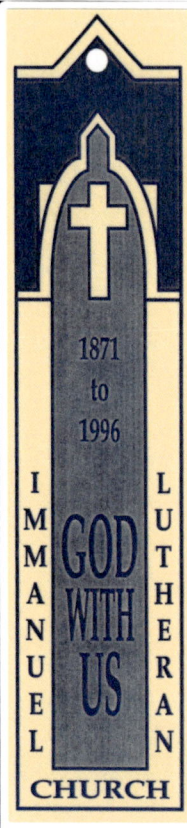

1-22. 125th Anniversary bookmark (1996)

Continuity

Although congregation members come and go for various reasons, Immanuel has been blessed with many long-time members. Appendix D lists those who have belonged to Immanuel for 25 or more years. Tyson and Maria Reed and their children represent the fourth and fifth generation of the Reed family to belong to Immanuel. Larry Wilson (former organist) represents a different kind of continuity. He believes he may have the record for attending Immanuel the longest before becoming a member—he attended for some 40 years before officially joining in 2019.

1-23. 150th Anniversary banner on the front of the church (2021)

CHAPTER 2

Immanuel Facilities

Facilities

Immanuel Lutheran Church sits on the ancestral land of the Dakota people who lived here for hundreds of years before Norwegians and other settlers arrived. At this point in Immanuel's history, the congregation is studying the history of the Dakota in Minnesota and the role of settlers in the disruption of Native American society and the takeover of their land. Immanuel members have learned about the treaties that were made and broken, efforts by government and church organizations to assimilate Native Americans through boarding schools, the destruction of Dakota sacred sites, and the Dakota War of 1862. Through study, dialogue with Native Americans, and acknowledgement of this history of colonization, Immanuel hopes to come to a place of reconciliation with our Native American neighbors today.

Facilities and Improvements

Before exploring the various construction, improvement, and remodeling projects, understanding the traditional names of the parts of a church is useful. The nave is the central part of a church, stretching from the (normally western) main entrance or rear wall, to the chancel. The nave is where the congregation sits during worship. The chancel is the space around the altar. Next to the cancel on the left is the pulpit, the raised platform from which the sermon is delivered. The lectern is to the right and is the stand on which the Bible may rest and from which the "lessons" (scripture passages, often selected from a lectionary) are read during the service. A transept is an area set crosswise to the nave. Immanuel has a semitransept—half of a transept—on the south side, where the bellchoirs often play. The sacristy, also known as a vestry or preparation room, is the room for the keeping of vestments, sacred vessels, and other church furnishings. The narthex is the entrance or lobby area, located at the west end of the nave, opposite the church's main altar.

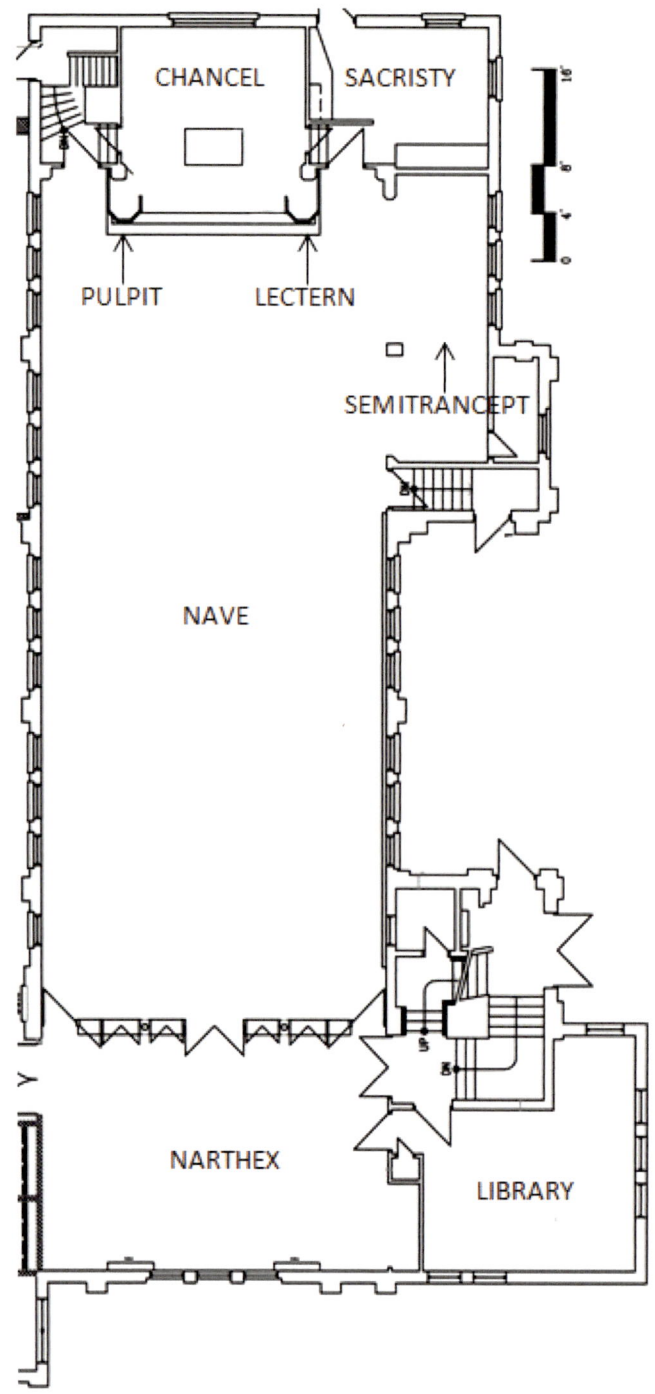

2-1. Immanuel Lutheran Church floor plan (drawn by Stephanie Alstead)

In 1925, Immanuel's current sanctuary was constructed above the basement, which had been built in 1923. The cost was around $20,000. The exterior walls are made of hollow Danville brick and cast stone trim. The architect was Edward N. Mohn and the builder was Peterson & Co. The new church was dedicated October 25, 1925, with Dr. Gustav Marius Bruce, a professor at Luther Seminary and former interim pastor (1917–1921), preaching. Immanuel's male chorus, *Nordmændenes* (The Norwegians), sang at the church dedication service in 1925. The Loyal Workers (one of the women's groups at the time) raised the funds for the light fixtures of wrought iron when the sanctuary was built.

2-2. Lutheran Church Herald *(Sept. 29, 1925) dedication of the "New Immanuel Church"*

One of the first funerals held in the new church presented a problem. The casket was mahogany and quite large. It would not fit through the door and up the stairs unless it was standing on end. After that, members were careful to choose smaller and less ostentatious coffins. A member shared another funeral story. Several years ago, a funeral was underway on a Wednesday at 1:00 PM. The tornado siren located on the roof of the Macalester gym went off in test mode. The siren was pointed directly at Immanuel and brought the funeral to a "dead halt." Since then, Immanuel has not scheduled a funeral at 1:00 p.m. on the first Wednesday of the month.

The bell tower on the Goodrich side never had a bell. For a few years, a recording of a bell chiming was played from inside the tower. The practice ceased because neighbors complained that the bell was too loud.

In 1951, Immanuel approved major expansion plans. Arthur Gordon chaired the finance board to raise the funds. The addition on the South Snelling side provided a choir room, narthex, Sunday School space, a stage area in the basement, 14 more pews (seven on each side), a balcony, and office space. This addition cost $117,000. The architect was Otto W. Johnson. The organ, which had been in the front of the church, was moved to the balcony, under which is written "Whosoever would be great among you, let him be the servant of all." The Women's Guild purchased a red carpet for the sanctuary. Boy Scout Troop 90 contributed money for the paneling and fireplace in the Scout room on the lower level. The new addition was dedicated in 1953. Dr. Elmer C. Reinerstson, President of the Southern Minnesota District Evangelical Lutheran Church, gave the dedication sermon. The building was often called "the church without a door" because the entrance from Goodrich was not visible from Snelling Avenue.

2-3. View of the choir loft

2-4. "The Church without a Door": View of Immanuel Lutheran Church and parsonage from South Snelling Avenue (1953)

Immanuel member Mark Anderson remembers when his father, Ernie Anderson, painted the gold design on the arches in the altar area in the 1950s. The paint was applied with a roller that had an image carved in it that had to be carefully matched. It took a long time to complete the project.

The congregation was growing. Three church services were held on Sundays. So many children attended Sunday School that classes met in shifts with two "sessions" held. In 1955, 278 students were attending Sunday School with 24 teachers. The Pre-K class was not split. At the request of the families, these little ones stayed with Mrs. Solfest J. Aalbue (Clara), their beloved Sunday School teacher.

Immanuel member Marvin Merrick remembered Mrs. Albue's class, "When she taught her classes about Jesus with devotion and sincerity, we knew the lessons were true and we believed."

It became clear that the congregation needed more space for Sunday School, a parking lot, and other improved facilities, and planning for an education wing started in 1959. In 1959, the property at 90 South Snelling between the parsonage and Lincoln Avenue was purchased for $14,500 with the intent of demolishing the house located there and using the lot for parking. Immanuel had no off-street parking before this time. For a short time, the house at 90 South Snelling was used as the temporary parsonage until the new parsonage on Summit Avenue was completed. The church voted to purchase the additional two lots between the parsonage at 104 South Snelling and 90 South Snelling as they became available, to sell and move the parsonage, and find a location for a new parsonage

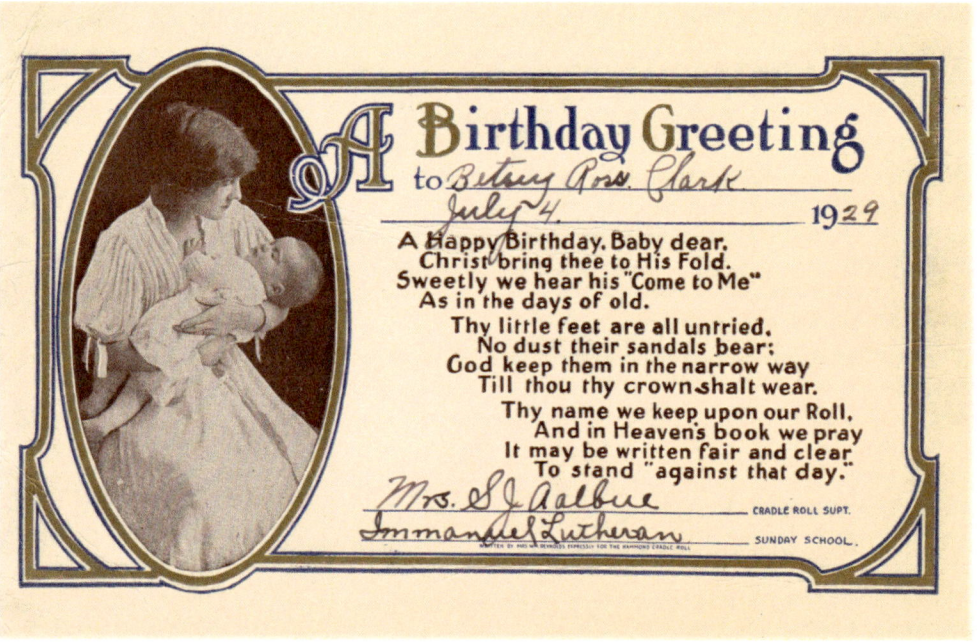

2-5. Birthday greeting from Mrs. Aalbue, Sunday School teacher (1929)

Two additional houses on this site north of the parsonage were purchased and removed. The last property purchased was 96 South Snelling in 1964 for $19,000. Once the parsonage was sold and moved, a parking lot for 80 cars was constructed.

The architect for the new education wing was Gerhard Peterson of Cone & Peterson, and construction began in 1960. The cost was $220,000. It was dedicated April 16, 1961, at a service at the Macalester Field House. The dedication was attended by 1,084 people despite a blizzard. Dr. Conrad Thompson provided greetings and installed Pastor J. Adrian Pfeiffer as Immanuel's Associate Pastor. Pastor Ruben Mostrom preached the sermon, and Dr. Richard Evenson, Executive Director for the Division of Parish Education of the American Lutheran Church, dedicated the Education Building. After processing across Snelling Avenue back to Immanuel, a Service of Entrance was held.

2-6. Groundbreaking for Education Wing with Sunday School children (1960)

2-7. Rendering of the education wing addition (1961)

First through the door into the new foyer was Elvina Loftness, junior high Sunday School teacher, holding the hands of two students. The new wing provided 26 classrooms, offices, pastor's study, a women's lounge, and a fireside room. Some of the Sunday School rooms have special names: Mrs. S.J. Aalbue (Immanuel's long-time Pre-K teacher), Miss Theodora Martinson, and Mrs. Roy Woestehoff. At this point, the address changed to 104 South Snelling Avenue, when the entrance moved to Snelling.

2-8. Elvina Loftness, who was first through the door of the Education Wing (1961)

In 1978, cushions were installed on the sanctuary pews for the first time.

The elevator project, "Give Faith a Lift," was the first step in making the building handicapped accessible. Planning began in 1987 and the project was directed by a Building Committee headed by Alan Robbins-Fenger. The architect was Jafvert Mueller & Mundt. The initial cost estimate was $255,000. The ground-breaking was held on May 15, 1988, and commemorative mugs were distributed. The project was completed in the spring of 1989. The total cost was approximately $376,903, which included supplemental work (repairs on the stone, brick, and mortar; interior remodeling and decorating; and landscaping). The amount pledged for the total program was $299,900. The mortgage for the elevator project was paid off in 1991.

In 1988, one pew was taken out on each side of the front of the church to allow the altar rail to be moved down to a lower level to provide handicapped accessibility. In the same year, the altar rail was removed and the altar moved out from the back wall of the chancel. The pastor continues to face the altar while celebrating Holy Communion, but is now also facing the congregation. Instead of kneeling to receive the Sacrament and blessing, those coming forward stand. This is advantageous for those who have difficulty kneeling and rising.

In 1993, stained glass windows donated by the Needels family were repaired and installed in the youth room on the upper floor. These windows were moved to the new East Lounge in 2006 as part of the remodeling project.

Because of persistent leaks, new roofs were installed in 1999. A new heating system was installed at the same time. Fun fact: In the late 1990s and early 2000s, a mallard duck family lived in the inner courtyard.

2-9. Mallard ducks in the courtyard (2002)

In 2004, planning began for a major renovation that would add additional space for gatherings, upgrade the education wing, relocate the nursery, improve accessibility, and facilitate ministry and outreach. During the first quarter, the "Building Bridges, Moving from a Rich Past to a Bright Future" capital campaign raised $718,000 in contributions and pledges toward moving ahead with the project. Based on this indication of commitment, the congregation voted in June to approve the project with a budget of up to $2.11 million, the balance to be funded with a 20-year mortgage from the ELCA Mission Investment Fund. SMSQ, the architectural firm that had created the Master Plan in 2002, was selected to complete a detailed design and manage construction. A Remodeling Committee headed by Immanuel member Harvey Jaeger was commissioned to oversee the project.

SMSQ completed the detailed remodeling plans in 2005. New features included a more welcoming entry, a central gathering space, and a dedicated youth area. The inner courtyard was removed and the basement adjacent to the kitchen was expanded. Staff offices were located together. Improved traffic flow, critical life safety improvements, and some deferred maintenance were incorporated. In preparation, many volunteers relocated staff offices to other parts of the building and moved furnishings and other items to on- and off-site storage. Some office equipment, such as the copier, was located in the women's bathroom, which continued to be used for its original purpose. Groundbreaking took place in June 2005.

On June 11, 2006, the renovated space was dedicated after the morning service with a blessing from Pastor John Marboe and a greeting from Saint Paul Area Synod Bishop Peter Rogness. A community open house was held September 17. Between services, coffee hour moved upstairs to the new "Gathering Space." Pastor John Marboe shared the story of a 12-year-old boy bounding up the steps to the new gathering space and exclaiming, "I love my new church!"

This project cost $2.11 million and has been funded by seven capital campaigns. These campaigns were:

2004–2007 Building Bridges, Moving from a Rich Past to a Bright Future.
2007–2010 Forward in Faith
2010–2013 Positioning Immanuel for New Opportunities
2013–2016 Gathered Together, Giving to God
2016–2019 See What God is Doing
2019–2022 Pathways to the Future
2022–2023 Rejoice! This campaign will pay off remaining debt and fund new initiatives.

2-10. Groundbreaking for the Building Bridges remodeling project—Sandy Anderson, Greg Knopff, Pepe Kryzda (project manager, SMSQ Architects), Harvey Jaeger, Pastor John Marboe, June Husom (2005)

2-11. Construction of the Gathering Space as part of the Building Bridges project (2005)

2-12. New Gathering Space (2006)

2-13. Jeff Schmidt and Dale Fierke Singing "If I Had a Million Dollars" for the Building Bridges Capital Campaign (2004)

The Building Bridges project installed air conditioning in the new and remodeled spaces, but not in the sanctuary, which became very hot in the summer. Often it was so hot that pastors did not wear their robes and some families decided not to plan summer weddings. Air-conditioning of the sanctuary was generously funded by Immanuel member Ken Fick in 2007.

In 2008, the transept (on the south side of the sanctuary by the lectern) was remodeled by church members. Remodeling rectified earlier water damage, removed the cramped pews, and provided a platform for musical performance.

In 2009, the Property Committee decided to remove the carpet in the chancel around the altar (it had become worn and stained) and then refinish the wood floor. Committee members handled the project with Immanuel member Stephanie Alstead as project leader. The carpet was not replaced.

In 2011, the Property Committee was responsible for purchasing an Automatic Exterior Defibrillator and coordinated training sessions. In 2013, the closet in the narthex was remodeled to provide a new space to showcase library books, art, and other displays.

In 2014, new wallpaper was installed in the sanctuary and new carpeting was installed in the sanctuary, narthex, and sacristy. Immanuel member Curt Hogenson led a project that removed a few pews and increased the remaining spaces between pews in the sanctuary. The changes were implemented by the Improvers.

In 2015, the balcony was remodeled. The existing risers and pews were removed and replaced by new risers and new individual chairs, and new flooring and lighting were installed. The result is a more flexible and safe balcony area. Immanuel member Stephanie Alstead did the design work, and volunteers did the demolition and construction.

In early 2017, the Property Committee initiated an energy audit by Xcel Energy consultants to convert existing fixtures to LED lighting. Harvey Jaeger coordinated the project. In 2018, the major lighting upgrade to LED bulbs was executed with Tillges Electric, an electrical contractor, doing most of the installation, with some assistance by the Improvers, a group of mostly retired members who handle many church facilities projects. Several fixtures were replaced. The estimated cost of the project was $31,230. Immanuel received engineering help from an Xcel-funded program and a $7,900 rebate from Xcel. The church Council provided funding because of the favorable payback to future energy (estimated at approximately $5,000 annually) and maintenance savings by using new LED fixtures and retrofitting existing figures with LED bulbs. The work was completed in the spring of 2018. The Improvers also did some LED conversions in earlier years.

2-14. Stained glass window above altar

Immanuel Furnishings and Decorative Elements

Immanuel's furnishings and decorative elements have changed over the years in response to changing tastes and the need to refurbish and replace as furnishings, wall treatments, carpets, etc. became worn and faded. Changes to the sanctuary are evident in wedding photos taken over the years and make this clear; see the wedding photos on pages 69–72.

Stained Glass Windows

The large stained-glass window above the altar on the east end of the sanctuary shows Christ ascending to heaven. The Ladies Aid raised $800 to purchase this window for the new church in 1925.

Immanuel has stained glass windows on the north and south sides of the sanctuary with pictures and Scripture verses telling the Gospel story. They have been lovingly donated by Immanuel members. Some of the windows have plaques that identify the donors and whom the windows honor. The first window in the semitransept is a picture of Jesus holding a lamb and a staff with the verse, "The Lord is my Shepherd I shall not want." The second window on the south side has Jesus blessing a child, with the verse "Suffer the little children to come to me and forbid them not." The third window on the south is a picture of Jesus holding the Holy Bible, with "Let your light so shine before men that they may see your good works and glorify your father which is in heaven." This window indicates that it was given by the Junior League, which may have donated all the windows on the south side.

The first window near the pulpit on the north side is of Jesus with John the Baptist and the verse "Behold the Lamb of God." It was given in memory of Sarah Marie Grove. The second window is of Jesus riding the donkey into Jerusalem with people waving palms with the verse "Hosanna in the Highest." It was donated by Marvel, Ove, and Miles Wangensteen. Doug Wangensteen recounted that he heard the following story about the "Wangensteen" window.

My grandparents, Martin and Agnes Wangensteen, were early members of Immanuel, I believe. Martin emigrated from Norway in 1902, was a baker, and owned a bakery on Snelling Ave, a few store fronts south of St. Clair. While their three children (Marvel, 1915–2015; Ove [my father], 1917–2002; and Miles, 1922–1982) were growing up, they were paid to work at the bakery. When Immanuel decided to raise money for the stained-glass windows, my grandfather thought the family should buy one of the windows. One evening at dinner, he told Marvel, my dad, and Miles that the three of them would buy the window and the window would be in their name. He would loan them money to give to Immanuel and would take a certain amount from each of their wages until the loan was paid. (My dad didn't say how he and his siblings responded, but they knew they had no choice.) So, the kids' names went on the brass plate below the window, and my grandfather took earnings from their weekly pay. My dad did not remember how much was taken or for how long this went on; however, it ended one Christmas when, as part of their gifts, my grandfather announced that he would forgive the remainder of the loan. This story reflects one of the ways, about 80 years ago, that a Norwegian immigrant taught his children not only about the value of money, but also that they should use some of their money to support important causes. My father and Miles went on to have careers as social workers, and Marvel became a high school teacher.

The third window depicts Jesus praying the Lord's Prayer. It was presented by the Sunday School in honor of Superintendent H.G. Grove in 1930. The final window on the south side has the words "Sing praises to the Lord" and depicts a man playing a lyre. It was donated in memory of William Martin Knudsen.

By 2001, the stained-glass windows in the sanctuary had gradually fallen into disrepair—the wood had deteriorated and the glass was broken and loose. The congregation generously responded, providing more than $80,000 to rebuild the windows with a sealed pane of glass on the outside to protect the stained glass and improve energy efficiency. Similar work was done on the window above the altar at the same time.

Statue of Jesus

The large statue of Jesus behind the altar was purchased by the Sunday School in 1925 when the sanctuary was completed. The statue is a copy of an original in Carrera marble carved by the Danish sculptor Bertel Thorvaldsen (1770–1844). Thorvaldsen's tomb monument of Pope Pius VII is the only work by a non-Catholic in St. Peter's Basilica. The original sculpture of Jesus, called Christos, is in the Church of Our Lady in Copenhagen. Jesus is portrayed as the resurrected Savior and shows his victory over death. Before this, most statues of Christ in churches were of the crucifixion. Copies of Thorvaldsen's statue were made in various sizes for many Protestant churches. Thorvaldsen himself made smaller copies beginning in 1835.

2-15. Stained glass window donated by Marvel, Ove, and Miles Wangensteen

2-16. Statue of Jesus behind the altar

In 1933, Immanuel paid $40.00 to August Klagstad for altar statue work. It is likely that Klagstad painted the hair and beard on the statue of Jesus brown and added color to his robes. Immanuel member and Norwegian immigrant Sverre Hanssen (1891–1968) painted the panels surrounding the statue of Jesus in 1945 with sky and clouds. (Hanssen also did much of the painting in the Minnesota State Capital.) In 1953, when the church was remodeled, the paint was removed from the statue of Jesus, returning it to the more original marble appearance. One Confirmation student recalled looking up at the statute of Jesus in the 1960s and feeling "inspired to be good."

Painted Seals on Either Side of the Chancel

Two seals representing the sacraments adorn the walls to the left and right of the chancel. To the right is a representation of the Eucharist with images of a cluster of grapes, a sheaf of grain, and a Communion cup, above which appear a Communion wafer with the letters IHS for the Latin *Iesus Hominum Salvatore* (Jesus Savior of the People). To the left is an image representing Baptism. The shell and drops of water are the washing of Baptism and the Holy Spirit is shown as a dove descending on the baptized.

The Banner Committee ("Precious Little Tucks Club")

Early in Immanuel's history, felt banners were made and displayed in the sanctuary. Sandy Anderson explained the history of the Banner Committee:

Banners have been a part of Immanuel's worship since 1973. Even before that, the interior was enhanced with felt banners. In 1973, I decided to make red and blue round banners to hang in the space between the sanctuary windows. Using the Prayer of St. Francis of Assisi, I sewed a verse on each banner. After the passing of Allie Pratt in 1979, her husband, Richard, donated money to buy materials for several new banners in memory of Allie. That started the PTL ("Precious Little Tucks") Club, otherwise known as the Banner Committee, comprised of Marcia Hanson, Arlene Storeby, Mary Sue Howes, Barb Minor, and me. Shirley Evans was our groupie, following us wherever we went, a different home each week. In true Norwegian fashion, we always had a wonderful little treat to cap off the evening. We solved a lot of world problems, shared stories and laughs. By 1980, we had created the Christmas Angel banner (Gabriel), the Easter butterfly banner, the Pentecost banner, the Thanksgiving batik banner, the Good Friday banner, and the Noah's Ark Baptism banner, all in memory of Allie. We ceased meeting weekly after I delivered my first child in 1980.

2-17. Statue of Jesus with painted hair and clouds behind the altar (ca. 1950)

2-18. Sandy Anderson sewing banners (1991)

Technology

To help with outreach, keep the congregation connected, support staff, and ensure building security, technology usage has evolved at Immanuel over the years. An early improvement occurred in 1939 when the Lutheran Daughters of the Reformation (LDR) and the Ladies Aid paid for a telephone to be installed in the pastor's office. In 1948, a "wire recorder" was presented to Immanuel. *The Messenger* reported, "It is a fine radio, phonograph and loudspeaker, and wire-recording facilities." Immanuel began broadcasting worship services over the radio on Station KEYD that year.

The Membership and Evangelism Committee facilitated "ministry" audio tapes of Sunday morning services, which were delivered to home-bound and hospitalized members. This ministry was started in 1993. Tape cassette players were loaned and audio tapes on services were delivered. For example, in 1995, 615 tapes were delivered to 26 recipients. For many years, Immanuel member Jerry Sandahl, the first real-time court reporter for the State of Minnesota, created a written transcript of the sermon. He diligently made an audio recording of the service with a cassette recorder, took the recording home, and used a stenograph machine to produce the sermon transcript. He also made duplicate cassettes and had those available, as well. As the technology evolved, Jerry provided audio CDs of the services along with the transcript. This amazing effort was retired when the pandemic of 2020 moved the services to Facebook, Zoom, and YouTube, which were recorded and posted on the Immanuel website.

Desktop computers have been used by the pastors and staff since the early 1990s. Annual reports frequently note purchase of one or more computers, facilitated by the work of computer task forces. In 2019, five Dell computers were purchased to support the staff with up-to-date and reliable workstations. These two desktops and three laptops running Windows provided a significant productivity gain. At this time, Immanuel had only three WiFi access points that provided staff and youth areas with adequate wireless coverage.

The COVID pandemic, which began in 2020, necessitated a significant evolution in the various technologies used in the church. To support the IP-based video stream equipment and enhance WiFi capability and coverage, a number of upgrades were completed in the fall of 2021. First was to utilize one gigabyte per second internet service to the church, which included installing fiber optic cable to the premises. Next was the addition of an Ubiquiti Dream Machine controller and two managed 24-port Ubiquiti switches. The Improvers installed an enclosure high on the wall in the copier room for equipment. One switch handles the office workstations and nine WiFi Access Points, and the other 24-port switch handles the streaming system. This system provides for separate staff, guest, and streaming virtual networks, ensuring isolation between them for performance and security. More than 90 percent of the church gained good WiFi coverage.

Sanctuary Audio

By early 2005, the sound system in the sanctuary needed to be updated or replaced. The Property Committee was to spearhead the effort, with input from the Worship and Music Committee. Assuming about a $15,000 cost, half was to come from committee budgets and the remainder coming from the designated memorial fund from Elvina Loftness' bequest.

Three companies were brought in to make suggestions and bid on the work. Eventually, the Property Committee decided that, since construction was underway for the addition, it would make sense to work on the sound system while walls were open, making it easier to interconnect the sanctuary system with the new Gathering Space, the sound system in the new East Lounge, the new Music Room, and Lower Commons along with the existing Fellowship Hall in the basement.

The bids came in higher than originally anticipated. Immanuel's pastor at that time, John Marboe, spoke with the preferred vender EMI, explaining that the church had a specific amount of money available, and just simply did not have more. EMI graciously lowered their bid to Immanuel's maximum amount available, and work moved forward.

By February 2006, installation of the system was complete. This was a new technology. The new Bose line array speakers allowed for a more consistent sound throughout the sanctuary and had an easier user interface. This allowed for the removal of the giant horn-type speaker that had been above the altar arch area and the complicated soundboard that had been in the overcrowded choir loft. It also created a way to record services digitally, making it easier to make recordings available on CD to those who missed a service. Periodic software and hardware updates to the system over the years have improved the quality of the congregational experience and made it possible to use it as part of the new streaming setup.

Building Security

For many years, Immanuel did not lock its doors during normal daytime hours. This changed in around 1990. Several factors contributed to the daytime locked door policy. One was individuals entering when the doors were open and then using the building for overnight shelter, often surprising staff and members when they were happened upon. Some individuals were found sleeping in the pews, which led one member to ruefully comment that that happened on Sunday mornings, too! Another was petty theft during the daytime.

Once the doors were locked during Saturdays and weekdays, Immanuel member Peter Draine installed an intercom system in 1994 that allowed visitors to speak to the church office and be "buzzed in" by staff remotely opening the door for them. This system was handicapped by the fact that church staff could not see who was at the door or where they went in the building after they entered. A design feature of the 2006 Building Bridges remodeling project was to relocate the church administrator's office and provide it with large windows so the church administrator could visibly monitor both the South Snelling Avenue and parking lot entrances.

Another part of the 2006 remodeling was the installation of a security alarm system that covered the church office wing where most of the church's valuables were kept. When the alarm is tripped, Per Mar Security contacts one of several Immanuel member volunteers on the "call list" who makes the decision to investigate the alarm themselves or to have the Saint Paul Police called.

Relocation of the church administrator's office helped in monitoring the entrances, but visitors entering from the parking lot could only be seen after they had already entered the building and come up the stairs. This led to instances of "piggybacking" where one individual would speak on the intercom and come to the church office after being buzzed in, while a second unannounced accomplice would slip into the lower level undetected looking for items to steal.

The inability of staff to visually identify visitors before granting them entrance led to the investigation of a video security system for Immanuel in late 2019. The initial plan was to have video coverage of the two entrances, but Saint Paul Police recommended a system covering key stairways and passageways. Coverage also included children program areas and areas of potential theft, including coat racks, offices, and the parking lot. While video security companies were being interviewed, Immanuel members learned that the State of Minnesota was offering grants to nonprofits to improve their building security. Immanuel applied for a $13,380 grant to install a video security system and provide church security training for staff and key church volunteers.

The grant was awarded in January 2021 and, in November 2021, a 14-camera video security system with recording and remote access capability was completed. Respecting individual privacy was a key concern with the video security system. No audio is recorded and only public areas are viewed. The church council approved a use policy to closely control who has access to the system and how recorded images are to be used. Immanuel member Ron Struss oversaw the project from grant writing to aiming of cameras to drafting the policy on access and privacy.

Connecting during the COVID Pandemic

When the COVID pandemic shut down the facilities in March of 2020, Immanuel utilized an Apple iPhone to live stream from the sanctuary via Facebook. This setup had a number of challenges and had to evolve quickly. This transition required both creativity and coordination, and stretched everyone involved. Initially, Pastor Bullock preached to a camera from her home, and developed a whole new concept for structuring a worship service online.

Zoom (a video conferencing software) was initially used to provide access to the worship service, with people "signing in" as attendees (with their microphones turned off). A virtual "coffee hour" followed the service, allowing members to turn on their microphones and chat with each other, thus helping to maintain a sense of community. Emily King (Director of Children and Family Ministry) became a Zoom live stream producer and technician; Chris Cherwien (Director of Worship and Music) became both a recording engineer and choir director while recording hymns and special music on GarageBand software. Church members set up a safe and well-ventilated recording studio for choir members in the East Lounge, and Immanuel families often went outside their comfort zones to participate online from home. It was sometimes a stressful process, but one that helped Immanuel members worship together as a church community while the pandemic was keeping members apart.

2-19. *Screen shot of Pastor Cindy Bullock leading worship from home via Zoom (2020)*

2-20. *Setup for Pastor Bullock leading Zoom worship from her basement (2020)*

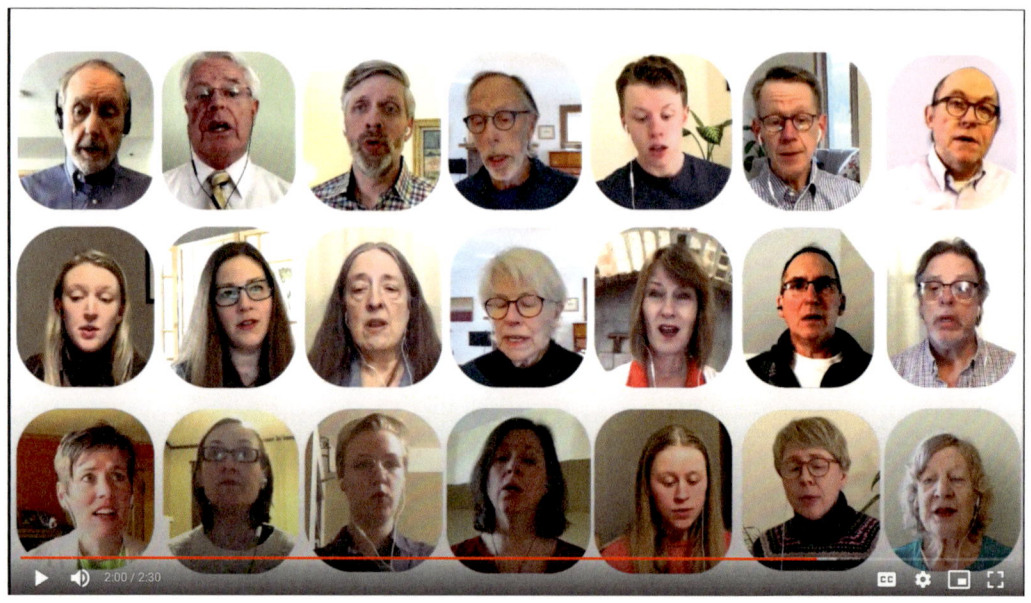

2-21. Choir singing for worship via Zoom from their homes (2020)

In the spring of 2021, it was evident that the pandemic was not going to be over soon, and that full Sunday in-person attendance was still far in the future. In the meantime, a partial opening, with restricted in-person attendance (100 people in the sanctuary) and a continued on-line service was the most viable direction. The Stream Team of members Brian Bullock, Joe Maniaci, Dale Fierke, Mark Thompson, and Mark Erickson took on the mission of researching, designing, testing, and implementing a system. The Team installed an operator's station in the conference room on the south side of the office corridor. In only a few months, the system was live, broadcasting to Immanuel's YouTube channel on Sunday mornings. The effort produces a very professional broadcast, and has already been mentioned by a family in the neighborhood looking for a church home after the pandemic. The technology allows Immanuel to live stream and record worship services, funerals, weddings, and other church events via the Immanuel website. The live stream network also is routed to existing equipment in the East Lounge, Gathering Space, and lower level Music Room. In June 2022, Ella Schmeits was hired to help the Stream Team.

Immanuel Facilities

2-22. Stream Team operators' station—Mark Thompson and Ella Schmeits, paid assistant (2022)

To support pandemic's social distancing guidelines, sanctuary overflow spaces have been made utilizing the East Lounge projector and Gathering Space TV by streaming audio/video feeds.

The system, as of November of 2021, consisted of three cameras, tally lights, analog to digital audio splitters, web cameras in the balcony, new microphones, a hand-built very robust computer, and miles of cables run to the control point in the conference room across from the staff offices—all controlled by VMix software.

Improvers

Interim Pastor Dana Nissen was the catalyst for starting the Improvers in 2000. He had started a similar group at his previous church in Chicago. While initially a group of men, participation is not limited by gender. Most Improvers are retired. The group, often called "The Imps," meets regularly on Thursdays, starting at 9 a.m. for coffee and sweet rolls, and working until noon. The primary purpose of Immanuel Improvers is to perform small, important maintenance projects that do not need to be hired out or contracted to an outside firm. The Improvers provide an opportunity for fellowship among Immanuel members, and save Immanuel a considerable amount of money during the year. The group has had a summer steak fry each summer for several years.

During the COVID pandemic, with the church building closed, the Improvers received permission from Immanuel's Reopening Committee to enter the building and provide regular maintenance while wearing masks. An important job was to help maintain the building's infrastructure so it would be a safe place to continue normal use when the building reopened. Following a protocol developed by the Property Team, the Improvers regularly ran water in drinking fountains and in all sinks, flushed all toilets, operated exhaust fans and air conditioners, poured water in all floor drains, ran the kitchen dishwasher, and checked refrigerators and freezers. In addition, they continued most of their regular tasks.

2-23. Improvers during COVID pandemic (2021)

Planting and Gardening

Over the years, church groups, families, and individuals have donated funds and volunteered time for church planting and gardening. In 1925, women in the church provided funds for shrubbery and flowers that were planted around the new church at Goodrich and Snelling Avenues.

At present, the grass, plants, and trees that are on three sides of the church building are cared for by the Property Committee, the Improvers, members Jerald (Jerry) Sandahl and Lee English, and a commercial mowing service. Of particular interest is the Joanne Sandahl Memorial Butterfly Garden, also known as the Peace Garden. It is located to the right of the entrance on South Snelling Avenue. Erik Mayre, Jerry's grandson, described the project in the *The Messenger* (Oct. 2003, v. 6, no. 10). In the center of the garden is a "peace pole" with "Peace" written in German, Norwegian, Danish, Swedish, Chinese, English, Braille, French, Hebrew, Dutch, Finnish, Korean, and Spanish. Jerry continues to tend to this wonderful garden, planting annuals, weeding, and replenishing the mulch as needed.

2-24. Peace garden

Many of you may remember Joanne Sandahl, better known to me and my brother as Happy Grandma. It was quite a loss when she died August 2, 2002. It left a big void in all our hearts. Happy Grandma loved butterflies and what they symbolized, "Transformation." So to remember her, we thought it would be good to create a butterfly garden here at Immanuel, where she loved to spend time worshipping God and making others "happy" with her hugs.

I was also at the time looking for an Eagle Scout service project. I wanted to do something that involved architecture or landscaping. I bought landscaping software and did research on butterfly garden plants. I came up with a plan and the church Property Committee approved it. The plan was also approved by the Eagle Project Council.

I then got a group of scouts and dug out the existing plants and shrubs and started to dig out the circle for the patio. We had the patio installed professionally so it would look nice. My Grandpa Jerry, an old Scoutmaster and master gardener in his own right, helped me buy the 52 butterfly attracting plants, including a number of plants called "Happy Return." With family, friends, and members of my Troop 31, we then planted the flowers and spread the mulch. You may have noticed the foot of the peace pole is in cement and there are pennies and rocks in it. The pennies represent that when we need help or feel low that Happy Grandma sends us a penny from heaven to lift us up. The rocks came from the north shore near Split Rock Lighthouse, which she loved very much.

Thanks for the memories, Happy! May Peace Prevail on Earth!

—Erik Mayre

In 2007, Lee English was chair of the Property Committee and noticed that the large planter (in front of the South Snelling entrance in which the sign is located) needed attention. He filled the planter with annuals and kept them weeded and watered—and has done so every year since then. He also began to maintain the two smaller planters of annuals on either side of the north entrance.

2-25. Planter in front of South Snelling Avenue entrance (2021)

2-26. Youth Bus Trip—Pastor John Lohre, youth, and chaperones (1980)

Immanuel Buses and Van

Immanuel had at least three buses over the years to pick up neighborhood children and bring them to Sunday School, take church women on social outings, and take youth on mission trips and to national Lutheran youth conventions. In 1950s, an Immanuel bus picked up children along Goodrich to bring to Sunday School. In 1961, Immanuel had two buses bringing children to Sunday School. The Lyngblomsten Circle bought a bus in the early 1970s. Immanuel member Eunice Baker drove the bus in 1985 when the Immanuel Lutheran Church Women went on a retreat to Green Lake Bible Camp. The old bus was retired in 1993 and a new (used) bus was purchased. Immanuel members Craig Fohrenkamm and John Gislason found the bus, and Craig painted and refurbished it at his body shop in 1994. Immanuel members Dick Sarafolean and Peter Draine drove the bus for many years on both long and short trips. A van was purchased in 1999 to facilitate outreach transportation, particularly for youth and seniors. The bus was sold in 2000. The van was sold in 2002.

CHAPTER 3

Worship, Music, and Art

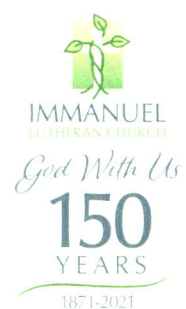

Worship Services

Church records suggest that services were held on Sunday and Wednesday evenings in the 1880s. In 1921, worship services were Sunday mornings at 10:45 with Sunday School at 9:30. Sunday morning services alternated between Norwegian and English. When the merger with Macalester Park and Trinity Lutheran churches was being considered, joint Sunday evening worship services alternated among the three locations for a time.

In 1945, Immanuel moved to two worship services on Sunday mornings. Communion was offered once a month alternating between the early and the later service.

In 1966, Immanuel began having three Sunday services. In 1977, six Lenten services were held at Macalester's Weyerhaeuser Chapel. In the fall of 1989, Immanuel tried two services with Sunday School at the same time as the first service. Students attended the 8:45 service with their parents for the first 15 minutes and were then dismissed to their classes.

Immanuel experimented with Saturday evening (Wednesdays in the summer) contemporary services beginning in 1993. Attendance was never more than 30 and usually only around 10. This supplemental service was discontinued in 1995.

In 1993, Immanuel moved to two Sunday services with an hour between services for education. There was some concern about children disrupting the services, but this was outweighed by parents wanting their children to attend the worship service and freeing pastoral staff for adult education opportunities at the same time as Sunday School.

In 2020, in response to the COVID pandemic, Immanuel moved to a single service, initially offered online only and, as gathering in-person restrictions eased, to a single hybrid service offered both online and in person.

Liturgical Year

Immanuel's worship services adhere to the liturgical year, with the colors of the altar and pulpit paraments and pastor's stole changing with the liturgical seasons. Immanuel's liturgical practices have evolved and changed over the years. The specific practices described below are examples of the manner in which Immanuel has observed the liturgical year over time.

The church year begins with Advent, the season of waiting and preparation for Christ's birth, which is observed the four Sundays before Christmas Day. The color is blue—for hope. For several years, an Advent wreath, with candles symbolizing the passage of the four weeks of Advent, has been located near the nave. An additional candle is lit on each subsequent Sunday until, by the last Sunday of Advent, all four candles are lit. A fifth Christ candle is lit at Christmas Eve.

The liturgical color of Christmas is white; all festivals and high holy days are white, symbolizing joy and celebration. Immanuel has celebrated

3-1. Christmas Eve at Immanuel

Christmas Eve with a candlelight service for many years. Those attending are given small candles, which are lit near the end of the service and the sanctuary lights are extinguished. Lit only by these candles and those on the altar, the congregation traditionally sings "Silent Night."

Epiphany concludes the 12 days of Christmas and is the traditional end of the Christmas season. White remains until after Epiphany. The time after Epiphany continues until Lent. Most of the Sundays during this time are "ordinary" Sundays, from the word "ordinal" or "counted," as in "the 3rd Sunday after Epiphany." All ordinary Sundays are green, the color of growth and representing growth in the Christian faith.

The penitential forty-day season of Lent begins with Ash Wednesday, when ashes, representing mortality, are applied to the forehead of those attending the worship service if they wish. Immanuel holds Wednesday evening service during Lent. Lent hymns and services do not use the joyful expression "Alleluia." Flowers are not placed on the altar. An Immanuel tradition is for the children to hide the Alleluia banner until the Easter vigil when it is used to lead a procession into the sanctuary. The liturgical color for this season of the church year is purple—the color of penitence.

Holy Week starts with Palm Sunday. Immanuel begins the Palm Sunday service by assembling outside or in the Gathering Space and processing into the sanctuary waving palm branches. The altar is stripped at the end of the Maundy Thursday service and will remain bare through the Good Friday service until it is re-dressed with white for the celebrations of the Saturday evening Easter Vigil and the Easter Sunday Festival Worship that marks the beginning of the Easter season. Immanuel holds an Easter Vigil service the Saturday evening before Easter Sunday. It consists of a "Service of Light," Bible readings, often a Baptism, and Holy Communion. The 50-day Easter season is celebrated with white or gold (or white and gold) paraments, symbolizing joy and celebration. For many years, Immanuel members have ordered blooming spring plants that decorate the nave and can be taken home after the service.

The Easter season ends with Pentecost, for which the liturgical color is bright red. The red paraments are a reminder of the fire of the Holy Spirit. All the Sundays after Pentecost until Advent are designated the 2nd, 3rd, 4th, Sunday after Pentecost, etc., and the color returns to green.

3-2. Easter Vigil (2015)

3-3. The sanctuary at Christmas

Sacraments

Lutherans recognize two sacraments—Holy Communion and Holy Baptism, which are called the means of grace. Immanuel offers Communion at every Sunday worship service and occasionally at other services. All are welcome. Those that do not take Communion may come forward and receive a blessing. If someone is unable to come forward and wishes to receive Communion, the ushers notify the pastor, who takes the sacrament to the individual where he or she is sitting.

Lutherans baptize by sprinkling or pouring water on the head of the person or infant. As part of the sacrament of Holy Baptism, the sponsors and the congregation affirm their own Baptism. The Baptism of infants is a joyous service at Immanuel. The pastor invites all children present to come forward so they can see what is happening. At the conclusion, the pastor usually walks up and down the aisle and presents the newly baptized infant to the congregation.

3-4. Pastor Cindy Bullock inviting the congregation to Communion (2019)

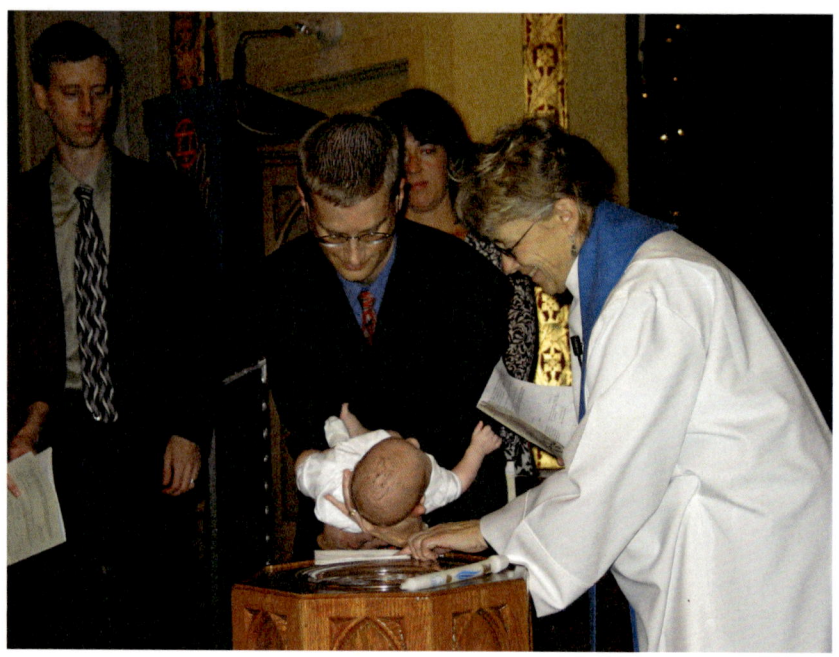

3-5. Pastor Joy Bussert baptizing infant (2006)

3-6. Pastor Cindy Bullock walking with newly baptized infant (2015)

Weddings

Weddings are a covenant made between two people—a lifelong promise of faithfulness made before God and the community. Immanuel welcomes any couple wishing to be married in the sanctuary, provided they complete a pre-marriage course with or approved by the pastor and have a legal marriage license. Immanuel offers wedding coordinators for consultation about wedding details such as use of church facilities, the order of service, decorations, receiving lines, etc. The coordinator helps with the rehearsal and is available to make sure the service runs smoothly on the day of the wedding. The Immanuel sanctuary has been the site of many joy-filled weddings over the decades.

Immanuel weddings over the years

3-7.1 David Lindgren and Ragna Wangensteen (1939)

3-7.2 Lester Leonardson and and Maxine Franson #1 (1946)

3-7.3 Lester Leonardson and Maxine Franson #2 (1946)

3-7.4 Pastor Einar Roald Carlson, Vernon (Bud) Jorgensen, and Betty Peterson (1958)

3-7.5 Vernon (Bud) Jorgensen and Betty Person #2 (1958)

3-7.6 Lee English, Peggy Johnson, and Odell and Virginia Johnson (1978)

3-7.7 Paul Larson & Julie Bentley with Pastor Elder and Esther Bentley (1994)

3-7.8 Joe Dufresne and Lori Hogenson (1996)

3-7.9 Steven King and Emily Smith (2006)

3-7.10 Kristopher Evenson and Sonja Forhenkamm (2010)

Ushers

Immanuel's ushers are essential for smoothly running worship services. Currently under the oversight on the Worship and Music Team, the ushers greet people as they arrive for service and distribute Sunday bulletins and the weekly "News and Notes." They pass the offering plates during the service and guide people forward for Communion. On Easter and Christmas, they work diligently to find seating for all. Ushers normally serve for a month at a time.

3-8. Immanuel ushers—Lyle Baker, Dean Hughes, John Kubesh, George Koerner, Doug Wangensteen, Jerry Sandahl, Bill Short, Bernice Maas, Millie Chapman (2007)

Both men and women usher and sometimes their children assist. Ushers are trained to deal with emergencies quietly and effectively. Before Immanuel added air conditioning to the sanctuary, people occasionally fainted during summer services. Ushers would get the individual out of the sanctuary in a wheelchair and alert one of the physician members in the congregation, who quickly determined if more care was needed. Most often, the rest of the attending congregation were unaware of the activity

Immanuel Membership

The definition of "members" has varied over the years. The data below are taken from Immanuel Lutheran Church annual reports and church records. Sometimes, the information specifies simply "members" or "confirmed members." Immanuel periodically reviews the membership and removes members who have died, transferred out, or become inactive—and adds new members as they join and youth as they are confirmed.

1871	9 members
1880	28 members
1925	328 confirmed members
1935	625 confirmed members
1950	1000 confirmed members
1957	882 members
1959	937 confirmed members
1960	1195 confirmed members (merger with Highland Park Lutheran added 248 confirmed members)
1966	1165 confirmed members
1967	1591 confirmed members
1970	1674 confirmed members
1980	1177 confirmed members
1983	1166 confirmed members
1989	1112 confirmed members
1992	1022 confirmed members
1996	896 confirmed members
2007	641 confirmed members
2020	568 confirmed members

Declining membership over the last 30 years reflects national trends. The Evangelical Lutheran Church in America reported the loss of more than 425,000 members and 450 congregations between 2011 and 2017.

Altar Guild

◦ *They that wait upon the Lord shall renew their strength, they shall mount up with wings as eagles. They shall run and not be weary, and they shall walk and not faint. Isaiah 40:31. (quotation in the original Altar Guild secretary's book)*

The original Altar Guild secretary's book, covering January 1955 through January 1961, begins with a brief history, noting that the Immanuel Altar Society was organized by women in the church in January 1945 and was first called "The Immanuel Altar Guild." In December of that year, the Immanuel Ladies Aid Society changed its name to "The Immanuel Women's Guild." Later to avoid confusion, the Altar Guild was renamed "The Immanuel Altar Society." At that time, the stated purpose of the organization was "to care for the altar, the various appointments pertaining thereto, and to be of assistance to the Pastor." This organization represented the first time anyone other than the pastor was allowed to prepare the altar. The original officers were: Pastor Conrad Thompson, president; Mrs. H.A. Arne, vice president; Mrs. R.S. Frigstad, treasurer; and Mrs. H.A. Daum, secretary. Flowers for the altar were provided by a local florist or by members' contributions from their gardens. After services, flowers were distributed to shut-ins or members who were hospitalized.

The Altar Society consisted of 12 members and usually met monthly either at a member's home or at the church, where the group cleaned and prepared the church for church holidays (primarily Easter and Christmas). Meetings included a devotion and often a "dessert luncheon." The group made decisions about ordering additional Communion glasses, purchased robes and stoles for the pastors, selected furnishings for the sacristy, and made linen baptismal towels. They scheduled members to prepare the sanctuary and wash up after Communion on Sunday, and ensured that flowers were on the altar and delivered to recipients (shut-ins and ill) after services. The Altar Society minutes report two contentious topics. Should artificial palms be used one Palm Sunday when the florist could not provide real ones? The decision was "no." Should plastic covers be used on top of the altar cloth to protect it? This was discussed for several months, but the topic was tabled and no decision was recorded. The name of the Altar Society was changed back to the Altar Guild in 1961 when the various women's groups at Immanuel and Highland Park Lutheran Church merged and changed their name to the Immanuel Lutheran Church Women (ILCW).

WORSHIP, MUSIC, ART

3-9. Altar Guild—Ina Kubesh, Jan Thorson, Bonnie Edhlund (coordinator), and Margaret Le Bien (2007)

Today, the Altar Guild (now consisting of men, women, and sometimes families) continues to prepare the "holy things" used during worship. Duties include purchasing supplies (wine, wafers, candles, etc.) in conjunction with the Worship and Music Team. They prepare for Communion and set up the altar each Sunday and before other services at which Communion is served. They prepare and maintain the altar paraments, candles, and other accessories used during worship services. For several years, the Altar Guild has coordinated a "spring cleaning" of the sanctuary, usually a couple weeks before Easter. It is a time to polish the silver, brass, and woodwork, dust everything, shine windows, etc. For many years, the Altar Guild has coordinated flowers (donated by congregation members) on the altar each Sunday and handled the Easter blooming plants and Christmas poinsettias (member-purchased) that decorate the chancel.

The Altar Guild Secretary's Book, referenced above, lists the following Altar Guild presidents (1955–1961): Mrs. Frank Lawson, Mrs. James Forchtner, Bertha Sorem, Prudence L. Fon, Isabel Korsmo, Mrs. Ken (Beryl) Berg, Cora Oss, Mrs. Leora Grinde, and Mrs. Morgan Anderson. In recent years, the following have been coordinators of the Altar Guild: Eunice Johnson,

Betty Jorgensen, June Husom, Rachel Husom, Angela Lewis, Margaret LeBien, Sue Browender, Diane Valure, Bonnie Edhlund, Jan Johnshoy, and Tenley Johnson. The management of roles for the Altar Guild have recently been reorganized. The original single coordinator position was split into multiple roles: altar prep coordinator (Kari Olson), altar flowers coordinator (Kathleen Raiter), and supply coordinator (David Stark).

Music

❦ I would gladly see all arts, especially music, in the service of Him who has given and created them. —Martin Luther, quoted in Leslie P. Spelman, "Luther and the Arts," Journal of Aesthetics and Art Criticism *10, no. 2 (Dec. 1951):167*

Music has been an important part of Lutheran worship from the time of Martin Luther. When Luther reformed the liturgy, he accorded full importance to the sermon and to community singing. He is credited with writing more than 40 hymns, the most famous of which is *Ein feste Burg ist unser Gott* (*A Mighty Fortress is Our God*). Community singing, called "choral singing," was defined as an assertion of faith, and a spiritual commentary on biblical texts. It could be backed by an organ (chamber organs at the time) or by an instrumental group.

Hymnals

Revisions of worship resources for congregations have taken place intermittently over the three centuries Lutherans have been on the North American continent. Lutherans came in waves of immigrants from different parts of Germany and Scandinavia, settling in many parts of North America. Each group brought their own doctrines, structures, and worship practices. Over the past few centuries, these small church bodies have gradually merged in various configurations. In the twentieth century, the consolidation of various immigrant Lutheran church bodies and those more established in the United States was reflected in the primary worship books used by the mid-century, namely *The Lutheran Hymnal* (1941) and the *Service Book and Hymnal* (1958).

In 1978, *Lutheran Book of Worship* was published, the fruit of an ambitious inter-Lutheran project that sought to unite most North American Lutherans in the use of a single worship book with shared liturgical forms and a common repertoire of hymnody. In 1988, the Evangelical Lutheran Church in America (ELCA) was formed from three predecessor churches, resulting in the largest Lutheran church in North America. In the fall of 2000, the Church Council

3-10. Rebekah Schulz, Minister of Music, with Evangelical Lutheran Worship, *the new "cranberry" hymnal (2007)*

of the ELCA authorized a church-wide effort to define and develop a new and common approach to primary worship resources to be supportive of the entire ELCA for the next generation. The result was the *Evangelical Lutheran Worship* (2006). One member remembers Ray Peterson standing in the lectern at one worship service when the new hymnals were introduced and explaining how to care for them. He held up an older hymnal and first folded a page corner, then wrote on a page, then tore a page—to an audible gasp from the congregation.

Immanuel has used many different hymnals over the years. The office of the Director of Worship and Music contains an extensive collection of hymnals, many used by Immanuel and some of which came from Highland Park Lutheran Church and were likely used before the merger. Others came from other churches or were gifts, and are retained as resources. The following is a list of hymnals and song collections likely used for services and in Sunday School at Immanuel and Highland Park.

The Lutheran Hymnary, published by authority of the Norwegian Evangelical Lutheran Synod, The Hauge's Evangelical Lutheran Synod, and the United Norwegian Lutheran Church of America. Decorah, IA: Lutheran

Publishing; Red Wing, MN: Hauge's Synod Book Department; Minneapolis: Augsburg Publishing House, 1913. (navy/black)

The Lutheran Hymnary, Including Symbols of the Evangelical Lutheran Church. Minneapolis: Augsburg Publishing, 1913 and 1935. (blue)

School Carols: A Collection of Hymns for the Sunday Schools. Columbus, OH: Lutheran Book Concern, 1914. (tan)

Hymns for Church Schools. Minneapolis, Augsburg Publishing, 1929. (softcover, blue)

The Concordia Hymnal: A Hymnal for Church, School, and Home, 7th edition. Minneapolis: Augsburg Publishing, 1937. (navy blue)

The Lutheran Hymnal, Authorized by the Synods Constituting the Evangelical Lutheran Synodical Conference of North America. St. Louis, MO: Concordia Publishing, 1941. (blue) Note: At the time of publication, members of the Evangelical Lutheran Synodical Conference of North America were: the Lutheran Church–Missouri Synod, Wisconsin Evangelical Lutheran Synod, the Synod of Evangelical Lutheran Churches, and the Evangelical Lutheran Synod (formerly the Norwegian Synod).

Songs for Children: A Collection of Hymns and Other Songs for Smaller Children to Be Used in Church School and Home. Minneapolis: Augustana, 1942, 5th printing 1947. (red)

Junior Hymnal Containing Sunday School and Luther League Liturgy and Hymns for the Sunday School and Other Gatherings. Rock island, IL: Augustana Book Concern, 1938, 15th printing 1957. (green)

Songs of Praise for Sunday School, Church Societies, and the Home, edited by Emmanuel Poppen. Columbus, OH: Wartburg Press, 1935. 22nd printing 1957. (light green)

Pilgrim Hymnal. Boston: Pilgrim, Press, 1931, 1935, 1958.

Hymns and Songs for Church Schools, edited by Ruth Olson. Minneapolis: Augsburg Publishing, 1962. (red)

Service Book and Hymnal of the Lutheran Church in America, authorized by the Lutheran Churches cooperating in The Commission on the Liturgy and Hymnal. Minneapolis: Augsburg Publishing, 1958, 12th printing 1969. (red) Note: The churches involved were: The American Evangelical Lutheran Church, The American Lutheran Church, The Augustana Evangelical Lutheran Church, The Evangelical Lutheran Church, The Finnish Evangelical Lutheran Church in American, The Lutheran Free Church, The United Evangelical Lutheran Church, and The United Lutheran Church in America.

Living Praise Hymnal, compiled by John W. Peterson. Grand Rapids, MIL Singspiration Music, 1974. (red)

Lutheran Book of Worship, prepared by the churches participating in the Inter-Lutheran Commission on Worship: Lutheran Church in America, The American Lutheran Church, The Evangelical Lutheran Church of Canada, The Lutheran Church—Missouri Synod. Minneapolis: Augsburg Publishing 1978. (green) Immanuel's copies for the sanctuary were purchased by members.

With One Voice: A Lutheran Resource for Worship. Minneapolis: Augsburg Fortress, 1995. (softcover, dark navy/black) Three hundred copies of this supplemental worship book and song collection were purchased in 1995 through individual family sponsorships.

Evangelical Lutheran Worship. Minneapolis: Augsburg Fortress, 2006. "commended for use in the Evangelical Lutheran Church in America . . . [and] a . . . approved for use in the Evangelical Lutheran Church in Canada." (cranberry) Immanuel began using this book in 2007. It was funded by members, who purchased volumes as dedications or memorials.

Choirs

Immanuel has had choirs since at least 1917, when church archives report that David Anderson was the choir director. When Immanuel's current building was built in 1925, seating for the choir was planned for the semi-transept. At that time, the choir had 35 members.

Immanuel has had a "senior" choir of adults and a children's choir for several decades and, at different times, a men's choir and a women's choir. Often the senior choir and the children's choir had different directors. The various choirs have had different names over the years: Cherub Choir (the youngest singers), Junior Choir, Senior Choir, Treble Choir, Youth Choir, Maranatha Singers, Chapel Choir, Carol Choir, Cantorei Choir, Choristers Choir, KinderChor, Hosanna Singers, and perhaps others.

3-11. Norman Heitz, Choir Director, with Senior Choir (ca. 1979)

3-12. Hosanna Children's Choir (2013)

3-13. Chorister Children's Choir (2012)

3-14. "Rejoice—A Witness" complete cast (1977)

Directors have had the title Choir Director, Music Director, Minister of Music, and—more recently—Director of Worship and Music. Directors often also have directed the handbell choirs. In 2010, Rebekah Schulz, who was hired as part-time Director of Music and Worship in 2006, became the fulltime Minister of Music. David Stark has had one of the longest, although intermittent, tenures as choir director: from 1984 to 1993, and then as interim director in 2005–2006 and again in 2011–2012. Appendix F lists Choir Directors, Ministers of Worship and Music, and Directors of Music and Worship.

In 1955, the Senior Choir was invited to appear as a solo choir at the St. Olaf College Music Festival. In 1975, the High School Choir had 22 members.

Connie Youngdahl, choir director beginning in 1976, formed the Maranatha Singers (9th through 12th graders), who performed "Rejoice—A Witness," a 32-minute cantata. The music was composed by Immanuel member Dawn Villars Hilbert. It was described as a musical witness to Christ with each of the 12 original musical offerings preceded by scripture passages. The songs were accompanied by piano and two flutes. From early 1977 to late 1979, "Rejoice" was presented in more than 25 churches (Lutheran, Catholic, Episcopal, Methodist, and Congregational) and rest homes. The group traveled to Stewartville and St. Peter, Minnesota; Sioux Falls, South Dakota; and Shell Lake, Wisconsin. The Wisconsin performance was broadcast. Tapes were prepared and sold with proceeds given to cancer research at the University of Minnesota. During the almost three years of its existence, older members graduated and went off to college and younger Immanuel members joined. "Rejoice" is a remembered as "treasured highlight in the lives of those Immanuel youth who were able to participate."

In 1995, the Immanuel choir joined with the choirs of Macalester Plymouth and Pilgrim Lutheran Churches to perform the Handel's *Messiah*.

Andrew Birling, choir director 2000–2005 and organist 2004–2005, also composed choral music, hymns, handbell music, and music for the responsive singing of psalms during Sunday services. He gave several organ recitals.

In 2010, Immanuel had the following choirs and ensembles: Cantorei (adult choir), Jubilate Ringers, Seraphim Ringers, and Choristers. Increasing numbers required splitting the Choristers (children's choir) into two groups: a Kindergarten/1st grade choir and a 2nd–6th grade choir. Due to an already-full-Wednesday evening rehearsal schedule, these choirs rehearsed simultaneously, with the organist, Megan Engel, conducting the Kindergarden/1st grade choir and Rebekah Schulz, Minister of Music, conducting the older choir.

During Rebekah Schultz's tenure (2006–2011), Immanuel offered additional music opportunities for children in the church and the larger community. Kindermusik offered music classes for children from birth to age 7. Although tuition was charged, Immanuel provided financial support, and classes were offered at a fraction of the normal tuition rates. In 2010, Kindermusik offered five classes attended by 23 children (21 families). Fifteen of the 21 families were not members of Immanuel. Rebekah also provided a "music club" for elementary students and offered a summer "choir camp."

Also in 2010, Immanuel provided music outreach through an intergenerational "sing and ring" for three hours on December 4, when 22 Immanuel musicians of all ages were stationed outside the Kowalksi's grocery store on Grand Avenue to sing carols and ring chimes for the Salvation Army. In many years, Immanuel has held an intergenerational caroling event with members of all ages bringing Christmas cheer to homebound members.

At the present time, Cantorei, Immanuel's adult choir, leads worship on most Sundays from September to May as well as at festival services. The choir learns a wide variety of choral repertoire from many different genres, hymns, and liturgy as needed to lead worship. The Cantorei choir practices once a week September to May. The senior choir was part of ecumenical Thanksgiving services for many years, ending in 2015. The Cantorei choir sang Bach's "Dona Nobis Pacem" with 120 others at the Cathedral of St. Paul in 2001.

Brass players (grade 9 and up) usually play four times a year. Immanuel has a Flute Choir (also grade 9 and up) that provides music in worship three to four times throughout the year. Soloists also provide music during worship, playing lute, guitar, marimba, oboe, and clarinet.

3-15. *Seth Harris playing the marimba (2021).*

The Choristers Choir is for children in 2nd–6th grades. Games, singing, vocal technique, and music theory are part of their time together. The Choristers have performed a musical each spring for several years, usually performing at the church and at Lyngblomsten for senior residents. These have included:

2013 "The Rock Slinger and His Greatest Hit"
2014 "Malice in the Palace"
2015 "Rescue in the Night"
2016 "Oh, Jonah"
2017 "A Technicolor Promise"
2018 "Malice in the Palace" (2nd time)
2019 "The Rock Slinger and His Greatest Hit" (2nd time)
. . .   No cantatas because of the COVID pandemic
2022 "The Sailor's Bible"

3-16. "Malice in the Palace" (2014)

Teens continue their musical growth in the Middle C Choir for youth in 7th–12th grades. This group leads the congregation in worship once a month and prepares a larger work in the mid-winter. The Middle C Choir presented the following cantatas in the early spring:

2016 "A Tale of Three Trees"
2017 "Life of the Party"
2018 "Welcome Back, Billy Best" (as a dinner and show)

This choir also rings handbells occasionally.

3–17. *"A Tale of Three Trees" (2016)*

Kinderchor is for children in kindergarten and 1st grade and is a part of the Sunday School hour each Sunday. The children explore their emerging singing voices through games and other activities. Kinderchor sings in worship occasionally at the Sunday service.

Hosanna Singers (preschool choir) meets during the Sunday School hour. Rhythm, pitch matching, and singing songs are a part of this beginning choir. Hosanna Singers sing in worship four times a year.

Immanuel choirs have joined other local choirs for special performances. In 1992, The Immanuel choir joined with choirs from St. Paul's Episcopal Church and Macalester Plymouth United Church to perform Dvorak's *Mass* at St. Paul's. In 2002, the choirs of Immanuel, Pilgrim, and Macalester-Plymouth combined for a performance of John Rutter's *Requiem*.

The Cantorei and Middle C Choirs, along with instrumentalists and soloists, performed the cantata, "A New Creation," by Rene Clausen on Sunday, February 24, 2019.

Organs

The women of Immanuel contributed $100 to a pipe organ fund in 1907. At that time worship was being held in the brick church in downtown Saint Paul at 14th and Canada. This is the first mention of an organ in Immanuel's church records.

In 1926, a self-contained reed organ was installed in the new church building at Goodrich and Snelling Avenues. In 1929, a Page theater pipe organ was installed with the organ console located in the chancel steps area. The Senior League helped with the organ fund. By 1929, they had raised $3,000 by selling organ pipes at $10.00 each. The women purchased 20 pipes for the organ with a donation of $200. The choir loft was located to the right in the semitransept area. The organ pipes were located in the ceiling about five to six rows of pews from the front of the sanctuary. The organ sound emanated through a grilled opening (still present) in the ceiling. Immanuel member Mark Anderson remembers that when he was a child in the 1960s, children would get to the church early Sunday morning, climb a ladder up into the bell tower behind the grate, and listen to the sermon from there. They had to be very quiet.

In 1952, the organ console and choir were moved to the rear balcony, while the pipes remained in their sanctuary front ceiling location. The organ console was placed on the right-hand side of the balcony as one is looking up from the lower congregation worship area.

In 1969, a new M.P. Moeller organ was installed in the balcony, having eleven ranks of pipes, which were later increased to fourteen ranks. It used both leather and plastic mechanical valves, with an electro-magnetic action. The organ console was relocated to the left side of the balcony. Since the upper ceiling was so low, some of the long bass pedal pipes had to be "bent" over (mitered) in order to fit into the limited space. Over the years, some of those large pipes began to split and collapse under their own weight.

During the late 1980s, the organ was revamped, and new pipes were added. While the organ was not operative, Immanuel members Vernon (Bud) and Betty Jorgensen lent their own organ to the church. On November 5, 1989, a renovated organ, rebuilt by Karl Eilers, was re-dedicated. The mitered bass pipes were straightened out and relocated to the "peak" of the ceiling where there was more room. All the pipes were raised up to permit them to sound out into the sanctuary area more effectively. The entire pipe swell chamber was completely redesigned. Seventeen electronic "ranks" of sounds were added. Unfortunately, over the years, the electronic sounds broke down, and became unusable.

In 2009, rather than repairing the electronic sounds, the entire organ was discarded and replaced with the present Allen digital electronic organ. It was installed in October and dedicated on Christ the King Sunday November 22, 2009.

Immanuel has had several talented organists over the years. Chelsie Heiden Jorgensen played the organ from 1925–1966, with numerous breaks for health issues. Vernon Jorgensen remembers that Harold Jacobson (organist from 1967–1978) often played two verses of a Sunday hymn and then stopped playing while the congregation continued in four-part harmony without accompaniment. Other organists have done the same in the intervening years. Larry Wilson, who served from 1978–1998, is likely the longest continually serving organist. He had a rule that no one could talk to him during the liturgy. He reported that one Sunday, someone said something to him and he got totally lost. Pastor Elder Bentley called up to him in the balcony, "Larry, we are on page 77." Appendix G lists Immanuel organists.

3-18. Chelsie Heiden Jorgensen, organist (1946)

Handbells

The worship services at Immanuel have been greatly enriched by handbell choirs over the past 41 years. The congregation has purchased five octaves of handbells and three octaves of choirchimes in this period. This is remarkable, given that handbells in the United States were first manufactured in the early 1970s. Immanuel's handbell choir began in 1980 with the purchase of three octaves of bells. Norm Heitz was the first director. The original five ringers were Barb Columbus, Shirley Evans, Chris Otteson, Terri Peterson, and Claire Taylor Sherman. The handbell choir met in a small room outside the balcony. In 1985, Janet Cruse took over as the handbell director. Deb Ahlquist joined the original five with baby Elsa in tow. The choir was expanding and needed more room, so it started rehearsing in the Pine Room. In 1993, Sarah Birkeland became the director, and the group expanded to ten ringers. This choir recorded a CD, "Lord, I Ring My Praise to Thee," and participated in two bell festivals. Rick Paulsen became the fourth director in 1999, followed by Andrew Birling in 2000 and Rebekah Schulz in 2007. Chris Cherwien was hired in 2012 and is the current director.

3-19. Handbell choir (2006)

The addition of choirchimes at Immanuel in 1993 allowed for the expansion of the bell program to the children and youth. Choirchimes have a different tone than handbells and are perfect for children and youth because they are very durable. They also provide a wonderful contrast in a musical piece.

In 1998, Immanuel had Junior High Bells, Children's Bells, Glory (afternoon) Ringers, and Jubilate (evening) Ringers.

In 2002, Immanuel made a large purchase of 37 bells with cases, tables, and pads to replace a mismatched set of handbells from two manufacturers, which were sold. Since then, Immanuel added to the number of handbells and choirchimes. The latest addition was in February 2020 when Immanuel purchased four large bass bells plus the case to store them in, a table, and table pads.

Many children, youth, and adults have participated in the handbell program since it began. Jubilate Ringers is a bell choir for high school students and adults. This group prepares handbell anthems as well as occasional accompaniments for hymns and psalms. The Jubilate Ringers were part of a Bell-Fest in 2002, a massed bell choir directed by Bill Alexander, handbell director at First United Methodist Church (Duluth), and director of Strikepoint, an international touring handbell ensemble. In 2021, the Jubilate Ringers joined the National Lutheran Choir for the 36th annual Christmas festival at the Basilica of St. Mary in Minneapolis. At the time of this writing, the Jubilate Ringers play in worship once a month.

Art

A "hobby and art show" was held in the courtyard in 1967. The current spring art show was started in 2002 by then choir director Andrew Birling. Congregation members of all ages are invited to display their creative works. The Spring art show took a pause during the 2005/06 remodeling project and resumed in 2007, under the guidance of Immanuel member David Alstead. The art show was "virtual" in 2020 and 2021 during the COVID pandemic. In 2022, the show was both onsite and virtual.

In the fall of 2002, Immanuel started an "Arts at Immanuel" series (later called "Arts and Music") of monthly events to share music, spoken word, and visual arts with the congregation and the larger community. The first event, Jazz and Java with the Things Quartet, transformed the fellowship hall into a coffeehouse for an evening of hot java and cool jazz, benefiting Rezek House for homeless teens. One performance by Andrew Birling (Immanuel organist), called "The Killer B's," offered an afternoon of organ music at Macalester-Plymouth United Church featuring Bach, Buxtehude, Barber, and others. In 2004, the series included outside musical groups, a children's performance of "O Jonah," and an "Open Mike Night." Open Mike Night continued for many years. Immanuel member Bernice Maas sang "I'm only a Bird in a Gilded Cage" at an Open Mike Night. Bernice, who was famous for her hats (many made for a special occasion), wore a hat that looked like a birdcage and covered her entire body. Bernice was the hit of the evening.

3-20. Art show (2002)

Immanuel has been fortunate to be able to provide space for an "Artist in Residence," Chillon Leach, beginning in 2009. Chillon has designed covers for church bulletins; paraments for the altar, pulpit, and lectern; and stoles for the pastors. She also created a cremation urn pall to be used during Immanuel's funeral services. She has made line illustration artwork for children and choir members to color and paint, as well as original artwork that is exhibited in the church public spaces. She works with various church committees that need creative input or artwork for various projects, such as the hand-painted supply bags for the Dementia Friendly team. She also gives presentations, leads forums, offers classes, helps with the annual Music and Arts Camp, and offers support for Immanuel members' personal creativity. While in residence most weekdays, she also has been on hand for any volunteer support the Immanuel staff may need on short notice. In addition to this type of broader arts ministry, Chillon utilizes the studio space creating artwork and hand painted textiles that she exhibits in various locations and events around the Twin Cities, giving publicly expressed exposure to Immanuel's support of having an artist-in-residence. Chillon completed an inventory of Immanuel's art and its provenance as part of the 150th anniversary of Immanuel.

3-21. Bernice Maas wearing a Christmas hat with working lights (1991)

3-22. Easter altar paraments and banner created by Chillon Leach (2016)

CHAPTER 4

Christian Education and Programming

Children and Youth

Sunday School

Sunday School has been an important part of Christian education at Immanuel since its beginning. The need for Sunday School classes closer to family homes in the Summit and Snelling area was the impetus for forming Macalester Park Lutheran Church, which soon merged with Immanuel. It was also a factor in the building of the East Immanuel church as an extension of the downtown Immanuel congregation in 1886. The need for more space for Sunday School rooms was the primary reason for construction of the 1961 Education Building, which added 23 classrooms.

The June 1919 Immanuel newsletter, *Hyrderösten (Shepherds' Voice)*, reported that Sunday School would be held every Sunday throughout the summer. In 1933, Immanuel started providing envelopes for student offering to train children for church giving later in life. In that year, Sunday School was held every Sunday except for six Sundays in the summer. There were 180 students, with 18 teachers and two seminary students assisting. In 1936, there were three weeks of religion school during the summer. In 1947, a house was purchased at 104 South Snelling to be used as a Parish House for additional Sunday School space.

4-1. *Children's' Sunday School (ca. 1930)*

Immanuel ceased summer Sunday School in 1950. The 1950s and 1960s were blessed with larger numbers of children in Sunday School. In 1955, there were 278 students and 24 teachers. Sunday School had to be conducted in two shifts, except for Pre-K, all of whom stayed with Mrs. Solfest (Clara) Aalbue, who was very popular. By 1958, three sessions of Sunday School were held—at 8:30, 9:30, and 11:00. The basement was divided into four classrooms; classes also met in the kitchen, the pastor's study, the church office, the stage, the balcony, and rooms on the second floor. Some classes were held in various Immanuel parish houses near to the church building over the years.

Mrs. Nellie Berry taught Sunday School for more than 50 years. In 1963, she received a plaque and a Bible from the Lutheran Council. She also taught release time Christian school on Wednesdays.

A Miss Christiansen (first name not known), who had been a member of Macalester Park Lutheran Church, appears to have served as co-superintendent of the Sunday School at the time of the merger in 1920. Rachel Husom was the first woman solo Sunday School superintendent (1964–1973). June Husom was Sunday School secretary and treasurer for 40 years—1956–1996.

In 1949, the Sunday School children donated $100 to a mission school in South Africa. They used their new "Light of the World" bank in the form of a lighthouse for collecting money.

For many years, the opening Sunday School music worship was led by the choir directors or directors of worship and music. Immanuel member Kathy Brudevold served as accompanist for K–7th grade Sunday School for several years. In the 1980s and 1990s, Immanuel members Judie Prayfrock and Sandy

CHRISTIAN EDUCATION AND PROGRAMMING

4-2. *Nellie Berry receiving service award—Pastor Roald Carlson, M.H. Thornton, Nellie Berry, Pastor John Adrian Pfeiffer (1963)*

4-3. *Rachel Husom teaching Sunday School (1962)*

4-4. Sheryl Goldberg teaching Sunday School (1980)

Hamburge were in charge of the Sunday School Christmas programs and wrote at least one of them. Programs included :
    1990 "Hark, The Herald Angel"
    1991 "God's Rainbow Promises of Christmas"
    1993 "Wise Guys and Starry Skies"
    1997 "He Is Coming Soon!"

Judie and Sandy also directed a spring Easter drama, "This Man Jesus," with Janet Cruse (children's choir director) in 1990 and 1991. In 2000, Sandy filled in as interim children's choir director. When Rebekah Schulz became Director of Music and Worship in 2006, the Christmas program was separated from Sunday worship and became a stand-alone Epiphany pageant. The pageants in 2021 and 2022 were "virtual" because of the COVID pandemic.

CHRISTIAN EDUCATION AND PROGRAMMING

4-5. Christmas Pageant (1979)

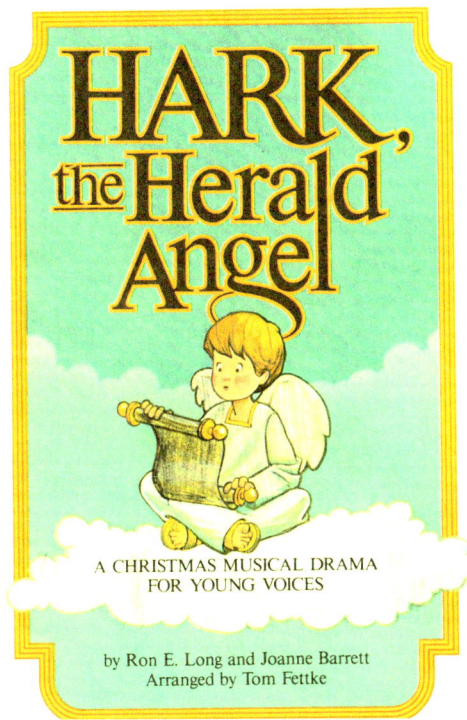

4-6. Sunday School Christmas program "Hark, the Herald Angel" (1990)

4-7. Sunday School Epiphany program (2013)

Sunday School is now held September through May and begins with a Rally Sunday. It serves ages three though senior high school. The children frequently have an annual meeting at which they decide what causes to support with the offering money. Projects funded in this way vary from year to year and have included Southeast Asian ministry, Alex's Lemonade Stand to fight childhood cancer, Common Hope in Guatemala, Sharing and Caring Hands, Heifer International, Keystone Community Services, Feed My Starving Children, ELCA Disaster Relief, and Tanzania scholarships.

Immanuel has had Sunday School superintendents since at least 1915, and for many years had Sunday School treasurers and secretaries. In 1994, the title of the position was changed from superintendent to Director of Christian Education and became a part-time, paid position. Over time, the position transitioned from ten to 24 hours a week. In 2017, the title became Director of Children and Family Ministry. See Appendix E for a list of those who held the positions of Sunday School superintendent, secretary, and treasurer; Directors of Christian Education; and Director of Children and Family Ministry.

Sunday School enrollment over the years reflects the size of the congregation and demographic trends. For example, Baby Boomers swelled the number of Sunday School students into the early 1960s. Following are data about Sunday School attendance and number of teachers for selected years.

    1933   180 students and 18 teachers
    1947   203 students
    1955   278 students and 24 teachers
    1960   372 students
    1992   200 students
    2004   110 students
    2013   85 students and 15 teachers
    2019   75 students

Release Time for Religious Education Classes

In 1940, the city of Saint Paul began offering church school release days every Wednesday afternoon. In the early 1950s, Nellie Berry started teaching release time classes at Highland Park Lutheran Church. She also taught at the Assembly of God Church in Highland Park. Immanuel provided funds to the churches where "Release Time School" was held. Students from nearby public schools attended religious training once a week. Students received Christian education, which included memorizing Bible verses and the names of the books of the Bible. Nellie Berry taught these classes well into her 80s, taking the bus from Lyngblomsten Care Center to schools. Church school release days were held at Immanuel into the early 1960s.

Presentation of Bibles

In 1945, Immanuel decided to give Bibles to students in their first year of Confirmation classes. This practice continues today. More recently, the 3rd graders have received Bibles from their parents at a special ceremony during the Sunday morning services. The presentation was skipped in 2021 because of COVID and Bibles were given to 3rd and 4th graders in an outdoor presentation in 2022.

4-8. Presentation of Bibles (2012)

Fed & Forgiven Communion Instruction

For many years, only youth who had been confirmed could receive Holy Communion. This changed in the late 1960s when the American Lutheran Church (of which Immanuel was a member) voted to permit children age 10 and older to receive Holy Communion. After consideration, Immanuel decided to implement this change and, in 1972, launched a program to prepare children who were ten years old or in the 5th grade to receive Holy Communion. By 1992, "First Communion" classes were held for 4th graders and their families. For several years, students made personal banners, which hung on the pews on "First Communion Sunday."

In 2011, an effort was made to align Immanuel's educational program with Immanuel's existing Communion worship practice of serving Communion to all ages when parents or sponsors determined a child was ready. At that time, Immanuel began offering Fed & Forgiven Communion instruction classes once a year for any age that wanted to begin receiving Holy Communion. These classes were taught every year through 2017.

Christian Education and Programming

4-9. Fed & Forgiven instruction (2005)

Preparation for Confirmation

Confirmation is a public profession of faith prepared for by careful instruction. It also is called an Affirmation of Baptism. It is an opportunity for people to affirm for themselves the promises that their parents, sponsors, and congregation made for them at their Baptism. At their Affirmation of Baptism, confirmands are asked to make this promise for themselves: "to live among God's faithful people, to hear the Word of God and share in the Lord's Supper, to proclaim the good news of God in Christ through word and deed, to serve all people, following the example of Jesus, and to strive for justice and peace in all the earth."

Immanuel's Confirmation records go back to 1883, when three 15-year-olds were confirmed. Early Immanuel registers were in Norwegian, and confirmands were given evaluations of very good, good, fair, and poor. Classes have varied in size over the years with the largest Confirmation class numbering 31 in 1964. Immanuel archives also contain the names of the two members of the 1920 Confirmation class at Macalester Park Lutheran Church (before the merger with Immanuel) and the names of those confirmed at Highland Park Lutheran Church beginning in 1927 and continuing until the merger with Immanuel.

4-10. Confirmation class with Pastor Bennie Duckstad (1925)

When Highland Park Lutheran and Immanuel Lutheran Churches merged in 1960, the two churches' Confirmation classes also merged. Sandy Bauer was part of the group from Highland Park and Mark Anderson was in the Immanuel group. A few years later, the two married and remain Immanuel members.

Assistant Pastor Jim Tangen instituted a three-year Confirmation program, which started in September of 1967. By 1974, the Confirmation training was changed back to a two-year program. In 1995, the Confirmation program transitioned from 8th and 9th grade students to one covering 7th and 8th grade students. In many years, beginning in 1999, the 7th and 8th grade Confirmation students went to a week-long Bible camp as part of the curriculum for the Confirmation program. For example, eleven 7th graders attended Green Lake Bible Camp in 2000. Confirmation students returned to Green Lake Bible Camp for several years, switched to Bay Lake Bible Camp in 2007, to Luther Crest Camp in 2012, and to Good Earth Village in 2015 and 2016.

Matthew Tingler (a fourth-year Luther Seminary student) was hired to teach 7th and 8th grade Confirmation students in 2009. In addition, Immanuel became a partner congregation with VIBE: Urban Youth Ministry. VIBE was a collaboration of Saint Paul congregations whose mission is to unite

Christian Education and Programming

4-11. Largest Confirmation class with Pastor Raymond Charles Boyens and Bishop Melford Knutson (1964)

congregations, transform urban youth, and strengthen communities. Immanuel 7th and 8th grade Confirmation students met with other VIBE churches for a joint Confirmation class on the second Sunday evening of the month. This partnership was discontinued in the fall of 2010. Matthew Tingler continued to teach Confirmation classes through 2011.

Currently, Immanuel 7th and 8th graders meet Wednesdays to learn about the Bible and what it means to be Lutheran. These foundational discussions aim to both strengthen the children's faith and encourage them to question their beliefs in a safe space. These gatherings are open to members and non-members alike. A third year (9th grade) was added in 2005. The third-year Confirmation students meet regularly with a mentor from the congregation to prepare their hearts and minds to publicly affirm their faith. The Confirmation service traditionally occurs in May, at which confirmands present their credos (statements of faith).

4-12. Preparation for Confirmation with Pastor John Lohre (1980)

Vacation Bible School

The origins of Vacation Bible School (VBS) in the United States can be traced to 1890s. Modern programs usually consist of a week-long program of religious education that may employ Bible stories, religious songs, arts and crafts, skits, or puppet shows, catering to elementary school-aged children. While the date that Immanuel began offering VBS is not known, a two-week "Summer Bible School" was offered in 1940.

Immanuel's VBS was offered in partnership with Pilgrim Lutheran Church for several years. Traditionally, VBS was during mornings, Monday through Friday, and open to children from Pre-K through 6th grade. A fee was charged, but scholarships were available for those who could not pay.

4-13. Pastor Cindy Bullock at Vacation Bible School (2012)

4-14. Chris Cherwin, Director of Worship and Music, with Vacation Bible School children (2013)

Faith and Science Adventures, and Junior Adventures!

Faith and Science Adventures is a new camp model replacing Vacation Bible School and was started in 2022. It is a five-day, 9 a.m. to 4 p.m., program for children who had completed grades 2–8. Junior Adventures! is a four-day, 5:30–7:30 p.m. program for Pre-K through 2nd grade children and their families with dinner and activities.

Music and Arts Camp

Immanuel's Music and Arts Camp was started in 2015 by Chris Cherwien, Director of Worship and Music. Chris serves as camp director and choir time leader. This week-long, summer day camp, is a place where faith and creativity connect in a God-centered environment. The camp's mission is to offer children who have completed kindergarten through 8th grade the opportunity to participate in a wide variety of visual and performing arts. This camp was created both for Immanuel's children and those in the community. While a fee is charged, financial assistance is available for those with need. Each elective is taught by highly qualified teachers who engage the youth in exciting and fun ways. Electives have included African drumming, photography, SAORI/Japanese weaving, Gamelan/Indonesian percussion, handbells, clay creativity, Nigerian dance/movement, creative writing, sculpture, script writing, ukulele, and yoga. Camp was cancelled in 2020 because of the pandemic but resumed in 2021. Enrollment reached a record full-capacity in 2022.

4-15. Music and Arts Camp drummers (2017)

Saint Nicholas Intergenerational Event

For several years in the late 2000s, Immanuel celebrated the season of Advent with an intergenerational event learning about Saint Nicholas. It was an evening to hear the legends of Saint Nicholas, the 4th century saint, who supposedly left gold coins and tangerines in the stockings and boots of the poor children in the towns and villages under his charge as Bishop in Asia Minor. Saint Nicholas made an appearance in full regalia. Those attending ate treats, sang songs, made holiday decorations, and, one year, made cards for the children in Immanuel's partner congregation, Mkimbizi Lutheran Church, Tanzania.

4-16. Saint Nicholas Intergenerational Event—
Saint Nicholas and Kate Bussert (2007)

Youth Programs and Activities

Youth have come together in various venues since the early days of Immanuel. The groups have had various names depending on the age group—Junior League, Intermediate League, Confirmation League (for 8th and 9th graders), Luther League, and Hi-League. In the 1920s, young people formed their own Junior League for 12-year-olds until Confirmation and Senior League (past Confirmation age) because there was no youth director at that time. The youth wanted to help purchase a pipe organ and held plays to raise money. Immanuel member Martin Wangensteen loaned them the money they needed and a used organ was purchased.

The Intermediate League was organized in November 1941 for confirmands until they became Senior League age. Sometime in the 1950s, the Senior League became the Luther League, and then became the Hi-League. For many years in the 1980s and 1990s, the Hi-League collected paper and cans that were sold to raise funds. One exceptional year was 1988, when $2,443.98 was raised.

Norwegian Lutheran youth have attended national conventions since at least 1919, when the Hauge Synod held a convention in Red Wing, Minnesota. Immanuel youth raised money to send two delegates to the June National Youth Convention in Saskatoon, Canada. Records of the national youth conventions Immanuel's youth have attended are incomplete, but attendance at the following is documented:

- 1957 Evangelical Lutheran Church's Luther League convention in Missoula, MT
- 1960 Milwaukee, WI (constituting convention of the ALC Luther League)
- 1961 Miami Beach, FL—"Christ Is Living" Speaker: Martin Luther King, Jr. The Hi-League took the church bus and made stops at Chicago, Gettysburg, Williamsburg, St. Augustine, Atlanta, and Lookout Mountain, Tennessee, while traveling to and from the convention.
- 1964 Detroit, MI—"Jesus Is Lord"
- 1967 Seattle, WA/Dallas, TX (split sites)—"We Are a Peculiar People"
- 1970 New York, NY—"And We Say We Care"
- 1973 Houston, TX—"With Eyes Wide Open"—1st All-Lutheran Youth Gathering (with Lutheran Church in America and Lutheran and Church Missouri Synod)—music: Johnny Cash, speaker: Fulton J. Sheen
- 1976 New Orleans, LA—"For All the Saints"—2nd All-Lutheran Youth Gathering
- 1979 Kansas City, MO—"Called to be Servants"

Christian Education and Programming

1982   San Antonio, TX—"In Christ, A New Creation"
1985   Denver, CO—"Proclaim, Him Lord of All"
1988   San Antonio, TX—"Rejoice in the Lord Always"
1991   Dallas, TX—"Called to Freedom"
1994   Atlanta, GA—"2 Be Alive"
1997   New Orleans, LA—"River of Hope"
2000   St. Louis, MO—"Dancing at the Crossroads"
2003   Atlanta, GA—"Ubuntu" (Do Life)
2006   San Antonio, TX—"Cruzando" (Crossing)
2009   New Orleans, LA—"Jesus, Justice, Jazz"
2012   New Orleans, LA—"Citizens with the Saints"
2015   Detroit, MI—"Rise Up Together"
2018   Houston, TX—"This Changes Everything"

4-17. *Youth in the Boundary Waters (2006)*

Because of the COVID pandemic, the national meeting planned for 2021 was rescheduled for 2022, and then cancelled.

Immanuel youth trips have run on a three-year cycle for many years. Former Assistant Pastor John Lohre reported that during his time at Immanuel (1977–1993), the three-year rotation cycled through the national youth gathering, a trip to a national park, and an outing in the Boundary Waters Canoe Area. Summer trips tended to be two weeks long and they used a huge tent Hi-League had made. Sometimes a trip to a national park was combined with a trip to the national youth gathering. After one trip to Big Bend National Park, the bus engine had to be replaced. In 1992, the Hi-League went on a Habitat for Humanity mission trip to Baldwin, Wisconsin, and then to Chicago.

Now, in addition to attending the national conference every three years, in non-convention years the youth usually have either an "adventure" week or a service mission trip. Adventure weeks might be a week at a dude ranch and, more recently, camping and canoeing in the Boundary Waters. Recent service mission trips have been to the Appalachian Mountains (2002), Benton Harbor, Michigan (2005), Youth Works! Mission trips to Chicago (2011) and Leach Lake (2013), and to the Pine Ridge Reservation in South Dakota (2019).

The high school youth group continues to meet. They gather at various times and days of the week for activities. The students in middle school have Confirmation education Wednesday evenings and have occasional fun "hang out" times. The high school group and Confirmation students hold a silent auction in the late winter or early spring and they assist with the lutefisk supper as fund-raisers for their summer trips. Both age groups have Sunday School. Before the COVID pandemic, Immanuel had separate classes for each group. Because of the pandemic, they started meeting as a single group.

4-18. Junior High Sunday School with teacher Paul Mattessich (2006)

4-19. Silent auction (2016)

Appendix H lists Immanuel's youth directors, youth ministers, and directors of youth and family ministry.

Young Adult Programs

During Immanuel's history, various groups have been created to meet the needs of young adults by providing social and service opportunities. In 1917, the Young People's Society had meetings on the second and fourth Sunday evening. A new program was started after WWII for young adults. "The Active Young People" put on a play for two nights (probably in the 1950s) at the Faust Theater, directed by Theodora Martinson, called *Charlie's Aunt*.

"Avenues" was started in 2000 as a ministry to and with young adults in their 20s, and to offer an opportunity for this group to socialize. For example, in 2004, Avenues was engaged in a "People Serving People" service project and a Sponsor-a-Family service project, worked with Inner City Kids program at the Marie Sandvik Center, held a progressive dinner and holiday party, and watched and discussed a movie about Martin Luther. Avenues was phased out in 2007, when the youth director reverted back to part-time position.

Adult Education and Programs

In Immanuel's early years, the various women's and men's groups routinely had Bible studies at each meeting, often with the pastor leading the discussion. Adult "Sunday School" is a relatively recent development in Immanuel's 150-year history.

4-20. Adult Forum meeting in the West Lounge (1978)

4.21. Program for 49'ers in the East Lounge (2006)

In the fall of 1975, an Adult Bible Class was held at 9:45 at the same time as Sunday School and the second of three Sunday morning services. The Adult Forum was started in 1972 between the services, but the forum was suspended in 1974 because of the difficulty lining up speakers for a reasonable price. It had resumed by 1977. By 1994, so many adults attended the Adult Forum that it was expanded to offer two different classes, each lead by a pastor. For a few years in the early 2000s, the Adult Forum was called "Food and Faith."

Immanuel member Roger Forman made recordings of the adult forum presentations for many years. He recorded the presentations using a digital video camera that recorded to MiniDV tapes. He dubbed these to the more popular VHS tape format and provided them to the church library for lending.

Immanuel has hosted two Bible study series: Bethel and SEARCH. The Bethel Bible Program was started in 1969 and involved 135 participants. It was led by Nancy Granrud. The SEARCH Bible Series for adults began in 1985 with nearly 80 adults participating.

Today adults have a number of educational options throughout the year. Pastor Cindy Bullock has offered Bible studies, book studies, speakers, personal devotions, and workshops. The Social Action Team hosts regular opportunities to learn about justice and equity issues. See Appendix I.

49'ers

At the time of the merger of Immanuel and Highland Park Lutheran Churches in 1960, Highland Park members had an organization called "After Fifty" for members over the age of 50. A new group, called the 49'ers (for those 49 and older), was created at Immanuel to enable the members of the two churches to get acquainted and socialize together. In February 1962, the new organization met for the first potluck dinner as the "49'ers." Attendance ranged from 50 to 75 participants. Pastor John Lohre and his wife, Mary, added their ages together so they could attend.

Monthly meetings, except during July and August, usually included an evening meal and a program, which might be a guest speaker or a music program. Immanuel youth washed dishes and did clean-up to raise money for their summer trips. The group usually had a picnic in June. Attendees gave a freewill offering, which was used to reimburse speakers, cover modest expenses, and also (when sufficient) disbursed for benevolence. For example, in 1966, the 49'ers gave $25.00 to Pastor Merrill Clark for New Guinea educational material. Pastor Clark was a missionary in New Guinea and the son of

Clayton and Violet Clark, who had been members of Highland Park Lutheran Church. In 2007, the head chaplain of the Minnesota National Guard spoke about helping veterans of the Iraq War adapt to civilian life. A collection at that program raised $350, which was supplemented by the Men's Club and donations from other Immanuel members. In 2011, nearly $2,400 was distributed to Loaves and Fishes, Keystone Second Harvest, Lyngblomsten Foundation, China Venture, The Parable fund, Feed My Starving Children, Tanzania Tree Project, and Wilder grocery boxes.

The 49'ers ceased in 2013, due to changing demographics and the fact that many seniors were attending Aging Splendidly events.

Aging Splendidly

A monthly lunch and speaker series called Aging Splendidly began in 2007 and provides social and educational opportunities for older Immanuel members and the larger community. One aim is to prevent isolation. It normally meets at noon on the first Thursday of the month October through June. A free will offering covers lunch expenses. Topics often include health, the arts, education, or a local social service. A favorite event is December's Christmas

4-22. Aging Splendidly lunch (2014)

Carol Sing-along which has been led by Immanuel member David Stark. David noted that he changes to a lower key when playing hymns for this group—making them easier for senior voices. Aging Splendidly is coordinated by Immanuel members Dave and Sue Klevan. Aging Splendidly paused during the COVID pandemic.

Church Library

"Ever since we had arrived in the United States, my classmates kept asking me about magic carpets. 'They don't exist,' I always said. I was wrong. Magic carpets do exist, but they are called library cards."—Firoozeh Dumas, Funny in Farsi: A Memoir of Growing up Iranian In America *(New York: Random House, 2008), page 220. (call # 979.4 Dum))*

The church library opened in May 1961 and was dedicated during the Sunday worship service on January 7, 1962. The following is an excerpt from *The Messenger* at that time:

> "Immanuel congregation has the advantage of having in its membership a fine corps of unusually well-trained individuals to take care of its new church library, which is located on the middle floor of the new Educational Building. The display of new books that was then placed about the Church Lounge was the finest any congregation could hope to have. These, added to the fine array that had come from both the former congregations, make our Immanuel Church Library an outstanding establishment."

The library was originally located across from the offices on the second floor of the education wing. Adelaide Norgaard, a graduate of St. Catherine College who had served as librarian in several positions in Saint Paul, was named director of the Immanuel library. The library moved to the former pastor's office on the south side of the narthex in 1966, where it is housed today.

In the following years, many more Immanuel members were enlisted to organize, maintain, and publicize the growing collection. It took a dedicated cadre of volunteers to type and file all the cards in the card catalog, shelve books, send over-due notices, and staff the library before, after, and between the several church services. The names of some of the volunteers who have been either librarians or dedicated library helpers follow:

Adelaide Norgaard* Irene Schilling Inez Bethke*
Dorothy Dohman Al Forman Nilla Osten
Laura Miller Gloria Dahlen Christine Otteson
Chris Knopff Hilda Haugen Jackie Kelly
Chuck Gierke Kathleen Jents Marjory Pesek O'Neil
Eunice Baker Morgan Anderson Esther Bentley
Ethel Smith Edna Harris Alpha Van Voorhis
Andrew Urness Myrtle Anderson Pearl Odland
Barbara Minor* Marguerite Hamre Ragna Lindgren
Beret Hanson Carole Needels* Roger Forman
Caroline Thompson* Diane Valure* Phyllis Bentley*
Mrs. Robert Janssen* Beryl Berg Mary Gwen Thompson
Shawne Osborne

*Individuals whom church records identify as Immanuel head librarians.

4-23. Phyllis Bentley in the library (2006)

Over the years an outstanding religious reference collection has been built and many of these books have been used for large congregational Bible studies such as SEARCH and the Bethel Bible Study Series. Many books dealing with life and faith have been added for personal use, including those for children and teens. The library currently has more than 1,800 books and videos for children, youth, and adults. The collection is curated regularly and includes copies of current popular fiction and non-fiction. The library is a member of the Lutheran Church Library Association.

The mission of the Immanuel Church Library is to provide an educational resource to all members and groups of the Immanuel community that will enhance their faith and understanding of their Christian identity and help them to obtain a better understanding of today's world. Titles are selected for their potential to enrich worship life; increase effectiveness in Christian service; support the total ministry of the church; provide inspiration, counsel, and prayers for specific issues; provide information about social and economic issues and other religions; and to provide an appreciation of good literature.

In the 1990s, the rapid proliferation of personal computers prompted public libraries to begin providing their catalogs online in order to allow patrons more independence and easy access from any internet connection. In the early 2000s, Phyllis Bentley and Diane Valure were asked by the Education Committee to serve as librarians and undertake a similar process with Immanuel's library.

4-24. Boy Scout history display on shelves outside the library (2022)

An entire inventory of the collection was necessary. The library required computers, a printer, lockable cabinetry, and wiring changes, all with a very limited budget. Roger Forman, member of the Education Committee, greatly assisted by locating used computers and everything that was needed to begin.

Phyllis and Diane wanted congregation members to have library access whenever the church was open, so the old-style cards and pockets in books were retained. The library relies on a "do-it-yourself" sign-out honor system.

In the 2000s, Diane and Phyllis made efforts to publicize the library in a number of different ways. They hosted several coffee hours between services with books on display. Carts of new books were parked in the narthex or Gathering Space during the time between services. Sunday School classes were invited to the library to hear a story and check out books. A carton of books was taken to a women's overnight retreat. Short book resumes occasionally have appeared in *The Messenger*.

In 2011, the Immanuel Foundation granted funds to build a showcase in the narthex to be used to promote library materials, but which also would be available for other displays. It was completed in 2013.

The library holdings were converted to LibraryThing (an online system for small libraries) in February 2017. Immanuel member Sue Klevan added a link to Immanuel Lutheran's website so that everyone in the congregation could access the online catalog by cell phone or computer to find an item by title, author, or subject.

CHAPTER 5

Building Community

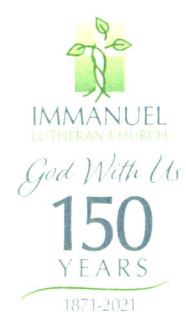

Congregation News and Publications

Budbaereren (*The Messenger*), was a widely read 16-page weekly religious periodical in Norwegian, published in Red Wing, Minnesota, by the Hauge Synod until 1916.

In November, 1914, the Men's Society of East Immanuel and West Immanuel began joint publication of the *Hyrderösten: Menighedsblad for Immanuels og Östre Immanuels Menigheder i St. Paul* (*Shepherd's Voice: Congregational Magazine for Immanuel and East Immanuel's Congregations in St. Paul*))—a congregational magazine that was written in both Norwegian and English. It was primarily a monthly parish paper. The editor was Immanuel's pastor, Dr. Gustav Marius Bruce. The Minnesota Historical Society has selected issues for January 1917–1919 (v. 3–5).

The Immanuel *Messenger* was published from 1921 to 1933 by the Ladies Aid. The Men's Club took over the publication of the parish paper in 1935 and called it *The Messenger*. The volume numbering of *The Messenger* has been inconsistent and seems to have started renumbering with volume 1 several times. In 1948, Pastor Conrad Thompson edited *The Messenger*. In the 1950s and 1960s, *The Messenger* was published by the women. Immanuel member June Husom often is listed as the editor. In the 1950s and 1960s, *The Messenger* provided a wealth of information to the congregation. It often included photos and reported upcoming and past church events and activities; numbers of people taking Communion and attending services; memorial gifts; births, baptisms, marriages, and deaths; members' travel outside the United States; youth attending colleges; news of past pastors; new members; names and addresses of members serving in the military; and address changes. When space permitted, an issue might include poetry or an inspirational message.

Hyrderösten

Hans navn skal kaldes Immanuel, det er udlagt: Gud med os. Matt. 1: 23.

Menighedsblad for Immanuels og Östre Immanuels Menigheder i St. Paul.

Udkommer en gang i maaneden.   Subscriptionspris: 25c for aaret.

Aargang IV.   ST. PAUL, MINN., OCTOBER, 1918   No. 10.

IMMANUEL NORSK LUTHERSK KIRKE
St. Albans St. and Aurora Ave.

G. M. BRUCE, S. T. D., Editor.
1328 Keston St.
Tel.: T. S. 831027.

President, H. G. Grove, 1398 Breda St.
Vice President, O. H. Oace, 662 Rondo St.
Secretary, J. M. Jorgensen, 727 E. 6th St.
Treasurer, John Christensen, 453 Sherburne Ave.
Trustees, C. Holm, S. Pettersen, M. Johnsen, O. H. Oace, J. Pettersen, A. Martinsen.
Menighedens Äldste, A. J. Ohnsager, C. Holm O. H. Oace.

Owing to a resolution passed at the synod meeting last summer, forbidding theological professors to serve as regular pastors in addition to their work as professors, the pastor was obliged to resign as regular pastor of the congregation at the business meeting held October 1. Both he and his family will nevertheless retain their membership in the congregation. Regular services will be provided and the work in the congregation will proceed uninterrupted until a regular pastor can be called. Let us therefore not slacken in our fervor and loyal support of the chuch, but let us work together for the building up of the kingdom of God in our midst.

RAPPORT FRA DELEGATEN TIL SYNODEMÖDET.

Til Immanuels menighed, St. Paul!

Som eders delegat til Den Norsk Lutherske Kirkes aarsmöde i Fargo, N. D., i Juni, 1918, finder jeg det som en kjæ pligt at rapportere som fölger:

Vi ankom til bestemt tid til mödets aabning og var vidne til at samme var utfört höitideligt og med anstand. En stor skare med prester og delegater var allerede ankommet og forhandlingerne blev udfört i overensstemmelse med forudfattede bestemmelser, hvorved der sparedes tid. Da der i aar ikke var valg paa embetsmænd, havde vi kun at vælge en nominationskomite. Naar denne var valgt, rapporterede den straks navnene paa dem, som den ansaa skikkede til at tjene paa de forskjellige arbeidskomiteer. Disse blev uden undtagelse godkjendt af den store forsamling.

De indberetninger som omfatter förste samfundsaar forelaa i pamflet form og blev overrakt til hvert stemmeberettiget medlem. Dette kom vel med, da det ofte var vanskeligt at höre hvad det blev talt; thi 1274 medlemmer trænger et stort rum, og da der ved siden af var mange besögende, saa blev det en stor forsamling.

Sessionen fra 8—9 morgen var, efter mit syn, den bedste. Paa denne tid holdtes bönne- og vidnemöde, i hvilket 2 @ 300 deltog med sin nærværelse.

5-1. Hyrderösten—*Immanuel's newsletter in Norwegian and English (October 1918)*

The Messenger was succeeded by a new publication called *The Vine*, which had its first quarterly issue in February 2022. *The Vine* has a goal to help members of the Immanuel community to get to know each other and to tell stories of where they see God around us.

In 2011, Immanuel began preparing a weekly "News and Notes," which supplemented the Sunday bulletin and replaced the information section that had previously been part of the bulletin. "News and Notes" includes announcements, a calendar, a list of people to remember in prayer, and names of worship assistants for the next Sunday.

In 2018, a video monitor was added to the wall of the upper Gathering Space above the foyer to provide better communication of upcoming events and to showcase events just completed. Immanuel member Sarah Brainard Marsh prepared a PowerPoint presentation loop weekly. In 2021, the monitor began to be used to stream the worship services.

An essential source of congregational information has been the church directories, published at regular intervals since at least the 1940s. The directories have provided names, addresses, and telephone numbers. The 1967 directory appears to be the first to include photos. Directories often included names of church staff and organization charts with names of church officers and committee members. Some listed the schedule of activities each week—dates and times, for example, of choir rehearsals, women's and men's group meetings, confirmation classes, etc. Later directories have been enhanced with photos of church activities. By the late 1980s, the photos changed to color. Often a commercial professional photographer was hired and members could purchase professional prints if they wished. In 2016, Immanuel stopped printing directories and moved the content (names, addresses, phone numbers, e-mail addresses, and photos) online using the "Instant Church Directory" software. Content is password protected and searchable; it can be printed upon request.

Website, Social Media, and E-Mail

Immanuel's first website was created by Immanuel member Carson English, as a service project when he was in high school in 1998. The site was hosted by Visi.com. Russ Carlson, parish administrator, maintained and updated the website until 2010, when Immanuel formed a small communications task force to revamp the website and begin using Mailchimp to manage the congregation's e-mail. Mailchimp started building a distribution list with people registering via the website. This was accomplished with the help of an independent contractor, Kurt Indemaur. Mailchimp was used to send "News

5-2. First issue of The Vine (February 2022)

and Notes" to parishioners weekly, *The Messenger* newsletter monthly, and other notices as they occurred. About the same time, Immanuel staff began using e-mail with [name]@immanuelstpaul.org addresses for each staff person, including a generic webmaster@immanuelstpaul.org e-mail address to accommodate responses.

The original website, Immanuelstpaul.org, became corrupt so it was retired, and the website and staff e-mail communications were unavailable for a time. The e-mail distribution list and Facebook were available and were used to communicate Immanuel news during this period. Immanuel took this as an opportunity to redesign the website and communication systems reflecting modern trends. A committee including Pastor Cindy Bullock, Lynnette Zika, Hannah Bartholic, and Sue Klevan met to define the requirements and design the new website ilcsp.org. Pastor Cindy's daughter Kim assisted with the programming. At this point, staff assumed full responsibility for updating the website and a volunteer continued creating and sending the e-mails. Staff assumed full responsibility for sending e-mails in 2021.

Immanuel created its first Facebook page in August 2011. In 2018, the church added an Instagram account. Both have helped share photos from events, communicate last minute updates, and provide faith-based content to the church community and beyond. During the pandemic in 2020, Facebook was used to live stream services from Pastor Cindy Bullock's home. In 2021, Immanuel also began offering the live service stream to its own YouTube channel to provide better sound and image quality.

Outreach and Community Engagement

One goal of the Building Bridges remodeling project of 2006 was to increase outreach and, since the project's completion, Immanuel has shared its building with:

Kinderstube, German Immersion Preschool (2008–2010). *Kinderstube* is a German language immersion preschool program of the Germanic-American Institute, a Minnesota non-profit organization.

Art with Ellen, preschool art classes with Ellen Ferrari (2007–2020)
Al-Anon
Winged-Heart Yoga
TOPS (Taking off Pounds Sensibly)
Girl Scout Troops 57386 and 52727
Boy Scout Troop 90, sponsored by Immanuel
Riverside Innovation Hub
Twin Cities Ancient Coin Club

North Star Ski Touring Club (until 2021)
Marcee Model Airplane Club
Breathing Group
At the Summit Preschool (2015–2018)
Aliro Voices
Lute Café
Business Networking International (BNI)
MOMS Club
Macalester College choirs
Mat Pilates class
National Lutheran Choir (renting a room for office space)

Immanuel has served as an election polling site and site of blood drives, often hosted in partnership with Gloria Dei Lutheran Church. Immanuel facilities have hosted multiple church bodies and activities, including House of Mercy Lutheran Church (2009–2011); Revelation Christian Church International (2010–2018); Youth Works! summer mission trips, during which the groups were housed in the church for several weeks (2011–2016); Living Gospel Believers Church (2018–2020); and the Ethiopian Church Conference (2021).

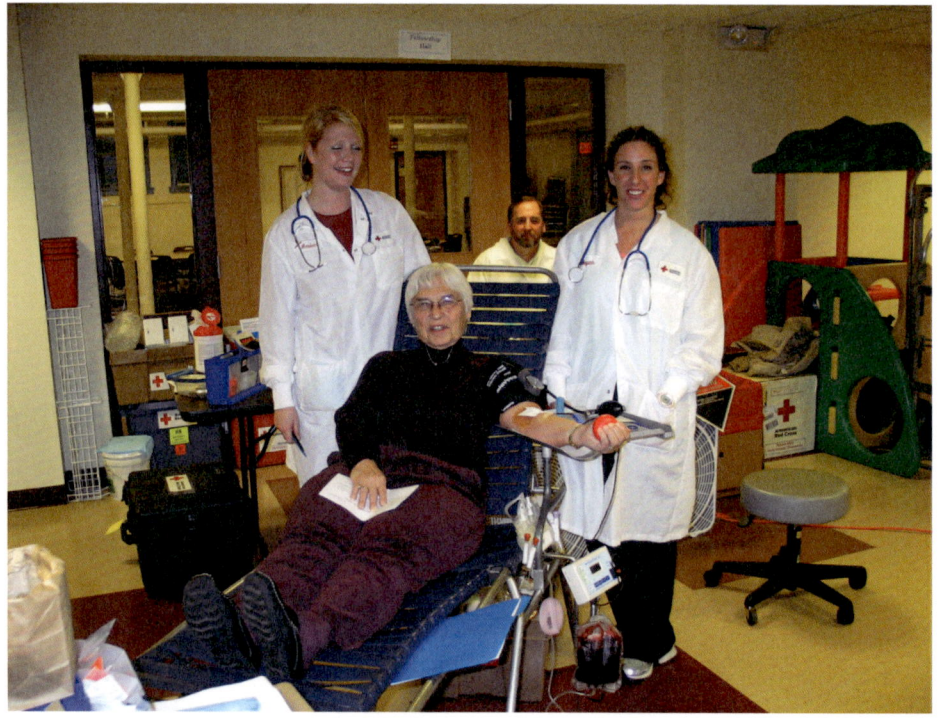

5-3. Kay Draine donating at the blood drive at Immanuel (2007)

Immanuel, Pilgrim Lutheran, and sometimes St. Luke's Lutheran Churches shared joint mid-week Lenten services in the early 2000s. Services rotated between the sanctuaries with the choirs singing together. In 2008, Immanuel member and well-known author and newspaper columnist Jim Klobuchar offered his "reflections" during the Wednesday evening Lenten services. Joint Ash Wednesday and Good Friday services were often held with Pilgrim Lutheran and, in 2010, a joint Good Friday service was held at Gloria Dei Lutheran Church with Pilgrim. The choirs of Immanuel, Pilgrim, and Gloria Dei offered many anthems to go along with the Tenebrae readings. Immanuel participated in citywide ecumenical Thanksgiving services in the late 1990s. Services were held at various churches in Saint Paul.

More recently, Immanuel has offered free emergency childcare during teacher strikes and snow days. Called Immanuel's Student Spot, the service is open to all community children. In 2020, childcare was provided for more than 70 students needing childcare during a four-day teacher strike.

Collaboration with Macalester College

Because of proximity, Immanuel and Macalester College have had a long-standing relationship. Macalester College was founded in 1885. The college is directly across Snelling Avenue from Immanuel. In 1941, the Macalester *College Bulletin* reported that the wedding of Marvel Wangensteen (class of 1936) and Perley Entzminger took place at Immanuel Lutheran church. Marvel is the aunt of current Immanuel member, Doug Wangensteen. In 1945, the Lutheran Student Association of Macalester was one of the largest student organizations on campus. Immanuel's pastor Conrad Thompson was the off-campus advisor to the group. Over the years, many Macalester students and graduates have become part of the Immanuel community.

Church records show that great numbers of Macalester students attended Immanuel between 1949 and 1957. Immanuel continues to be a church home for "Mac" students. In 1983, Immanuel gave $1,000 to the Macalester Ministry. In the 1990s, Immanuel had a part-time (10 hours per week) ministry representative, who worked with the Macalester chaplain, led a Wednesday evening Compline worship, and facilitated faith discussions.

The church parking lot is an ongoing collaboration. Macalester staff and students park in the lot on weekdays. In return, Macalester maintains the parking lot, including painting the parking "stripes," and keeps it plowed in winter.

Macalester students do many projects each year with Immanuel staff and members. Immanuel members have created volunteer opportunities and internships for "Mac" students. In 2020, Audrey Wuench, Macalester intern, helped with the 150th anniversary by interviewing and recording Immanuel members' memories of the church community on Zoom.

Macalester students have been hired to work in the Immanuel nursery during church services. The Macalester choir practiced at Immanuel during the remodeling of their music building space on the campus.

Many Immanuel events have been held at Macalester. Immanuel members worshipped in the Macalester chapel during some construction projects. Immanuel's church Council has held retreats at Macalester.

A few of the Immanuel events hosted on the Macalester campus include:

1945 Easter service held at the Macalester gymnasium
1960 Service of union of Highland Park and Immanuel at Macalester gym
1961 Dedication of the Education Wing
1971 Trip to the Macalester planetarium in the evening
1977 Reception at Macalester to celebrate the 25th anniversary of Pastor Elder Bentley's ordination
1992 Retirement reception held at the Cochran lounge for Pastor Bentley
2022 150th anniversary banquet and program

5-4. Dedication of Immanuel's Education Wing in Macalester Gym (1961)

Sports at Immanuel

Various sports activities have engaged members over the years. The chapel built in 1921 had a gymnasium. Members played kitten ball (an early name for softball) in the 1920s. There were boys and girls softball teams in the early 1960s and pick-up softball games were popular in the 1990s. At various times, Immanuel groups went bowling. One evening in 1954, the Immanuel Lutheran Brotherhood bowling team scored 990, the highest game total of any team in the league.

Both men and women had dartball teams. In 1954, the women's dartball team won the Good Sportsmanship Trophy in the Lutheran Dartball League. The women's dartball team won the second-place trophy in the Women's Lutheran League in 1961 and the men's team won the championship the same year. Immanuel had a men's basketball team in 1964 and in subsequent years. The team had uniforms and played in a YMCA league.

Immanuel sponsored boys' basketball teams for several years. In 1955, the Immanuel junior basketball team was undefeated and won the title in its division of the YMCA church league.

Annual Sunday School picnics often included games and sports competition. For example, footraces were started by a cap gun at the Sunday School picnic at Como Park in 1959.

In 1991, Immanuel had an "Everybody's Club," which had a co-ed softball team for 20–60 year-olds. The team played in the Emmaus Church League.

The Junior League and Hi-League have had many sports-related outings. The Hi-League had volleyball and softball teams and, in 1991, placed third in the Faith Volleyball League. In 1993, these groups went snow tubing and horseback riding, played volleyball, and went canoeing.

Boy Scouts

Troup 90

The association of Boy Scout Troop 90 with Immanuel began in May of 1934 when the Immanuel Men's Club sponsored the Troop. The Troop was 24 boys strong and was led by Scoutmaster Herbert Page. By 1942, Troop 90 had its first two Eagle Scouts. Some of the event ribbons earned by the Scouts during this time have survived and are stored safely in the Scout room in the church basement. The Troop was disbanded due to "no boys or leadership" in May 1947.

In 1952, under the guidance of Immanuel members Al Forman and Everett Needels, Troop 90 was restarted at Immanuel, sponsored by the Immanuel Brotherhood. Dave Birt, who represented the Saint Paul Area Council, presented the Boy Scout Charter to Morgan Anderson, Immanuel's institutional representative. This began the continuous years of sponsorship by Immanuel Lutheran Church that endures today. The Troop started with 13 Scouts led by Scoutmaster Robert Pope. Since then, Troop 90 has had 26 Scoutmasters and has produced 86 Eagle Scouts. Included in that group of Eagle Scouts are these sons of Immanuel who attained Scouting's highest award: Eric Urness, Lars Teppo, Noel Teppo, Daniel Barbosa, Eric Edhlund, Austin Bentley, Justin Purves, Jake Sherman, Alex Kaardal, Charlie Bartholic, Nick Valure, Bram Valure, and Chris Thompson. In 2021, the largest group of Scouts in Troop 90's history earned Eagle Scout status: Owen Gifford, Connor Lehner, Lawrence Peterson-Ortega, Dan Ryna, Mario Schellenberger, and Logan Voigt.

The Pro Deo et Patria (For God and Country) is a special Boy Scouts of America award established in 1943 by the Lutheran Church, and was the first Protestant religious emblem program. It is awarded for 150 hours of Christian service to the church under the direction of the pastor, plus the completion of a special project. Six Troop 90 Scouts (John Pehling, Steven Flom, Eric Bentley, Roger Oss, Gordon Dahlen, and James Walden) received the award in 1967.

Over the years, the Troop has won numerous awards related to its excellent Scouting program. Many of its adult leaders have received awards at the district and Council level. Three Immanuel members involved in Troop 90 leadership received the rare Lutheran Lamb Award for service to youth in Scouting and the Lutheran Church bestowed by the National Lutheran Association on Scouting: Russ Edhlund (2004), Elmer Kaardal (2012), and Mark Thompson (2016).

In recognition of Immanuel sponsoring Boy Scout Troup 90, the Boy Scouts of America (BSA) Indianhead Council selected Immanuel as Chartered Partner of the Year in 2001. BSA North Star District again awarded this honor to Immanuel in 2004.

In 2009, one of Troop 90's Scouts, Richard Silverman-King, was awarded the Boy Scouts of America National Life Saving Medal of Merit when he used skills taught to him by older Scouts to save a classmate from choking.

Camping and high adventure are the cornerstone of Troop 90's program. Among the exciting destinations to which they have traveled are Isle Royale, the Boundary Waters Canoe Area, the Big Horn Mountains, Yellowstone National Park, the Superior Hiking Trail, the Porcupine Mountains, Philmont Scout Ranch, and Florida Sea Base. They have spent the night sleeping in such unusual places as a giant cave, a World War II submarine, and the outfield at the Metrodome. Appendix J lists Troop 90 Scoutmasters.

5-5. Boy Scouts selling herring at the lutefisk dinner (ca. 2006)

Troop 38

Troop 38 was started at Highland Park Lutheran Church in 1928 and was famous for having the most Eagle Scouts for many years. Known Scoutmasters were C.C. Clark and Art Kingsbury. Immanuel members of this troop who attained the rank of Eagle Scout were Kermit Uggens, Greg Norgaard, and two sons of Clarence Nelson. Troop 38 organized boys into "The Calumet Indian Dancers," who made their own costumes, learned authentic dances, and performed in Minnesota and across the United States, including on the steps of the White House. They had a bus tour in the western U.S. in 1958. With the merger of Highland Park and Immanuel in 1960, the assumption is that Troop 38 scouts merged with Immanuel's Troop 90.

Immanuel Foundation

The Immanuel Lutheran Church Foundation was established in 1991 as a non-profit corporation to support Immanuel Lutheran Church in its programs and endeavors, foster Lutheran education through scholarships, and advance Christian outreach in the community. The Articles of Incorporation were submitted by Immanuel members Jim Hagquist, David Swanson, Otis

Hilbert, Claire Taylor-Sherman, and John Otteson, and certified by the Minnesota Secretary of State on April 10, 1991. The original Board of Directors consisted of Stan Anderson, Mark Jacobson and Nancy Granrud.

The Foundation is managed by a Board of Directors, who are members of Immanuel, but not members of the church Council or church staff. Election of the Directors takes place at the annual congregational meeting. Additionally, an annual report of the Foundation is presented to the congregation during the same meeting. This is an opportunity for the Foundation to share its financial report and a summation of the funding provided in the previous year.

The Foundation has different sources of funding, including memorials, estate giving, special gifts, and annual giving. The Foundation makes grants from the investment income generated by the principal balance.

Donations to the Foundation began shortly after its incorporation. The Foundation has received and invested gifts, grants, bequests, securities, and other real or personal property. The first reported donation of significance was the Patricia Martin memorial. Another early donation came from the DuCharme Memorial Scholarship Fund when the Council approved of the transfer of these funds to the Foundation. In 1999, the Foundation placed special emphasis on encouraging additional donations by communicating the activities, the purpose, and the role of the Foundation. The themes emphasized were *Leave a Legacy* and *Where There is a Will, There is a Way*.

According to Foundation records, the Foundation had total assets of $6,412 in 1992, which grew quickly to $52,601 in 1995. A steady stream of donations and memorials, large and small, throughout the years has significantly increased the Foundation's total assets, which at the end of 2021 were $502,960.

Gifts from the Foundation are categorized into four areas of support:

1. Scholarships for Immanuel Members Attending Lutheran Colleges and Seminaries. One of the initial sizable donations to the Foundation was a gift specifically to provide scholarships to Immanuel members who attend Lutheran colleges and seminaries. The Foundation carries on this founding tradition each year with direct scholarships, often matched by the educational institutions where recipients attend. The initial scholarship amount granted was $250. In 2009, the scholarship amount per applicant increased to $1,000 per year and then eventually to a maximum of $4,000 per applicant, per year in 2019.

2. Bright Idea Grants. The Bright Idea Grant program was established by the Foundation's Board of Directors in 2006. Grants are awarded each year to innovative programs proposed by Immanuel members that meet the defined Bright Idea Grant criteria, such as a new initiative, an identified need, or opportunity within Immanuel. Such an initiative or program should be able to leverage other non-cash resources to help a group achieve its goals, be well-planned, and use high quality resources for implementation. Examples of projects supported by the Foundation Bright Idea Grants include a women's retreat, kid's carnival, art and music camp, author reading series, financial education for teens and parents, dementia educational/support packets, St. Nicholas festival, iconography class, puppet ministry, and the 2020 virtual flea market.

5-6. *Open Eye Puppet Theatre, funded by Immanuel Foundation Bright Idea Grant (2015)*

3. Poverty and Hunger Issues. In 2011, the Foundation received a generous bequest to open a new category of giving, specifically for hunger and poverty. This provided the Foundation an opportunity to move into a new and critical area of need. The creation of this funding category also provides the Foundation and the members of Immanuel with a challenge to support this exciting opportunity with future gifts directed toward the alleviation of hunger and poverty. The Foundation requests input from Immanuel's Social Action Team when making yearly gifts to this important mission.

4. Special Funding Requests. The Immanuel Lutheran Church Foundation also considers special, one-time funding requests of great importance to Immanuel. For example, a grant was given in 2009 to assist with the costs of redeveloping the Immanuel website, which provided the Church with a better tool for outreach. Other special funding grants included audio/visual equipment and funding for the 150th anniversary celebration activities.

Over its 30 years of existence, the Immanuel Foundation has had a significant impact by improving Immanuel's visibility in the community, enriching the lives of the congregation, supporting Immanuel's youth in attendance at Lutheran colleges, and assisting the poor by contributing to hunger and poverty-focused organizations. The distribution each year has historically been based on a percentage of the Foundation's earnings from investments; as of 2020, the target was to distribute 5 percent of the previous three-year average earnings.

The following individuals have served as presidents of the Immanuel Foundation since its incorporation:

Year	Name
1991	Mark Jacobson
1994	Roger Lilleodden
1996	Dean Hughes
1998	John Otteson
1999	Ralph Thrane
2003	Doug Wangensteen
2005	Peggy Johnson
2007	Sue Browender
2010	Jeff Schmidt
2013	Lori Dufresne
2018	Penny Norquist
2022	Heather Cordes

Women at Immanuel

The roles, activities, and treatment of women in Immanuel, Macalester Park, and Highland Park Lutheran Churches paralleled the situation of women in the United States over the decades. In the early years, gender norms prevailed, with men perceived as the breadwinners. They had an almost exclusive voice regarding public matters, such as voting. Single female immigrants usually worked in domestic services and supported themselves until they married, when their focus became the home, domestic chores, and caring for the sick and the needy in their communities—and sometimes around the world. Women in the 18th century and early 19th centuries set up social and service organizations, often revolving around church membership, which was the case in Immanuel, Macalester Park, and Highland Park Lutheran Churches.

Throughout the years, the various Ladies Aid societies, circles, associated groups, and guilds of Immanuel have supported mission work and made significant financial contributions to the church. These groups also provided the women in Immanuel a place to socialize and to grow and not only in a spiritual way. The various women's groups also taught them to speak in public, run a meeting, and organize a successful event, whether it was a church supper or a rummage sale.

A central goal of these groups was supporting the missions and missionary work of the church. In addition to providing money, the women made clothing, blankets, quilts, and other items that were sent to the needy. Dr. Gustav Marius Bruce (former Immanuel pastor and professor at Luther Theological Seminary) noted that the various women's groups of the Hauge Norwegian Lutheran churches in America supplied much of the funding for home and foreign mission work. The women raised funds in an endless variety of ways, many listed below.

Unfortunately, early mentions of married women in Immanuel church records seldom use their given names, referring to them only by the husband's names, for example, Mrs. John Nelson. This was the social norm and the practice in the media for decades. In 1967, Immanuel began listing women by their first name, last name, then their husband's first name. An article in the *Washington Post* traced that newspaper's changing practices, noting that only in 1989 did the *Post* stylebook recommend referring to a married woman by her first name and surname without the "Mrs." or listing her husband's name.

Initially, Immanuel women could not serve as deacons, trustees, or other officers in the congregation. One might posit that women began to create their own social and service groups because they could not participate in governance or other official church activities. However, Immanuel women were given the right to vote on church matters in 1917; note that the United States did not grant women the right to vote until 1920. Only in 1961 was the Immanuel constitution changed to allow women in leadership roles. In 1964, Rachel Husom was Immanuel's first female Sunday School Superintendent, although records indicate that she served as Assistant Sunday School Superintendent before then. A "Miss Christensen" is listed as one of several Sunday School officials immediately after the merger with Macalester Park Lutheran Church. It was clearly a transitional period and, by 1925, Solfest J. Aalbue is listed as the sole Sunday School Superintendent. Rev. Susan Smith was called to be Immanuel's first woman pastor in 1995. Nancy Granrud was the first woman Council president in 1980. Thirteen women have served as president between 1980 and 2022. See Appendix K for a list of Immanuel presidents.

5-7. Pastor Bennie Duckstad with women of the church (1932)

Women's roles in society began to change in the second half of the 20th century and these changes naturally affected the activities of women who were Immanuel members. In 1950, only 29 percent of all women in the U.S. were working outside the home and this increased to 56.8 percent in 2022. The most drastic increase was among working mothers, which went from a mere 11.9 percent in 1950 to 72.4 percent (of women with children under the age of 18) in 2022. These women were working outside the home and, for the most part, continuing to care for their children and homes—resulting in less time for church activities. They often found networking, support, classes, and volunteer opportunities in the broader community.

Early History

By 1881, five Immanuel women were meeting as the original "Ladies Aid." Their main objective was to support mission work. The group met on the first Wednesday of the month. They brought handwork (aprons and shirts to make and sell), and Rev. Fredrick Herman Carlson, Immanuel's first called pastor, read to the group from mission papers to keep them informed about activities in the mission work. They had no fixed dues, but usually had a child's bank on the table in which they put such offerings as they could afford. When the meeting was over, the lady that was to entertain next time took the bank home. Presidents of the Ladies Aid in the early years were: Mrs. John Nelson, Mrs. Trine Brekke, Mrs. Chr. O. Brohaugh, Mrs. Jens Johansen, Mrs. Andrew Martinson, Mrs. G.M. Bruce, Mrs. H.G. Grove, and Mrs. O. Christensen.

"So why do we Norwegian immigrant women of Immanuel Lutheran church come together on a cold January night in Saint Paul? We come to share devotions

that help us focus our minds and hearts throughout the next days. And we are able to get support and help from other women as we struggle to make our way in this new country with a new language and different ways of doing things. And together we have a way to help others by making money with our sewing. None of us are rich but see that we have good opportunities to make a living here in Minnesota. We want to follow the teachings of Jesus to help those in need and there are always others who have needs greater than our own. We are thankful for our wonderful newly founded church and our very own pastor and a chance to receive communion and worship together on Sundays—right in our neighborhood. We are truly blessed." —Karen Christensen (Mrs. Ole Christensen), 1881

As the membership grew, the women arranged for officers and had a sale once a year, usually on Thanksgiving Day. After the afternoon sale, the women would serve a well-attended supper. One year, the women prepared eight turkeys "with all the necessary trimmings." The money raised usually went to home and foreign missions and church schools.

In 1916, the group of women who had been instrumental in establishing the Sunday School in Bucka's Hall (1676 Grand Avenue) met to form the Macalester Park Ladies Aid. This was a year before Macalester Park Lutheran Church was formally founded. One of the first recorded acts of financial support from the Macalester Park Ladies Aid was providing $250 toward the purchase of the lot for the chapel on Goodrich Avenue in 1918, followed by another $345 in 1919. During World War I, the women of Immanuel made bandages for the soldiers. During this period, the women's groups met in homes.

When Immanuel and Macalester Park Lutheran Churches merged in 1921, the two Ladies Aid groups remained separate and did not merge until 1925. Before they merged, they worked jointly on many functions, conducted mission projects, and raised funds for the new church building at Goodrich and Snelling. In 1921, the Ladies Aid groups of Immanuel and Macalester Park had the same goal: "To be a spiritual and financial support to the new joined congregation."

In order to work together while operating as two organizations, both groups frequently sent speakers to address each other's meetings to discuss shared goals and projects such as the flower fund to provide cheer to returning missionaries, mission boxes, and Christian education. One of the most important projects for the women at this time was the organization of a multi-congregational Sunday school, which was formed prior to the joining of the congregations as a means of providing a sense of community, education, and support to their children, the "unchurched," and those in need.

By 1925, and with construction underway, these groups were working hard on resolving barriers so they could become one group. Through their activities, thriftiness, and savings, they collectively pledged more than $2,000 to provide pews to the new church. In addition, they contributed other items such as a new runner for the central aisle and dishes and silverware for the kitchen, remained committed to their mission efforts, and raised benevolence funds to support the Lutheran Girls' Rescue Home and the Mission Cottages, which provided temporary housing for missionaries while they were on leave. Two women were appointed to introduce visitors to members and a visiting committee made calls on members and friends. It was decided to read the women's group constitution every three months at meetings, but in 1928 the constitution was lost so a new one was written. Only three "treats" could be served at Ladies Aid meetings or the hostess would be fined $1.00. In 1926, there was discussion about allowing only two treats at meetings. There is a record of a rummage sale held in 1925 with a fish pond. A special event in 1927 involved watching a "moving picture" of the passion play with music provided by Cardoza & Company. The Ladies Aid found it difficult to distinguish West Immanuel from East Immanuel in written materials, so it was decided to add the name, "West Immanuel," "Macalester Immanuel," or "Midway Immanuel" along with the address of the church on correspondence.

Once the two Ladies Aid groups officially merged, they continued to meet the growing demand for financial support of the new building construction, including fundraising that paid off a note debt that others in the church could not meet. Throughout the remainder of the construction, the women increased their giving. They saw that shrubbery and flowers were planted on the new grounds. They performed essential ministry duties such as forming a committee to make visitors welcome and organizing membership events to help people become acquainted. Further, they painted the basement, varnished cupboards, gave preserves and donations to the missionaries, made Thanksgiving baskets for the needy, provided clothing to the Children's Receiving Home, and responded to the many needs of the growing congregation. In addition, they committed to buying the large stained-glass window that was installed above the altar.

In 1928, the women organized themselves into three circles divided alphabetically by last name. Each group was given autonomy to organize their own program for fundraising. This spurred increased activity that not only allowed for the gift of the stained-glass window, but the shrubbery, lawn, and other essential decor. The circles were dissolved once these projects were finished, but were reestablished along with the adoption of a new church constitution in 1929. For the ladies, the decade culminated with four new circles pledging to raise $40 each to be able to purchase a stove for the new kitchen. Results were beyond expectation and more than $400 was raised—enough for the stove and the beginnings of a new fund to pay for a church organ the following year.

By 1931, the Great Depression was affecting all parts of life. For the women of Immanuel, the response meant more effort to aid the congregation's financial obligations in these dire times. Thank-offering boxes were added as well as a self-denial giving initiative, and special membership drives aimed to add more women to the Ladies Aid. Records show the women were able to raise several thousand dollars over the decade. Funds were sent to the Rescue Home and Zion Auxiliary, and baskets of food were sent to the needy. The Ladies Aid paid $400 to the building fund and $553 toward the congregation's loan, installed a new sink in the kitchen, and added more dishes. In 1932, the Ladies Aid began to work more closely with the national Evangelical Lutheran Church's Women's Missionary Federation (WMF) and added the Cradle Roll program. The Cradle Roll was a ministry that provided a packet of information related to Christian child development to families of baptized children 1–33 months of age. The Cradle Roll became the Mothers Club in 1944 (in the 1950s, mothers graduated when their children passed six years of age), the Mary Circle in 1961, and then the "Stay-at-Home Mom's Circle" in 2000. The Baby Palooza program for mothers with infants and toddlers started in 2013.

The Mothers Club was both an outlet and escape for young mothers. Participants remembered—

Mother's Club was an opportunity to have an evening out (without the kids) and enjoy exclusively ADULT conversation. We made many life-long friends through Mother's Club.

One of my memories of Mothers Club was our annual 'auction.' We would all bring something we made: cookies, banana bread, etc. Martha Lindgren would bring things like handmade rugs, and she had six children!

My memories are of the wonderful support the women in Mothers Club were for one another in those pre-daycare days. Morning coffees, babysitting for one another, and good evenings together.

In 1945, we had our annual picnic—the only time we brought our kids.

The 1930s saw the beginnings of a new tradition for Immanuel. The women held the first lutefisk supper in 1932, which became an annual dinner in 1935. They again created a committee to make visitors feel welcome. The women formed sewing groups, which continued through the following decades, making blankets, baby clothes, and quilts. They gave money to the Red Cross for drought victims and to Immanuel Trustees to pay the insurance. They helped buy choir gowns. In 1935, the name was changed from the Ladies Aid to the Ladies Guild.

5-8. Charter members of the Women's Guild (1950)

Among the assorted projects to raise funds were ice cream socials, paper sales, vanilla sales (one year, the women sold 12 dozen bottles and netted $50.00), nuts and car freshener sales, and sales of Jell-O and "powders." Immanuel women were one of many church groups that had a stand at the Minnesota State Fair. They collected rags and sold them to Harvey Smart's gas station (Fairview and Grand Avenues) for 10 cents a pound. The women assembled, printed, and sold cookbooks in 1925, 1932, 1939, and 1943, when they sold 600 cookbooks for 35 cents each. They also prepared and sold a Scandinavian cookbook in 1949. Women collected discarded nylons and made animal toys for handicapped children in Minneapolis. Funds were collected to provide scholarships for Luther Seminary students and to give to the Lutheran Welfare Society, a precursor of today's Lutheran Social Service of Minnesota. For the duration of World War II (1942–1945), Immanuel women got together to knit and sew for the soldiers, provide dressings for the Red Cross, and make cookies for the USO.

After World War II

In 1945, the Immanuel Lutheran Ladies Guild changed their name to Immanuel Lutheran Women's Guild. There were four circles in the 1940s. The Mothers Club started a nursery in 1944. In 1949, rather than have a rummage sale, clothing was donated to displaced persons in Europe.

The 1950s saw growth in Immanuel's membership as well as in the women's groups. The women eliminated the debt on the kitchen remodeling and purchased carpeting for the sanctuary. In 1956, the Hospitality Committee made 108 calls. That same year, the women bought new kitchen equipment and new furniture for the pastor's study. For several years in the 1950s, the Women's Guild held a fall festival, with almost all of Immanuel's organizations having booths. Items sold included hand-sewn and knitted items, baked goods, Christmas tree trimmings, candles, and cards.

Following the merger with Highland Park Lutheran Church in 1960, the Highland Park Lutheran Church Women's Guild merged with the Immanuel Lutheran Women's Guild, which involved the joining all of the women's groups from both churches. Also in 1960, a new synod, the American Lutheran Church, was formed through a merger of the "old" American Lutheran Church, the United Evangelical Lutheran Church, and the Evangelical Lutheran Church. At this time, the name of the affiliated national women's group became the American Lutheran Church Women. Immanuel followed suit and, in 1961, Immanuel's various women's groups merged to become the Immanuel Lutheran Church Women (ILCW), with a new constitution and new guidelines. The mission of the ILCW was "To know and do the will of the Lord Jesus Christ." New circles were created. The ILCW met the first Thursday of the month with varying afternoon and evening meetings. Ten circles met at various times during the second and third week of the month. Esther Anderson (Mrs. Morgan Anderson) was the president of the ILCW during the year of the merger and Marguerite Hamre was the first president of the new combined group.

In 1960, the ILCW gave $1,500 to Immanuel to furnish the West Lounge in the new addition and provide dishes. This new room housed the archives of the various women's organizations at Immanuel and served as a meeting room for circles and other events. The 1960s saw the organization of the Lyngblomsten Circle to further the work of the Lyngblomsten Home. A nursery was started to provide care for little ones on Sunday mornings. Besides the 11 circles, there were two mission sewing groups with 125 women participating. In 1962, a coffee hour was introduced between services on the first Sunday of the month, provided by (of course) the women. In 1967, the Christmas celebration featured a "Festival of Nations" theme at the Christmas luncheon, with 11 nations represented. The circles prepared food from each country. The women presented a popular "Hobby Day" in both 1967 and 1968. Also in 1968, the women shared a Lenten Sacrificial Meal using food mentioned in the Bible.

5-9. *Faith and Joy Circle meeting in the West Lounge, which was funded by the ILCW (2007)*

A new ILCW constitution was accepted in 1971. A highlight of the activities of the ILCW in 1971 was an International Fun Fair. Booths representing the culture and food of several different nations were displayed and a talk was given by Betty Denny titled, "Witnessing for Christ." That year, the women were involved in 20 projects to either raise money or directly serve the community. In 1972, 29 projects were undertaken. Separate groups consisted of the Wedding Ring Circle, which served for weddings, and the Condolence Committee, which served for funerals. Other related groups included the Altar

Guild, two Sewing Circles, and the Lutheran Social Service Auxiliary. The men's and women's groups at Immanuel together provided subscriptions to "Campus Life" to all confirmands. The Lyngblomsten Circle had a successful boutique at the Lutefisk dinner in 1979.

In the 1980s, the ILCW women were fond of skits and plays, and several were written by Immanuel members. At the 1987 Christmas gathering, women were handed scripts for "A Christmas Carol" as they entered the Fireside Room and asked to read the part for one of the characters. Everyone said, "Yes!" The play was performed with no rehearsals and much laughter, However, Immanuel member Bernice Maas had practiced the role of Ebenezer Scrooge ahead of time. Women's groups often took day trips. Pastor John Lohre accompanied the ILCW on a bus trip to Duluth's Glensheen Manor in 1980. The women had a very successful parking lot sale in 1981.

5-10. ILCW Skit "How Can We Keep Them Down on the Farm after They've Seen Snelling Avenue," with Ron Hovick (Luther Seminary student), Janet Cruse (left), and Sandy Butler (right) (1991).

In 1986, Garrison Keillor sold tickets to "A Night at Lake Wobegon," which was held at Dorothy's Chatterbox Café (Immanuel's kitchen.) Immanuel women cooked hotdishes and Jell-O salads, and were the waitresses wearing hairnets and aprons with hankies in their pockets. The program included Fryda, the Goddess of Neatness; Lefse, Goddess of Unseasoned Food, and "Surprising, Inventive Jell-O." Larry Wilson provided piano music and David Stark sang a solo and led the audience in singing, "Amazing Grace." A good time was had by all.

The 1990s continued the good works, Bible Study, and fellowship of the ILCW. There were Valentine's Day parties, Christmas parties, a Fall Brunch in 1994 with the theme of "Here's to your Health—Body, Mind, and Spirit," musical performances, and a special Valentine's Day luncheon in 1996 celebrating the 125th anniversary of Immanuel Church.

In the 2000s, the ILCW had six circles, including a funeral circle, which provided refreshments after funerals held at Immanuel. The women assembled health kits to be distributed to refugees by Lutheran World Relief. Women's retreats were held yearly and focused on supporting the physical, emotional, and spiritual health of the women of Immanuel at a delightful spot miles away. Many programs had a focus on issues around the world. In 2007, *Noche de Colores*" was held at Immanuel—focusing on the sights, sounds, and tastes of Guatemala. There was a market with handmade Guatemalan items for sale, a demonstration of Guatemalan weaving, and Guatemalan-inspired foods. Immanuel member Ann Derr gave a talk about her volunteer work in Guatemala with cleft palate surgical teams and the Common Hope project. Janet Metcalfe, from the Saint Paul Area Synod, spoke on the ministries of the *Iglesia Luterana Agustina de Guatemala* (ILAG)

The 2010s continued a focus on ministries around the world and in the local community. Women baked bread for Communion at a retreat, made fleece blankets, knitted baby hats, learned about anti-bullying initiatives, and studied the lives and works of Franciscan nuns. Programs focused on the ministry with Native Americans in the East Metro with speaker Pastor Jennie Lightfoot. One entertainment highlight was a performance by the Hoang Anh Vietnamese Dance Troupe. The ILCW collected supplies for Lutheran World Relief layette kits. A new event was added to the yearly schedule called "Girls Night In." This event invited women of the church to an evening at Immanuel for pampering, junk food, games, laughter, yoga, and movies. Another annual event was the Spring Tea and Hat luncheon where mothers, grandmothers, children, nieces, and friends were invited to a luncheon and program, and were encouraged to wear a hat of their choice. Immanuel women prepared another church cookbook to sell in 2011.

5-11. Noche De Colores—Penny Nordquist, Karen Searle, and traditional Guatemalan weaver (2007)

5-12. Spring Tea and Hat Luncheon—JoAnn Hogenson, Sandy Butler, and Harriet Kidder (2011)

In 2020, the ILCW women's retreat at Mount Olivet Retreat Center had a presentation on Immanuel women's history, previewing Immanuel's 150th anniversary. The ILCW decided to try a new governing structure in 2021 that eliminated the president, vice president, and other officers, while still providing budgetary oversight.

Various Women's Groups

Busy Bees

The "Busy Bees" were organized in 1883 by Laura Nelson and Elizabeth Larson. Twelve "girls" participated. They were mainly single working women. They met twice a month in an upstairs room in a rented house on 13th Street. From there, meetings moved to the church on 14th and Canada Streets and then to the church on Aurora and St. Albans. In the early 1900s, meetings were conducted in English, but treasurer's reports were in Norwegian until 1908. Meetings included a devotion, a business meeting, conversation, and sewing items for an annual sale. Initially, the group had only two officers—a president and a treasurer. The dues were in no fixed amount, each member giving what she wished or felt she could. The annual sale was the chief source of income, but occasional lawn bazaars, parcel sales, and ice cream socials raised funds. Sometimes a supper was served in conjunction with the sale.

Money raised was primarily directed to mission work, but also given to Immanuel when it was in need of funds. They contributed to the pastor's salary, purchased a piano, and, as early as 1907, gave $100.00 toward a pipe organ fund. Funds were given to the Beresford Orphan's Home and the Children's Receiving Home, earlier known as the Colony of Mercy.

In the latter part of 1909, the Busy Bees began to meet monthly. Over time, a secretary was added, a flower fund established, and the dues were set at fifteen cents for regular members and ten cents for the younger women.

The Busy Bees changed their name to *De Unge Kvinders Syforening* (Young Women's Sewing Association) in 1915. This was later translated to The Young Ladies Aid. In 1918, the name was changed again to The Loyal Workers Society in response to World War I. There was pressure on immigrants in the United States at that time to give up using their native language and show their loyalty to their new country. As one member noted, "Loyalty to church and to country was the urge on every hand."

In 1924, the Loyal Workers pledged to purchase the electric light fixtures for the new church structure then being planned. They raised the needed funds through cake sales and Saturday afternoon "Tea Rooms." The members sold *McCall's Magazine* subscriptions on commission as another way of raising money.

In the spring of 1928, the Loyal Workers sponsored the first Mother-Daughter Banquet. The banquet continued annually for many years. In 1945, Loyal Workers charged 35 cents per person to attend the banquet. Because of food shortages during World War II, the party was held in the church instead of in a restaurant. It featured musical numbers, a dramatic reading, and a skit with "our own amateur talent." It was held with "deep appreciation and thankfulness to God for one of his greatest gifts—Mother." The Mother and Daughter banquet in 1954 was considered the 27th and 150 guests attended.

5-13. Mother-Daughter Banquet entertainment (1932)

Always concerned about raising funds, the Loyal Workers decided to tax each member $4.00. In subsequent years, the $4.00 pledge continued as well as suppers, parcel sales, and musical programs. In 1931, they implemented a birthday calendar, with space for fifteen dimes. They began sewing again and made articles (dishtowels, etc.) to sell to individuals and at the Ladies Aid fall sale.

Lutheran Daughters of the Reformation.

Lutheran Daughters of the Reformation (LDR) was a national initiative of the Evangelical Lutheran Church and was primarily composed of single business and professional women who were high school graduates and beyond. Married women raising families belonged to the Ladies Aid. Immanuel's LDR was among one of the first societies to affiliate with the Synod's national organization in 1932. Leaders in establishing Immanuel's LDR were Lena Christensen, Agnes Oliver Lindgren, and Constance Weswig Johnson, who later became the first president of the newly formed organization. The LDR had two arms: Fidelis and Dorcas Society.

They raised funds to support Jewish missions, missions in Alaska, and Immanuel's needs, including contributing to the pastor's salary and buying a piano. A Historical Department and a Reading Project was added to the national LDR work. The Immanuel LDR signified their cooperation with these two movements by adding a historian to their staff of officers and by selecting a committee to promote interest in the Reading Project.

The group was tireless in their work to support missions, missionaries, and the needy, and to help support the needs of Immanuel. This does not mean, however, that there were no social times. In early years, as well as in the years that have followed, the women enjoyed each other's company. They got together for picnics and other social hours, which fostered the friendships formed.

As we scan the life of the organization, from the beginning to the present time, one thing we can readily observe is that the ideal of service to the church and to fellow men has ever been present. In this spirit the girls have labored in this little corner of the Master's Vineyard and have gone forward under His leadership. In conclusion, let me say that I hope the blessings of God may rest upon us in the future as it has in the past, and that we may have grace to go forward as true daughters of the church. —Agnes L. Hansen, 1933

Circles and Special Women's Groups

Circles are small groups of women who meet monthly for Bible study, socializing, and to work on special projects. In 1928, Immanuel's Ladies Aid formed three circles, with each circle deciding on its own program for raising money for shrubbery and the stained glass window behind the altar. In 1948, there were four circles and by 1965, there were ten circles. Records from 2005 indicate there were three circles.

Immanuel has had many circles over the years and some have had a specific mission. One example was the Sewing Circles, which made blankets, baby clothes, and quilts for the needy. Another was the Lyngblomsten Circle, which had the primary goal of raising funds for the Lyngblomsten Foundation; it dissolved in December 2009. The names of the circles have varied over time. Names used and reused have been Joy, Faith, Hope, Peace, Unity, Courage, Patience, Love, Mary (which became the Stay-at-Home Moms), Sarah, Rebekah, Lydia, Naomi, Deborah, Elizabeth, Esther, Martha, Dorcas, Grace, Sofia, and Jael.

Today, Immanuel has six circles. Women may choose a circle based on when and where it meets. During the COVID pandemic, circle meetings were held on Zoom and attendance waned. Reinstating in-person meetings has increased interest and attendance.

Over the years, the women of Immanuel created other groups to address specific needs and interests. Among these were a Grief Coalition, a "scrap bookers" group, and women who met to work on quilts. The Quilters met every other Wednesday to make handmade quilts that were given to Plymouth Youth Center, Southeast Asia Ministry, Lutheran World Relief, and Birthright. In 1975, the group made 59 crib quilts, 127 baby gowns, 24 receiving blankets, and 103 quilts. The quilting group was dissolved in 2005.

Blessed are the Quilters, for
They are the piecemakers,
They know how to cut corners.
They keep you in stitches.
They make great comforters.
They patch things up.
They pick up the pieces.
They save you energy.
They put color into your life.
                    —*Ina R. Jacobs*

5-14. Gertrude Widsten working on quilts for Global Mission (1980s)

5-15. Pastor Elder Bentley, Sandy Anderson, and Esther Bentley with quilt made by the Immanuel women for his retirement (1992)

The PrayerFull Pantry ministry was started in 2011, building on an idea of the Grace Circle and supported with a Bright Idea Grant. Immanuel members are invited to prepare a meal or two for Immanuel members who are experiencing significant life events (births, deaths, illnesses, job losses, etc.).

Men at Immanuel

"I remember the first time I went to Immanuel [circa 1921]. It was on a Saturday and my Dad took me with him as he and six or seven other men were going to do volunteer work to complete some of the carpenter work and build shelves and cabinets. They joked and laughed with each other and were happy to contribute their time and talents to do what was necessary to improve their place of worship. The walls were unpainted, windows were plain frosted glass, bare wooden floors and folding wooden chairs instead of pews. I liked and was impressed with my new church. It took years to complete the church to the satisfaction of the congregation."
—Marvin Merrick, son of a founder of Macalester Park Lutheran Church

Immanuel men's groups have had various names over the years: Men's Club, Men's Society, Men's Group, and Lutheran Brotherhood. One of the early groups was organized in 1917. The first meeting of the Men's Club was held in 1938. For many years, the group had monthly dinners, prepared by Immanuel member Ferne Needels (Roger Needels' mother) for 100 men. Dinners continued into the 1960s. These dinners had a program, often a speaker (such as Paul Giel or Walter Mondale) and might have included a sports movie.

In 1925, the men installed the furnishings in the chancel. In 1935, the group took over publishing and financing the *Immanuel Messenger* (newsletter). Starting in 1946, the men's group published an Immanuel business directory for several years.

The men hosted Father and Sons banquets from the 1940s through the 1960s. In April 1948, *The Messenger* reported, "The program being planned will enable any boy who can stay awake after 7PM to attend the banquet with his father. Men who do not have sons may call the church office to receive the name of a boy without a father able to take him to the banquet." Governor Luther Youngdahl spoke at the 1951 Father and Sons banquet. Eighty-five men and boys attended the 1952 banquet. That year, the Immanuel Junior Basketball Team was presented with the YMCA Junior Championship Trophy at the banquet. Immanuel women's groups prepared the dinner and served.

5-16. Lutheran Brotherhood members carving at a one of their banquets (1960s)

In the 1940s and 1950s, the men's group sponsored teams that played dartball, kittenball, shuffleboard, bowling, and basketball. The men's group provided the basketball teams with sports jerseys.

Before the creation of the Improvers in 2000, the men's group handled many projects around the church, including repairs in the basement and furnace room, work on the church grounds, and more. The men's group agreed to pay part of the expense for a $80,000 loan in 1952 for the church expansion on the South Snelling side. They pledged $1,000 over two years and raised $500 at a dinner that year. They converted the parsonage garage into a Boy Scout room, spending $75.00 and doing the work themselves.

In August 1951, the Men's Brotherhood sponsored their fifth annual ice cream social. *The Messenger* reported, that "Everett Needles, manager of Needles & Co., has guaranteed mosquito control, so come on out. You won't have to worry about mosquitoes!!!" Tickets cost 35 cents.

Fishing trips have been a favorite activity. In 1947, 38 men and boys went to the Tjornhom Lodge on Ottertail Lake. Forty men and boys went on the 1949 fishing trip. Fishing trips continued into the 21st century, but the fishing trips were paused during the COVID pandemic.

5-17. Men's fishing trip (2014)

The current group, called the Men's Club, began in 1992. This group meets on the second Saturday of the month for breakfast, fellowship, and sometimes a speaker. The men's breakfasts were paused during the COVID pandemic. The Men's Club hosts the annual lutefisk dinner. At the time of this writing, the men's group supports a student in Guatemala through Common Hope and a high school student in Tanzania through Bega Kwa Bega.

5-18. Men's Club breakfast (2006)

Lutefisk Dinner

Immanuel Church women began annual lutefisk smorgasbord dinners in 1935 with lutefisk suppers recorded at least as early as 1932. Two lutefisk dinners were held in 1938 to raise money; the proceeds that year were $126. The dinners were suspended during World War II from 1942–1946. In the 1940s, the women and men put on the dinner together. By 1952, the lutefisk dinner was becoming too much for the women, so the men's group was asked to take over. In 1952, 350 people were served.

> *One of the traditional projects for the raising of funds, the annual 'smorgasbord' was dispensed with . . . due to the high price of food and the necessity for cooperating with our nation in conserving food for our armed forces.*
> —Ladies Aid, 1942

5-19. Lutefisk Dinner Committee in traditional Norwegian dress—Ann Munson, Alice Freeberg, Alida Merrick, and Hazel Hovelsrud (1934)

5-20. James Forchtner and David Lindgren boiling lutefisk in cheese cloth (late 1950s)

At the first few dinners run by the Men's Club, the lutefisk was boiled in cheese cloth. That created a rather distinctive and unpleasant aroma. Wiser lutefisk cooks convinced the men to bake the lutefisk. Ever since, Immanuel has been known to serve "the best fish in town."

Hundreds of meatballs are prepared before the dinner by Immanuel's "holy rollers." Early Immanuel member Marv Merrick stated, "Those delicious meatballs are my mother's Swedish meatball recipe. Of course, Dave [Lindgren] and Roger [Forman] refer to them as Norwegian meatballs." The meatball mix is now purchased, but continues to be rolled by hand. In the 1960s, one Immanuel woman made all the lefse. The Immanuel women provide a bake sale featuring a variety of Norwegian treats. Boy Scout Troop 90 sells many quarts of pickled herring. Guests enjoy wearing Norwegian sweaters to the dinner. Immanuel men and women help serve the tables. The youth clear tables and transport dishes to the kitchen for washing.

5-21. "Holy Rollers"—David Lindgren, Stan Anderson, and Robert Granrud (2001)

5-22. Lutefisk Dinner servers—Andrew Urness, Doug Derr, Russ Edhlund, and Doug Sherman (2006)

5-23. Women's Bake Sale at the Lutefisk Dinner (2006)

The sole purpose of the annual lutefisk dinner is benevolence. Income is dispersed to various organizations with an emphasis on feeding the hungry, improving the lives of youth, and recognizing veterans and those in active military service. Half of the money collected at the lutefisk dinner is given to organizations outside of Immanuel and the other half is used to support internal Immanuel needs. The success of these dinners is a tribute to the hundreds of Immanuel volunteers who have worked so hard over the years. The lutefisk dinner is a labor of love. From rolling meatballs and peeling potatoes to making baked goods for the bake sale to setting up, serving, and cleaning up, Immanuel members create a place of welcome and fellowship.

The typical menu consists of lutefisk and butter or cream sauce, meatballs and gravy, boiled potatoes and butter, peas, cranberries, lefse, fruit soup (a Scandinavian dessert of stewed fruit served cold), and cookies. Some guests are known to pour butter and cream sauce on everything. The food is served family style with bowls and platters brought to the table.

☙ *One year, Allan Forman was selling tickets for the lutefisk dinner. He had 1,200 tickets printed and sold them all. However, Allan ordered only enough food to feed 900 people! Do the math! Allan looked around. The pews in the sanctuary were filled with people. Chairs in the narthex were filled with people. The Sunday School rooms were filled with people. Roger had to come up with enough food to feed an additional 300 ticket-carrying people. He sent men out to the neighboring grocery stores to buy as much meat as possible. If they could get lutefisk, great! Otherwise, any other meat would be fine! In the spirit of the lutefisk dinner, people were fed and satisfied. After that, ticket sales were limited to 900 with 3 serving times—set at 5, 6 and 7 p.m.*

While waiting to be seated, guests assemble in the sanctuary and are entertained by music, often a group of traditional Norwegian fiddlers. For many years, Immanuel member Ralph Thrane greeted guests in the sanctuary and regaled them with stories of his North Dakota Norwegian ancestors while they waited to be called to dine.

5-24. Ralph Thrane welcoming guests at a Lutefisk Dinner (ca. 2010)

Between 2007 and 2019, 8,332 lutefisk dinner tickets were sold and $69,764 was disbursed to local and national charitable organizations and to meet needs within Immanuel. Funds have gone to Lyngblomsten, St. Mary's Home, Union Gospel Mission, Southeast Asian Ministry, Merriam Park Food Shelf (now Keystone Community Services), and numerous additional beneficiaries.

Several people have served as chairs of the lutefisk dinner, many serving in this role for several years: Arnold Jorgensen and Gunner Korsmo, David Lindgren, Jim Forchner, Dean Thorson, Allan Forman, Gene Evans, Walter Harris, Roger Forman, and currently Russ Edhlund.

No supper was held in 2005 because of construction. The COVID pandemic forced cancellation of the dinners in 2020 and 2021, although, in 2021, the men sold pickled herring and lefse and raised $300 for benevolence.

Immanuel's Veterans and War Efforts

Immanuel families have been impacted by several wars and have sent men and women to serve in the military throughout the decades. Immanuel church records indicate that during World War I, Immanuel sent 10 servicemen to war: Victor Westphal (descendent of an Immanuel founding member), Walter Knudsen, Carl Nicolson, Gudolph Grove, Harold Grove, Joseph Jorgensen, Henry Johnson, Walter Johnson, Möller Olson, and Albert Olson. All returned safely and were welcomed back into the congregation with much joy and celebration. The women of Immanuel at that time were dedicated to providing assistance by rolling bandages for servicemen. The Immanuel newsletter reported in 1918, "The Red Cross unit of our church reports that altho (sic) there was a shortage of yarn during September, 35 pairs of socks were turned in, making a total of 78 pairs sent to the Headquarters." Immanuel had a Liberty War Savings Society that sold War Savings and Thrift Stamps. In December 1919, Immanuel hosted a potluck supper to welcome Immanuel's servicemen home from World War I.

The country was shocked by the Japanese attack on Pearl Harbor and the outbreak of World War II. Immanuel sent 98 men and three women to serve in all branches of the military. A service flag was prominently placed in the narthex with a blue star for each man and woman in the military. Prayers were lifted up throughout the war. A poster was placed in the church with photos of service members and addresses were provided so that parishioners could write to them. The pastor sent issues of *The Messenger* to those serving in the military, which they greatly appreciated receiving. Three Immanuel members died during World War II: LeRoy Olson, killed in France; Walter Lamson, killed over England; and Robert Sorem, killed in Leyte in the Philippines.

Other Immanuel members were called up or volunteered to serve in military defense work, such Immanuel deacon, C.R. Raiter, who was called to work on U.S. Defense in Newfoundland in February 1941, and Pastor Bennie Duckstad, who resigned his call at Immanuel and enlisted to serve as an Army chaplain. Women, such as Immanuel member Phyllis Berg who served in the WAVES (Women Accepted for Volunteer Emergency Service--the women's branch of the United States Naval Reserve), were becoming an important and acknowledged part of the World War II war effort.

"I received the Messenger *today with the request to be remembered on Easter Sunday in the prayer for my folks as well as myself. I think that is a mighty fine gesture, as that is the only way many of us will be able to join our parents, loved ones, and friends in worship on Easter. We all would give almost anything to be there on that particular day . . . —S. Sgt. Edward C. Johnson, Italy, Feb. 25, 1945.*

"Receiving the Immanuel Messenger *has been a great source of pleasure for me. We in the Service are always pleased to hear the news from home and learn where some of our church pals have gone. We pray for you, our Immanuel, and for that final peace." —Harold Johns, April 1945*

During the difficult times of World War II, Immanuel was recognized as a church that provided outstanding support for Lutheran World Relief. When Norway was occupied by the Germans in World War II, Immanuel urgently searched for ways to get money to needy Norwegians. Immanuel continued to help those in need—missionaries in the field, soldiers in service, Jewish people abroad, and neighbors nearby who needed food. During World War II, the women of Immanuel sent cookies and cards to servicemen and women from the congregation. In 1943, the USO put out a request for 3,000 cookies and the women of Immanuel contributed to this goal. The women of Immanuel had been having lutefisk dinners for the congregation and friends since the early 1930s. Then in 1940, Swiss steak was prepared instead of lutefisk. Lutefisk dinners were postposed during the war, but they started up again when conditions normalized.

In November 1944, a candle lighting service was held for all the members of Immanuel who were serving in the military. Pastor Conrad Thompson officiated. As each name was called, a candle was lit. Each family with a service person was presented with a Certificate of Honor. A prayer service was held on Easter Sunday in 1945. The congregation prayed for all those serving in the armed forces; those serving were all contacted and asked to pray for Immanuel on Easter. Special worship services were held to commemorate Victory in Europe (VE) Day and Victory in Japan (VJ) Day, and the end of the war.

5-25. Pastor Conrad Thompson at WWII candle lighting service (November 1944)

In 1945, Immanuel's men's group (Lutheran Brotherhood) had a serviceman's committee, which planned an event to welcome home members of the armed services. The Christian Service Flag was lowered in May 1947. Joe Jorgensen, representing the Veterans of Foreign Wars (VFW), spoke to the Lutheran Brotherhood in 1945 on the topic of problems facing veterans on their return to civilian life. In his talk, Mr. Jorgensen encouraged church members to welcome returning servicemen and women, but discouraged them from bringing up the horrors of war. In 2020, five surviving World War II veterans at Immanuel were interviewed for an oral history. They were George Koerner, Ken Fick, Stan Anderson, Gordon Bauer, and John Arneson.

Over the years, 13 Immanuel pastors have served in various branches of the military, showing their dedication to God and country: William Beck, Elder Bentley, Einar Roald Carlson, Bennie Duckstad, Ralph Glenn, Rolfe Sven Johnstad, Melvin Kaatrud, Paul Frederick Metzger, Leif Ingvar Monson, Eugene Herman Pfeiffer, David Quarberg, Larry Rehlander, and Conrad Thompson. Pastor Duckstad was in his mid-40s when he resigned his call at Immanuel to serve as an Army chaplain in World War II.

5-26. Pastor Bennie Duckstad in U.S. Army Chaplain uniform

5-27. Pastor Elder Bentley in U.S. Navy Chaplain uniform

Following World War II, Immanuel members continued to serve in the military. In the 1950s and 1960s, *The Messenger* routinely published the names of service men and women, along with their APO addresses. Members were encouraged to write, offer support, and send Easter and Christmas greetings to each of them. Immanuel member Rev. Ed Maas was an Army chaplain who spent time in Germany and southwestern United States after World War II. He served as a chaplain at the Minnesota Veterans Administration hospital from 1984 to 1994 after he and his wife, Bernice, joined Immanuel.

In 1950, an Honor Roll was placed in the narthex for men who were called into service for the Korean War. The Ladies Aid sent gifts to servicemen in 1953 and 1954. Immanuel's Korean War veterans alive in 2020 included Andrew Urness, Gordon Bauer, John Skalbeck, and Lewis Dohman. Gordon Bauer and Andrew Urness have faithfully served in the Honor Guard at Fort Snelling for funerals. Roger Forman served in U.S. Military Intelligence in West Germany in the 1950s. Dick Sarafolean served in the U.S. Navy from 1955 to 1962 (during the Cold War), monitoring the Russians on the D.E.W. (Distant Early Warning) line. Vernon (Bud) Jorgensen served in the U.S. Navy in the early 1960s. Tom Cline served in the U.S. Air Force from 1963 to 1967, including time on the Auxiliary Airfield on Iwo Jima. Henry Seka served in the Gulf War and retired from the service after 20 years. His wife, Diane Laker-Seka, still serves in the military.

Immanuel members who served in the Vietnam War include Russ Edhlund, Craig Fohrenkamm, Wayne Veum, Jim Zika, and Marshall Storeby. Russ Edhlund was drafted through the lottery system to serve in Vietnam. He recalls that he was given a New Testament to take with him when he enrolled in the army. He was also given a Lutheran cross to wear with his dog tags.

Immanuel member, Marshall Storeby, served as a private in Vietnam. The story of his time there was made into a movie, *Casualties of War*, starring Sean Penn and Michael J. Fox. Fox played Private Storeby, who refused an illegal order to participate in the assault and murder of a civilian Vietnamese woman. In spite of threats to his life, he later reported the crime and testified against his squad leader and fellow soldiers. During the court martial, Storeby was asked why he made his decisions. His answer is testimony to his strong moral sense—"We all figured we might be dead in the next minute, so what difference did it make what we did? But the longer I was over there, the more I became convinced that it was the other way around that counted—that because we might not be around much longer, we had to take extra care how we behaved . . . we had to answer to something, to someone—maybe just ourselves." (Quotation from *Care for the Sorrowing Soul: Healing Moral Injuries from Military Service and Implications for the Rest of Us*, by Duane Larson and Jeff Zust (Eugene, OR: Cascade Books, 2017.)

When confronted with an unforeseen challenge, Immanuel has looked for solutions using the strengths of its members to help each other weather the storm and stay connected to each other and to God. Immanuel pastors have led the congregation with their strength and guided with the Word of God. Pastor Gustav Marius Bruce wrote to parishioners in 1919: "Be still and know that I am God." Pastor Conrad Mervin Thompson reminded parishioners in May 1945: "He will never give you more than you can stand."

CHAPTER 6

Benevolence and Social Action

Many do not know that Immanuel was a "mission plant congregation"—the goal being to "plant" a new church. Immanuel Lutheran Church received financial support from the Inner Mission of the (Hauge) Norwegian Lutheran Church Synod in America. In 1921, Immanuel received $100 a month. Early Norwegian Lutheran churches in the Midwest also received ministerial and financial support from Norway. Immanuel's Pastor Conrad Thompson, in his autobiography, recalled that Immanuel was located in "a vast mission field." The long-standing Home Mission loan from the national church was paid off in the 1940s. Despite receiving external support and experiencing occasional difficult economic times, the members of Immanuel have been incredibly generous with their time and funds. Immanuel has an impressive history of responding to calls for help locally, nationally, and internationally—and making long-term commitments to assist where there is need.

Immanuel's Early Outreach and Benevolence

Early issues of the *Immanuel Lutheran Messenger* and other Immanuel records note financial support for the following organizations, agencies, and initiatives both within and outside the United States:
- Lutheran Bible Institute
- Zion Society for Israel (missionary activity both among Jews in the United States and in other lands)
- Norwegian Lutheran Orphans Home, Beresford, South Dakota (est. 1896)
- Children's Receiving Home (Colony of Mercy—est. 1919)
- Lyngblomsten Care Center
- Lutheran Girls Rescue Home

Lutheran Welfare Society (originally Lutheran Inner Mission Society; merged with Board of Christian Service to become Lutheran Social Service of Minnesota in 1963)
Lutheran Committee for Indians living in the Twin Cities
Lutheran Children's Home at Como
St. Mary's Home
Plymouth Christian Youth Center
Augustana Academy—scholarship fund for minority students
Lake Park Wild Rice Children's Home
Norwegian Seamen's Mission
Ephahatha Mission
Lutheran Vespers
Gideon Society
Green Lake Bible Camp
Red Wing and Kenyon Homes
Lutheran Indian Mission
Golden Valley Lutheran College
Macalester College Ministry
Jewish Missions
Alaska Nome Church
Manafiafy Girls School, Madagascar
Bible School, South Africa
Pakistan Relief
Tubfrim, a Norwegian charity for disabled children
Bibles for India program

Foreign Missionary Support

It was common for churches in the Norwegian Evangelical Lutheran Church, then Evangelical Lutheran Church, then American Lutheran Church, and then Evangelical Lutheran Church in America, to have missionary committees, each church supporting one or more missionary units through direct funding of the central church's global missions and through efforts of the Ladies Aid, other women's groups, and men's groups. Missionaries on furlough were often invited to speak and then given financial and material support at these visits. Immanuel has a long history of supporting foreign missionary work.

The Immanuel Ladies Aid, as early as 1881, was apprised of foreign mission efforts by the pastors. The women made and sold aprons and men's shirts to provide money raised for home and foreign missions, and to support

Lutheran church schools. Beginning in the 1920s, church women were provided with mission boxes to take home. Spare coins were collected in the boxes, which were turned in at the end of each year. Funds from these Ladies Aid activities then were sent to the Women's Mission Federation. The practice of using mission boxes continued for at least 60 years.

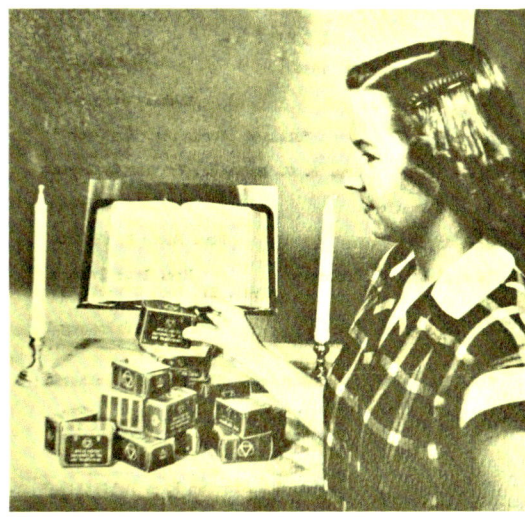

6-1. Mission boxes (1950)

In the 1930s, Immanuel provided support for the Shishmaref Lutheran Church mission on Sarichef Island, in the Chukchi Sea, Alaska. The Lutheran presence in Alaska dates back to the 1890s when Lutheran Pastor T.L. Brevig and his wife accompanied a group of Laplanders sent to Alaska to teach the native people reindeer husbandry. In the late 1920s and early 1930s, the newly formed Lutheran Daughters of the Reformation (LDR) planted a new church in Shishmaref. Immanuel women in the LDR mailed a Christmas box to the natives in Shishmaref in 1933, and they received a box of gifts in return. Shishmaref is a traditional Inupiaq village, just north of the Bering Strait and five miles from the mainland. Christmas boxes also were sent to Igloo and Teller, Alaska, with gifts and 36 testaments. The enrollment of babies in the National Cradle Roll supported the Alaska missions.

6-2. Deaconess Anna Huseth, missionary at Shishmaref, Alaska (ca. 1925)

Also in 1933, the Sunday School children of Immanuel sent money to the Christian Children's Fund to assist children overseas.

Immanuel supported many missionary families. For several years, the church women had a special fund to buy flowers for returning missionaries. In 1935, Rev. Joseph Paul Aalbue and his wife Iola Marie (nee Brennel) left to serve as missionaries in China. He was the son of Immanuel members Solfest and Clara Aalbue. He died Aug. 24, 1939, in the Matilda Hospital, Hong Kong, at the age of 31. See Appendix B. His wife spent four years in the Norwegian Lutheran Mission Field following his death.

In 1936, support was provided for the Rev. O.L. Hofstad family (missionaries who went to Madagascar in 1936). Their daughter Louise would go on to marry Ernest Midthun and serve several terms in Madagascar.

In 1945, support was provided for the Rev. Svein Steffenson Tverberg family. Rev. and Mrs. Tverberg were missionaries for 21 years in Madagascar. Their daughter, Swanhild (Swanee) Tverberg, married Immanuel Pastor Conrad Thompson, who served at Immanuel from 1945 to 1949. Mrs. Tverberg addressed the Immanuel Ladies Aid on being a missionary mother and spoke on several occasions. In the 1940s, missionaries who were home on furlough often came to speak at the Ladies Aid meetings. One of these was Minnie Waage, who spoke about her missionary work in Columbia, South America.

Immanuel also provided support for three foreign mission schools, and Immanuel women made quilts that were sent to the mission fields. In 1945, Immanuel provided funds for repairs of war-damaged mission stations in China through the Church Extension Fund. In 1946, Immanuel supported Jewish missions.

In various years, postage stamps were collected and sent to Germany and Norway, and eyeglasses were sent to foreign missions through Help for the Needy.

Immanuel supported missions in Columbia and Madagascar (1956), the South Africa Mission (1957), and the Brazil Mission (1960). Immanuel also sent support to Guinea, Madagascar, Zululand, and Kurdistan.

In 1961, Immanuel helped support the establishment of the American Lutheran Church congregation in Oslo, Norway, to minister to NATO forces and American Embassy staff stationed in Oslo.

In 1964, support was provided for Rev. and Mrs. Merrill Clark (missionaries to Papua New Guinea). Rev. Clark was the son of Clayton Clive Clark, Sr. and Violet (nee Geckler) Clark, members of Highland Park Lutheran Church and Immanuel after the merger.

In 1966, Immanuel supported a Hong Kong refugee children's school, a leprosarium in India, Brazil Bible Camp, a library in Cameroon, and missions in Japan, Ethiopia, Nigeria, New Guinea, Taiwan, Zion Society for Israel, and India.

In 1967, Carol Anderson was commissioned at Immanuel as a missionary nurse to Tanzania.

6-3. *Rev. and Mrs. Sven Tverberg, with Pastor Conrad Thompson and his wife Swanhild, daughter of the Tverbergs (1946)*

Historical Benevolence in the United States

Much of the benevolence in Immanuel's early years resulted from the diligent work of the various women's groups—the Ladies Aid (married women), the Busy Bees (single women; later known as the Loyal Workers), and the Lutheran Daughters of the Reformation (single professional women). They raised funds through donations and sales, and also made handwork that was sold or donated to the needy. The work of these industrious women is covered in detail in Chapter 5, "Building Community."

In 1942, the Loyal Workers "adopted" an eight-year-old boy, Donald Smith, who was a member of the Ho-Chunk tribe, referred to as Winnebago at that time. "Adoption" was a type of sponsorship where the women's group agreed to send him clothing each year. Donald was a day-student at the Bethany Indian Mission School, Wittenberg, Wisconsin. He lived with his family, who did not live on a reservation but in a community close to the school near many other Native American families. The Bethany Indian Mission Boarding School in Wittenberg was started in 1884 by the Norwegian American Lutheran Church and operated as a boarding school for Native American children until 1933, sometimes in partnership with the U.S. government. When the boarding school closed in 1933, Native children were encouraged to attend nearby public schools. Some families were reluctant to send their children to public school because the children did not have adequate clothing. The adoption program was started to provide summer and winter clothing to a child, which allowed him or her to attend public school. To maintain eligibility for this adoption program, a Native child had to attend both the public school and the Bethany Summer Lutheran Bible School. Immanuel received photos and thank you letters from Donald from 1942 to 1949. The Immanuel community is learning about the larger boarding school movement and its disruptive effects on Native American families and culture.

Support for Refugees

Immanuel supported many refugee families in the years following the end of World War II and the end of the war in Southeast Asia. These people were fleeing war and persecution, often coming from refugee camps and arriving in the United States with very little. Immanuel members met refugees upon their arrival to Minnesota, helping them settle in a new and very different country from the one they left. Some of the services Immanuel provided included help finding jobs, clothes, and apartments; completing paperwork; providing groceries and apartment furniture; obtaining driver's licenses; and navigating the bus system to get to work and to travel around the area. Immanuel served as a sponsor and sought to ensure success for the refugees in their new country. For the most part, Immanuel has lost contact with the families it sponsored, one indication that Immanuel met its goal of promoting their success. These families no longer needed the helping hand Immanuel provided.

In 1955/56, the Highland Park congregation sponsored the settlement of the Karl Schoene family from Bavaria, Germany. The family later opened the Gasthaus Bavarian Hunter near Stillwater. Around the same time, Immanuel sponsored the Ralph Horvath family, who were settled into their apartment home at 1124 Randolph. Mr. Horvath had been in a concentration camp in Hungary for two years and in a displaced Persons Camp in Vienna, Austria, for four years.

In 1973, Immanuel sponsored the Munshe family from Uganda. Originally from India, they were exiled by the Idi Amin regime. They owned their own school in Uganda and fled because Idi Amin was executing leaders in many fields, including education.

In 1975, Immanuel supported the Phu Lam family. The Lam family's oldest son, Ba Lam, shared their story. Ba was born in Vietnam and was three years old when his family immigrated to the United States. Father, Phu Lam, was a first lieutenant in the South Vietnamese army and a high school principal. Mother, Thom Vo, was a secretary for the United States Embassy in South Vietnam. Sons Tung Lam and Ba Lam were born in Vietnam; daughter Que Lam was born in 1976 in the United States. The family spent time in Thailand and Guam refugee camps before coming to America. They were in Arkansas for two and half months. While there, Ba's mother worked with the Red Cross doing paperwork to help families find churches to support them. During this time, she found three Minnesota churches to sponsor her family. The entire family from Ba's mother's side was able to immigrate to the United States, including grandparents, aunts and uncles, and cousins (five families). The Red Cross helped all five families move to the same state (Minnesota), which was so important to their well-being. Three Saint Paul area churches, including Immanuel, sponsored the families. The Lam family eventually bought a house in the Como Park area and attended Immanuel Christmas Eve services for many years. Elvina Loftness invited Ba's family for an annual Christmas Eve dinner. After they were established and working, they held a party hosting approximately 50 members of Immanuel Lutheran Church.

Immanuel members Dru and George Koerner lived on Lake Johanna and mentioned to Elvina Loftness, an eager supporter of Immanuel's refuge families, that a young Vietnamese dentist named Ba T. Lam was moving in next door. When Elvina said she knew him and his family, a new story began.

> "Thank you so much for taking the time to put this wonderful [history] together.... I'm sure many people will appreciate hearing the history of how Immanuel Lutheran Church has helped so many immigrant families achieve happiness and success in the US!" —Ba T. Lam, DDS, son of immigrants

During 1990–1991, Immanuel sponsored two families from Vietnam: the Cao family (husband Truoc Cao, wife Phan Vy-Thuy and daughters Yen-Ly and Vinh-Truong), and the Tieu-Ny family (sons Quang-Thang and Quant-Thinh). Mr. Cao served with American forces in South Vietnam. He spent several years in a prison camp. Support for these families included household goods and tutoring. Immanuel members were invited to many wonderful meals and celebrations at their homes.

6-4. Extended Cao Family (early 1990s)

In the spring of 2022, Immanuel began partnering with Christ the King Lutheran Church and Lutheran Social Service Circle of Welcome to support four Afghan refugees: Zalmay Habibzai, Ahmad Najim Ahmadi, Ahmad Samim Ahmadi, and Mustafa Safi. Immanuel team members involved in this initiative are Dave and Sue Klevan, Emily and Steve King, and Linda Carlson.

Benevolence in Recent Years

> *The life of a community is complex and mysterious. The most important thing to be said (even if our statistics were not as strong, nor our list of activities so full) is what I would most want to be said every year of every church: that God's Spirit has been among us, speaking, sustaining, reproving, forgiving, uniting, healing, creating, re-creating, calling, sending, inspiring, consoling, saving*

and serving us. Immanuel is alive because God in Christ has made us so. We are blessed. May we also be a blessing. —former Pastor John Marboe

Immanuel has donated to many organizations and agencies since the 1960s. These include delivering Christmas presents to the Union Gospel Mission, collecting food for the Salvation Army and Merriam Park Food Shelf (now Keystone Community Services), collecting food for HUNGER as part of the Lutheran World Federation, and providing financial support for WCAL Radio, a noncommercial Lutheran radio station at St. Olaf College, Northfield, Minnesota, with a daily devotional hour. Immanuel gave funds to "Treasure Chest," which supported scholarships, TV programs for children, college lay training, and parish education research. Immanuel supported the Community Study Center, which provided tutoring for elementary school children in collaboration with other churches in the early 1970s. Immanuel made a donation to St. Mark's Lutheran Church, Saint Paul, after it had a fire in 2014. Hope Circle coordinated the creation and delivery of kitchen kits for shelters in the metro area. Immanuel purchased cleaning kits to help with Fargo flood relief. For several years, Immanuel had an "Undie Sunday," on which new underwear was collected for the Union Gospel Mission. Immanuel provided support to the Evangelical Lutheran Church in America's Malaria Campaign and continues to support its Lutheran Disaster Response initiative.

For many years beginning in 1984, Immanuel had a giving tree (or gift tree) to collect Christmas gifts, which were distributed to Southeast Asian ministries, Lyngblomsten Care Center, and Wilder Child Care Center. Immanuel also provided Christmas boxes to the Saint Paul Intervention Project, Saint Paul Area Council of Churches Indian Affairs Ministry, and the Women's Crisis Center. Immanuel provided funds to Wilder Twin Cities Mobile Market, Minneapolis American Indian Center, Highland Area Leisure Center, and Congregations Caring for Creation, a Minnesota-based organization. Additional funds were provided to Agora (a program to train lay people to lead in ethnic specific and multicultural congregations), Daily Work (a service located at Christ Lutheran Church on Capitol Hill, which supports people looking for work by helping them locate and apply for jobs), and Open Hands Midway. The latter is hosted by Bethlehem Lutheran Church in the Saint Paul Midway area, and provides free meals Mondays and Wednesday, and clothing, household items, and groceries.

Several of Immanuel's former and current benevolence activities and benevolence partners are detailed below.

Meals on Wheels

In 1976, Immanuel began its involvement with Meals on Wheels, thanks to the initiative of long-time member Truus Ingebritson. Truus believed there were many elderly people in the area that did not have proper nutrition. She talked to Pastor Elder Bentley about her idea that Immanuel should help address this problem and he promptly agreed. They thought it would be possible if area churches would work together. The federal government had a Meals on Wheels program but the one Truus started was independent of it. She was the co-founder of SWAM (Southwest Area Meals) in 1976.

One of [Truus's] favorite sayings is, "Love is a basket with five loaves and two fishes. It's never enough until you start to give it away!" Truus says that she really doesn't run the program. She says, "Someone else does who can multiply the loaves and fishes." —Quoted by Saint Paul Dispatch *columnist Oliver Towne [Gareth Hiebert] in January 1984 article*

Truus coordinated her efforts with St. Mary's Catholic Church and St. Mary's Nursing Home located on Norfolk and Prior Avenues in Saint Paul. The area churches provided the drivers who delivered the meals to people's homes. Each church was designated one day a week to deliver the meals. Drivers received a route and index cards with information about each individual, such as name, address, directions to the residence, dietary restrictions, and health concerns. It took about one hour for the drivers to deliver their assigned meals. St. Mary's supplied nutritious, well-balanced meals keeping in mind special dietary needs of people. On Immanuel's assigned day, Rachel Husom, Betty Jorgensen, and Betty Ofstead rotated days taking turns filling the containers with nutritious meals. June Husom and Rachel Husom delivered meals out of the West 7th Street location. Phyllis Holmgren also delivered meals. On holidays, Truus would often help deliver meals and she added small gifts with these meal deliveries. One time she was short $200 to purchase those small holiday gifts. She went to church and prayed. That night, she got a call from a woman who said she had $200 to give to some worthy cause and wondered if SWAM could use it. (Source: Oliver Towne's January 1984 *Pioneer Press* column)

Immanuel visitation Pastor Ralph Glenn loved telling a joke before his report at Council meetings. This one relates to SWAM:

A family of mice died and went to Heaven. When St. Peter asked the mouse family how they liked Heaven, they squeaked, "We love it! But, it is a little bit too big for us to get around and see all of Heaven." St. Peter thought

6-5. *Phyllis Holmgren delivering Meals on Wheels (1979)*

for a little bit then gave each mouse roller blades. Delighted, they zoomed around Heaven enjoying the sights!" Months later, a family of cats died and they also went to Heaven. When St. Peter asked the cat family how they liked Heaven, they me-owed, "We love it, especially the Meals on Wheels!"

When Truus retired, Betty Jorgensen, Rachel Husom, and Betty Ofstead assumed the coordination of Immanuel's program. Eventually, St. Mary's took over the coordination of the program with locations in Merriam Park and on West 7th Street. The participating churches still provided the drivers. Immanuel's coordinated participation ceased in 2011, when St. Mary's closed. For a short time after this, Dick Sarafolean, June Husom, and Rachel Husom continued to deliver meals.

Christian's Toy Box

6-6. *Christian's Toy Box*

Donations are requested each year for Christian's Toy Box in memory of Christian Olaf Osen, who succumbed to leukemia in 1999. Christian was the eight-year-old son of Immanuel members John and Karen Osen and brother of Anders. Toys are collected and donated to Child and Family Services at Children's Hospitals and Clinics of Minnesota. Contributions include new, unwrapped toys, games, art supplies, books, other creative activities, and gift cards.

Wilder Child Development Center

Wilder Foundation Child Development Center provides full-day childcare services and early childhood education programming with qualified staff and age-appropriate curriculum that emphasizes multi-cultural and multi-sensory activities. By providing proficiency in personal and social skills, language and literacy, nutritionally sound meals, and family outreach activities, children are ready for school and life-long learning. Every Christmas, Immanuel provides gift boxes (sometimes called baskets) to the families in the Wilder preschool program. The program started as a way to provide a holiday meal to families facing financial pressures. However, the meal was not always culturally appropriate for the Saint Paul's diverse preschool families, prompting church leaders to ask what the families actually wanted. In 2016, Immanuel transitioned to buying gifts for families based on their needs and requests, such as a movie night basket, pajamas, and toys and games. In 2020, Immanuel members fulfilled the needs and wish lists of more than 70 families.

6-7. Immanuel youth collecting Wilder Christmas boxes (2007)

Keystone Community Services

Keystone Community Services (formerly Merriam Park Food Shelf) is a community-based human service organization in Saint Paul offering a variety of programs for all ages at multiple sites. Keystone includes free food shelves and emergency assistance; a comprehensive Seniors Program that provides Meals on Wheels and programs for active seniors; case management for seniors, the disabled and at-risk families; and a support program for Hmong youth and their families. Food and dollars collected at Immanuel are delivered to Keystone with a goal of providing 300 lbs. of food each month. Canned goods are solicited on an ongoing basis and through special events, such as Souper Bowl Sunday and Sunday School drives. In the past 25 years, Immanuel has seen a shift from donating massive amounts of canned goods to donating generous amounts of cash. The Social Action Team usually hosts a coffee hour once a month to raise funds for Keystone and also raises funds during March, Minnesota's FoodShare Month, although this was paused during the COVID pandemic.

Lyngblomsten Care Center

Lyngblomsten has received support from Immanuel members from its earliest days. It provides a ministry of compassionate care and innovative services to older adults in order to preserve and enhance their quality of life, including home-based and community-based services, senior housing, and skilled nursing care. The Lyngblomsten Society was formed in 1903 by a group of Norwegian women to care for older people without family or friends. The organization began to grow by establishing "branches" around the Upper Midwest. On February 17, 1906, they incorporated and began fund raising. The original facility was opened in December 1912. For several decades, these women, their daughters, and granddaughters ran the Lyngblomsten Home through the sponsorship of member branches. As women entered the workforce and had less time for volunteer work, along with increasing government regulations for board and care being established, this was no longer feasible. In 1960, Lyngblomsten was reincorporated and its grounds and assets were given to what was then the Saint Paul Conference of the American Lutheran Church. The women of Immanuel have been involved with supporting Lyngblomsten for many years and became a corporate congregation in 1960, meaning that Immanuel and other churches signed a covenant with Lyngblomsten affirming the mutual understanding and commitment. Corporate partners work with Lyngblomsten to strengthen ministry to seniors, such as Immanuel's Care Team Ministry. Immanuel supports Lyngblomsten by volunteering and providing financial support. For many years, Immanuel had a women's Lyngblomsten Circle with the primary purpose of raising funds for Lyngblomsten.

6-8. Visitation Pastor Paulus Pilgrim Visiting Lyngblomsten Resident (1970s)

Care Team

The current Care Team Ministry was preceded by a "Caregiver Program" organized in 1985 by Immanuel member June Husom.

In a joint partnership with Lyngblomsten, Immanuel members Karen Koch and Kitty Larson became the first coordinators in 2000 for "Care Team Ministry," a ministry to Immanuel members with special needs, especially those who are homebound. Between 16 and 20 Immanuel members go out in teams to visit and support members in their homes, give respite to caregivers, provide rides to church and appointments. and deliver the sacrament of Communion. Visiting teams provide friendship and practical support to those in need. Before the COVID pandemic, the group averaged close to 1,000 volunteer hours a year. The group usually delivers cookies in June and December and hosts a Friendship Gathering for the care partners, families, and friends. All Care Team members receive training (now online) from the Lyngblomsten Foundation and meet every other month for support and education. The Care Team sponsors a Rake-a-Thon to assist with fall lawn work. Youth, and their families, Confirmation students and their mentors, and others of all ages help with this work. Over the years, JoAnn Hogenson, Barb Columbus, Marilyn DuBay, Kay Draine, Elaine Jaeger, and Jane Tripple have served as Care Team leaders. During the COVID pandemic, the Care Team continued to meet via Zoom. Elaine and Jane retired at the end of 2021, but some Care Team members continue to connect with those served by the ministry.

6-9. *Care Team Leadership—Jane Tripple, Elaine Jaeger, Kay Draine (2015)*

6-10. *Rake-A-Thon—John Mattessich, Alex Sieg, Dave Alstead, Melanie DuBay, Stephanie Alstead (2006)*

Knitting for Warmth

Knitting for Warmth began in 2007, meeting monthly on Sunday afternoons at Immanuel. The group knitted hats, mittens, and scarves that were donated to numerous charities including Joseph's Coats, St. Thomas Moore Swap Shop, Dorothy Day, Ramsey County Public Health Nurses, and even the Seaman's ministries in Duluth. Knitted items were made and sold at the annual lutefisk dinner for two years. The money was then used to purchase shares of the Heifer International project's Knitter's Basket—four fuzzy animals (a llama, an alpaca, a sheep and an angora rabbit) that provide Heifer partner families with ample wool and opportunities to build a better life.

In 2014, Knitting for Warmth started a knitting group at Hart House, a 24-bed transitional housing program designed for women in recovery from chemical dependency located in Saint Paul. Knitting for Warmth members taught knitting and provided yarn and treats one evening a month. In the second year, the program transitioned to a monthly craft group to include more women who did not want to knit or crochet. This program met monthly and there were always visiting children joining their mothers on craft night. The group held two Christmas programs at Hart House with pizza and salad, and cookie decorating activities.

In 2015, Knitting for Warmth received a grant from the Paulson bequest and another $100 dollars in 2016. The group also received funds from the sale of knitted elves and a generous donation ($500) from the Immanuel Lutheran Church Women's bake sale at the lutefisk dinner. These funds were partially used to buy craft supplies and provide monthly treats and two holiday parties for the women who lived at Hart House.

Knitting for Warmth disbanded in 2016.

Interfaith Action

Immanuel joins other congregations to support Interfaith Action of Greater Saint Paul (formerly the Saint Paul Area Council of Churches; SPACC), which seeks to build a more just and compassionate society. Immanuel members Nancy Granrud and Tara Mattessich served as SPACC presidents, as did former Pastor John Lohre. Interfaith Action connects congregations, faith communities, and civic organizations to overcome poverty, promote peace, and dismantle racism and other barriers that divide the community. Interfaith Action initiatives supported by Immanuel include:

Crop Walk: The Saint Paul Crop Walk is an annual event to raise funds to fight hunger in Saint Paul and around the world. Twenty-five percent of the money raised goes to Interfaith Action's Department of Indian Work food shelf, and the remainder is used to support Church World Service's hunger relief efforts in areas most in need throughout the world.

6-11. Deb Ahlquist leading the Immanuel group at a Crop Walk (2011)

Project Home: Project Home provides 40 beds of emergency shelter for children and their parents in Ramsey County each night. Immanuel assisted in hosting at Cretin Derham Hall, hosted at Immanuel in 2007, and assisted at Messiah Episcopal Church on Friday nights in June beginning in 2008. Immanuel members have enjoyed interacting with families. In addition to volunteering, Immanuel supported Project Home financially through the annual Flea Market and collected supplies such as pajamas and personal supplies for the families.

School Tools: This initiative gives homeless and low-income children the tools they need to flourish in school. Immanuel collects new school supplies every fall to help local children in need.

Hearts and Hammers (formerly Paint-A-Thon): Volunteer teams paint the homes of seniors and people with disabilities. The program helps homeowners remain living independently in their own homes and improves neighborhoods throughout the Twin Cities. Each summer Immanuel members and Immanuel's affiliated Boy Scout Troop 90 complete a small house or garage painting project. The commitment is usually two evenings and includes sanding and painting.

6-12. Doug Derr helping with Paint-A-Thon (1993)

MICAH: MICAH is the Metropolitan Interfaith Council on Affordable Housing and envisions a metropolitan area where everyone without exception has a safe, decent, accessible, and affordable home.

Dorothy Day

Loaves & Fishes, founded in 1982, provides nutritious meals to people who are hungry in an atmosphere of hospitality. Loaves and Fishes serves meals at St. Stephens in Minneapolis and the Dorothy Day Center in Saint Paul, and jointly assists guests with mental health services, medical care, and basic needs key to becoming self-sufficient. Serving meals through Dorothy Day's ministry has been a long-standing outreach service of Immanuel. A dedicated, consistent team has served a noon meal to the homeless population in downtown Saint Paul on the third Saturday of the month since 1982. The program was first administered through the Loaves and Fishes program, then by Catholic Charities. Immanuel members Jerry and Joanne Sandahl were the original volunteer recruiters, grocery shoppers, and leaders. Member Nancy Reidel took responsibility for grocery shopping after Joanne's death. Jerry and Nancy continue in leadership at the time of this writing.

The fixed menu has always been Sloppy Joes on buns, "beans and weenies," homemade cookies, and milk. Hardboiled eggs and bananas are also offered as "pocket food" to take away for later. The meal begins with a prayer. Men, women, children, and families are served. Jerry has said the most difficult part of this ministry is seeing the children. Jerry began collecting Beanie Babies and stuffed animals to distribute to the children.

Over the years, cooking has moved several times including on-site at Dorothy Day on 7th Street downtown where clients were served. The new Dorothy Day Place opened in 2019. Food preparations returned to the site, making it much more efficient for volunteers who arrived at 10:00 AM and finished by 1:00 PM with a crew of 15. The team served 197 people per month on average in 2019 and close to 2,000 meals during the year. Immanuel's budget is $400 per month. Leftover food is reserved or repurposed by professional staff. In March 2020, the COVID pandemic caused the Immanuel team to cease physically volunteering, but Immanuel continues to provide $400–$450 for the monthly meal, which is prepared by the Dorothy Day staff. The volunteer team plans to return to serving Sloppy Joes at Dorothy Day once it is safe enough to do so.

6-13. *Immanuel's Dorothy Day Team (2002)*

Habitat for Humanity

Twin Cities Habitat for Humanity strives to provide decent, affordable housing by continuing to build and preserve homes, so hard-working families can own homes in healthy neighborhoods with access to jobs, transportation, and quality schools.

Immanuel joins Interfaith Builders, a coalition of Saint Paul churches and synagogues, on a two-week construction project in the summer, and also provides financial support.

6-14. Habitat for Humanity project—Sandy Butler and Russ Edhlund (2013)

Lutheran Social Service

Lutheran Social Service (LSS) is Minnesota's largest nonprofit social service organization serving children, youth, families, the disabled, and seniors. Its origins can be traced to the founding of Vasa Children's Home (Red Wing) in 1865 by Pastor Eric Norelius. Until the 1970s, LSS focused on the welfare of children. Since that time, LSS has expanded its mission. Immanuel provides funding for homeless youth programs that befriend youth on the street and provide emergency shelter, transitional housing, and independent living support. Programs include the following:

Rezek House is a two-year transitional living program in Saint Paul for youth ages 16–21 experiencing homelessness. Immanuel helped set up the house for occupants, helped create a backyard garden, and now provides meals, donates goods, raises funds, and donates time and professional dental and legal services.

LifeHaven is a transitional living program in Saint Paul for teen mothers and their children, who are experiencing homelessness.

Safe House is an emergency shelter for youth. Immanuel partners with Lutheran Social Service to coordinate weekly and holiday meals and collects funds for new clothing for residents of Safe House.

Joint Religious Legislative Coalition (JRLC) mobilizes Jewish, Christian, and Islamic communities to influence public policy in Minnesota. Immanuel members join other faith communities in action and advocacy.

ISAIAH-MN is a multi-racial, state-wide, nonpartisan coalition of faith communities, childcare centers, and other community-based constituencies in Minnesota. ISAIAH strengthens the ability of people of faith to address both local and regional community issues, including mass incarceration, immigration, healthcare, and racial inequity. One initiative of ISAIAH is encouraging citizens to vote.

Every Meal: Fighting Child Hunger (formerly The Sheridan Story) provides children in the metro area with meal ingredients for the weekend. The program now serves more than over 10,000 children across 400 locations. Immanuel families began packing food for the program in 2022.

Saint Paul Area Synod of the Evangelical Lutheran Church in America

The Saint Paul Area Synod is a geographic region of the Evangelical Lutheran Church in America (ELCA) that supports congregations in carrying out their missions. Comprising the eastern half of the greater metropolitan area of the Twin Cities, the Saint Paul Area Synod includes about 115 congregations and 145,000 members. It is one of 65 synods in the ELCA and the second largest in the number of baptized members. The Saint Paul Area Synod supports congregations and pastors by preparing candidates for ordination, helping with the call process, providing training for congregational leadership and staff, guiding mission congregations, etc. Part of synod benevolence goes to the church-wide ELCA that ministers around the world. Immanuel's annual benevolence budget includes an allocation for the Saint Paul Area Synod. In addition, Immanuel financially supports **Shobi's Table**, a ministry of the St Paul Area Synod. Shobi's Table, a pay-as-you-can cafe on wheels, serves a fresh, from-scratch, delicious, and nutritious lunch to everyone who comes to the food truck. The food truck is located in St Paul along the University Avenue corridor, serving on Thursdays in Frogtown and on Fridays in the Midway area.

Feed My Starving Children

Feed My Starving Children is a non-profit Christian organization committed to feeding children hungry in body and spirit by addressing malnutrition and associated diseases. Twin Cities volunteers hand-pack meals specifically formulated for malnourished children that are shipped to nearly 70 countries around the world. Immanuel's involvement with Feed My Starving Children has been organized through the Sunday School and offers food-packing opportunities for children and adults.

Immanuel's Flea Market and Carnival

6-15. Flea Market and Kids Carnival Sign

According to Immanuel records, the early congregation had flea markets as far back as the 1920s and 1930s. From their onset, they have been a source of funds for benevolence. In 1985, the Group Activities Committee sponsored an "All Church Garage Sale" in the church parking lot; all proceeds went to the American Lutheran Church World Hunger program. In 2004, the Flea Market idea resurfaced while John Marboe and Joy Bussert were Immanuel's pastors. Pastor Joy led the planning team, working with the Legislative Awareness and Social Action Committee. She wanted to take advantage of the rare asset of having a parking lot on South Snelling Avenue and the visibility to the community that it provided. This was an opportunity to work together, reach out to the community, and enable everyone to do some recycling. Music, games, and fair food provided by Immanuel member Ross Robey were essential to making the "blacktop" event a success. That year, the "New York-Style" Flea Market sponsored a street dance featuring Bend in the River Big Band in the parking lot. The joint event brought in $5,000 with the proceeds going to the Rezek House (Lutheran Social Service young-adult housing project) and Immanuel's capital campaign.

When Immanuel member Christine Danielson took over the helm in 2009, she was given one and only one directive, "You have to keep the sale outside to utilize the blacktop." Mother Nature had another idea. The forecast (and actual weather) was for heavy rain, and the one and only directive was ditched and a plan was quickly developed to move the sale inside. However, what seemed like a setback turned into a game-changer. Feedback for the indoor Flea Market was so positive that the planners decided to keep the sale inside for future Flea Markets.

6-16. *Sorting Flea Market donations—Stacey Von Wald, Shawna Boll, and Peg Wangensteen (2010)*

In 2010, Immanuel members Kari Moeller and Heather Cordes planned the first carnival in the parking lot to maintain the spirit and intent of the outdoor blacktop event. The Kids' Carnival was accompanied by live music and fair food. Thus the Fall Festival was born. During the 2010 recession, the Flea Market leadership team switched from giving 10 percent of proceeds to giving 100 percent. The Immanuel general fund was tight and no benevolence giving was budgeted. A seed was planted when the team applied for an $800 Thrivent grant that required 100 percent of the funds to be given away.

They proposed to and got approval from the church Council that 100 percent of the net profits be donated to benevolence to continue support to community partners. The Flea Market has donated 100 percent of proceeds ever since.

6-17. Kids Carnival (2015)

As the years went by, the benevolence list grew. The Flea Market leadership team narrowed the list, focusing on fewer partners so the gifts would have more impact. In 2019, advocacy organizations were added to the direct service organizations as recipients. This was done in keeping with the Social Action Team's purpose to live out the words of Micah 6:8 "And what do I ask of you? To love kindness [acts of service and benevolence], do justice [advocacy and action], and walk humbly with your God [spiritual growth and learning]."

Because of the COVID epidemic, no flea market was held in 2020. The flea market team raised funds through a coin drive, direct donations, and a Facebook live "telethon." A total of $11,780 raised and was given to community partners.

In 2021, with concerns about COVID and its variants still present, the Flea Market returned to its one and only original directive—to be outside on the blacktop. The planning group opted to move the sale outside again. Immanuel member Ross Robey again provided concessions. Just before the entrance was scheduled to open on Friday at 10:00 a.m., a fierce wind descended, tipping tents and racks, and creating great excitement. Volunteers worked together and quickly put the tents, racks, and merchandise to rights. The entrance opened and happy shoppers rushed in. Then the rain started. Plastic was spread over the tables, eventually the rain stopped, and volunteers dried and reorganized—and people again shopped. A live band provided music outside in the evening. A cake walk and other amusements were offered. The Saturday sale went without problems. The total income was $10,486 and given to Interfaith Action, Lutheran Social Service Metro Homeless Youth Services, and ISAIAH.

Spring Fest

For a few years in the 2000s, Immanuel also held a Spring Fest in the parking lot, at which pre-ordered flowers were delivered and a "flower shop" provided last-minute items for Mother's Day. The Robey family offered concessions.

Global Benevolence in Recent Years

Immanuel has continued initiatives to meet the needs of those around the world. Blankets have been collected for Lutheran World Relief and funds given to Heifer International Project and ELCA World Hunger. Immanuel member Roger Needels coordinated a soap drive for third world countries for many years. Soap donations from the congregation were matched by Needels Janitorial Supply Service. A total of 3,250 pounds was provided in 1990. Goods knitted and sewn by members have remained a tangible donation. For example, in 1993, the Immanuel Lutheran Church Women made and tied 82 quilts and 74 blankets for Lutheran World Relief.

For many years, the Sunday closest to Epiphany Sunday has been chosen as Global Mission Sunday to celebrate and raise funds for Immanuel's mission partners in Guatemala and Tanzania. Sales of coffee, chocolate, and other goods as part of Fair Trade ministries have been held in coordination with Global Mission Sunday. In February 2022, Lusungu Msigwa of Iringa, Tanzania, a student at Luther Seminary, was the guest preacher for Global Mission Sunday.

6-18. Spring Fest—Kay Draine and Dick Sundberg (2008)

6-19. Common Hope Vision Team from Immanuel in Guatemala in front of the house the team helped build (2003)

Guatemala

In 2003, Immanuel began partnering with **Common Hope, Guatemala**, a local mission organization established in 1986 that is devoted to securing education for the young and poor of Guatemala. Common Hope believes that education is the key to unwinding the cycle of poverty and that a child's success in school depends on his or her family's health, safety, and stability. The goal is to foster hope and opportunity in Guatemala, partnering with children, families, and communities to improve their lives through education, health care, and housing. Immanuel sent adult volunteers on mission trips to Guatemala with Common Hope in 2003 and 2008. In 2003, 12 people from Immanuel were Immanuel's ambassadors working with the poor near Antigua. The group built a house, helped in the library, the pharmacy, the gardens, the special education classrooms, and visited families in their homes. A second group went to Guatemala in 2008. Immanuel members who have travelled to Guatemala with Common Hope include: Ann and Doug Derr; Ray, Elizabeth, and Ashley Peterson; Peter, Kay, and Lori Draine; Pastor John Marboe and his wife Andrea; Lee Rife; Dick Sarafolean; Ellen Peterson; Jan Johnshoy; Dick Sundberg; and Immanuel friends Denise Joyce and Lico Aipo, Mary Gotz, Terry Lovaasen, Bill Smith, and Patricia Gromak.

Immanuel has collected children's shoes, school supplies, books in Spanish, office supplies, special education materials, and suitcases for this organization. Immanuel members have sponsored more than 25 students through Common Hope. Sponsorship supports children so they can attend school and gives their entire family access to medical and dental care, adult education classes, social work services, and more. Immanuel was designated a Common Hope "Faith Community Partner" in 2019.

The Saint Paul Area Synod has a companion synod relationship with *Iglesia Luterana Agustina de Guatemala (*Augustinian Lutheran Church of Guatemala; ILAG), a church that ministers to people from the margins of Guatemalan society, particularly the indigenous poor. ILAG is dedicated to sharing the gospel and carrying out the work of God, developing equitable pastoral and lay leadership, fostering theological, economic, and social self-sufficiency in vulnerable communities, and supporting development projects for the Lutheran community. Immanuel provides financial support for this relationship.

6-20. Dick Sarafolean meeting his sponsored Guatemalan child and family (2003)

Tanzania

Through *Bega Kwa Bega* (Shoulder to Shoulder, BKB), Immanuel partners with **Mkimbizi and Magubike Lutheran Churches,** two congregations in Iringa, Tanzania. Immanuel and the Iringa congregations exchange prayers and visits, and Immanuel provides funding for several projects including scholarships for secondary students, microfinance, and planting trees. Immanuel's *Bega Kwa Bega* story is one of "Prayer, Presence, and Projects."

Prayer: Each Sunday since 2005 Immanuel has prayed for Mkimbizi Lutheran Church, a parish on the outskirts of Iringa, Tanzania. In 2020, Immanuel added a second Iringa Diocese partner congregation, Magubike, a rapidly growing parish in farm country on the route to Ruaha National Park. Mkimbizi and Magubike parishes pray for Immanuel each Sunday. Prayer in Iringa is fervent and intense, an amazing experience.

Presence: In the 1980s, Saint Paul Area Synod and Iringa Diocese of Tanzania shared a dream of developing a seminary to train badly needed pastors. The seminary idea became the Iringa University College (now the University of Iringa). It was the first private university in Tanzania. The university needed students, which resulted in a high school scholarship program, pairing congregations in Saint Paul Area Synod with Iringa Synod parishes. Some 60 congregations or about half the Saint Paul Area Synod are partners. Several additional projects (affiliates) came into being. The secret to this astounding growth, according to Pastor Nayman Chavalla, Iringa Diocese leader, is "We do not ask for money. Come to visit us. You will fall in love with our country and our people. The projects and money will follow."

In 2005, Pastor Don Fultz and his wife Eunice came to Immanuel to talk about the partnership between his congregation (Holy Trinity Lutheran Church, New Prague, Minnesota) and the Ruaha Mbuyuni congregation in Tanzania. Immanuel was partnered with Mkimbizi parish near Iringa University and invited to "Come to Iringa!" A group of five committed to the trip. By departure time, the group was only two: Dave and Sue Klevan. The experience in Tanzania was awe-inspiring. The animal safari was delightful. Worship, home visits, and trips to BKB schools, Ilula Hospital, and Iringa University were priceless. Dave and Sue returned to Immanuel inspired to promote BKB. Soon other Immanuel members and friends travelled to Iringa on visits. These included Pastor Joy Bussert and her daughter Kate; Phyllis Holmgren's niece Terry, her sister, and son; Barb Columbus; Phyllis Bentley; Pastor Cindy Bullock; Peg Wangensteen; Kay, Peter, and Lori Draine; Jan Johnshoy; Lee Rife; and Pastor Carol Tomer (Pilgrim Lutheran Church) along with other Pilgrim Lutheran Church members.

Projects: Immanuel members have sponsored more than 200 high school students in Mkimbizi and Magubike parishes from 2005 through the present. These graduates are now healthcare professionals, teachers, and other community leaders. Immanuel members funded units (SACCOs—Savings and Credit Cooperative Organizations) as part of Iringa Hope, the very successful microfinance/agriculture affiliate. Immanuel led the Millions of Trees affiliate. More than a million Mexican pine seedlings are growing on Iringa district foothills. Thousands of grafted avocado seedlings have been planted to address malnutrition and to provide another cash crop. Immanuel has contributed to the Shoulder to Shoulder affiliate, which sponsors a district hospital and nursing school. Ilula hospital has major HIV, obstetrics, and trauma programs. Immanuel is part of Radio *Furaha* (Joy) affiliate, which broadcasts gospel music and health, financial, and agricultural information. Saint Paul Area Synod congregations send more than a million dollars annually for students and projects in Iringa district. The success of this program inspired the Evangelical Lutheran Church in America to pair each synod with an area of the world in need. BKB is their flagship program.

Immanuel hopes and prays that the progress in Iringa will make the people self-sufficient and that Iringa partners will continue to add hundreds of Lutherans each year. The people of Iringa pray for and inspire Immanuel. This partnership is a blessing to all.

6-21. Immanuel visitors to Mkimbizi Lutheran Church, Tanzania— Pastor Cindy Bullock, Kay and Peter Draine, Sue and Dave Klevan, Peg Wangensteen, and hosts (2013)

Increasing Financial Benevolence

One of the ways Immanuel serves in the community is by financially supporting community groups who are doing work that Immanuel cannot do. These are Immanuel's benevolence partners. The support of benevolence partners has changed greatly over the past 25 years as national charitable giving trends have changed. At one point, the majority of charitable giving was done through churches. Today most people give directly to their charities of choice, and churches see fewer of those dollars. Immanuel's practice has shifted, as well. Today some partners are supported through general fund giving, but fundraising occurs through an annual Flea Market and Fall Festival, MN FoodShare appeal, school supply drives, Christmas gift collections, and one-time appeals for families or individuals in need. The Immanuel Lutheran Church Women, the Men's Club, and the Immanuel Foundation also give generously to community partners. In 2015, an unusual year, several bequests were received and 10 percent of the bequests were given immediately to benevolence partners. As a result, more than $80,000 was given to outside benevolence partners in 2015.

CHAPTER 7

Governance and Organizational Structure

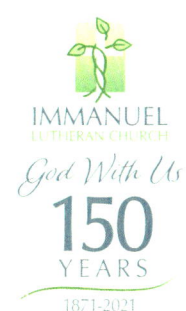

Constitution and By-Laws

Immanuel has had numerous constitutions and by-laws over the years; some are missing from the church's records. The earliest constitution has not been found. However, a 1921 draft model constitution was found in the Luther Seminary files of Dr. Gustav Marius Bruce (Immanuel's Interim Pastor, 1917–1921); it likely parallels Immanuel's constitution at that time. In this constitution, the officers of the congregation consisted of a president, vice president, secretary, and treasurer, a five-member Board of Elders, a five-member Board of Trustees, a three-member auditing committee, a Sunday School superintendent and assistant superintendent, a secretary and treasurer of the Sunday School, and an organist. The pastor served as ex officio president. The chairman of the Board of Elders was the ex officio vice president. The treasurer of the Board of Trustees served as treasurer of the congregation. The church Council consisted of the Board of Elders, the Board of Trustees, pastor, and secretary. Though not explicitly stated, it appears that the Board of Elders was charged with overall responsibility for managing the church and oversight of financial matters.

Typical constitutions over the years have addressed the following:
    Name of the congregation
    Confession of belief
    Synod affiliation
    Criteria for membership and voting
    Responsibilities of members

Grounds for disciplinary action
Officers and committees
Procedure for calling a pastor and the duties of the pastor
By-laws governing congregational meetings and elections and how the by-laws may be amended.

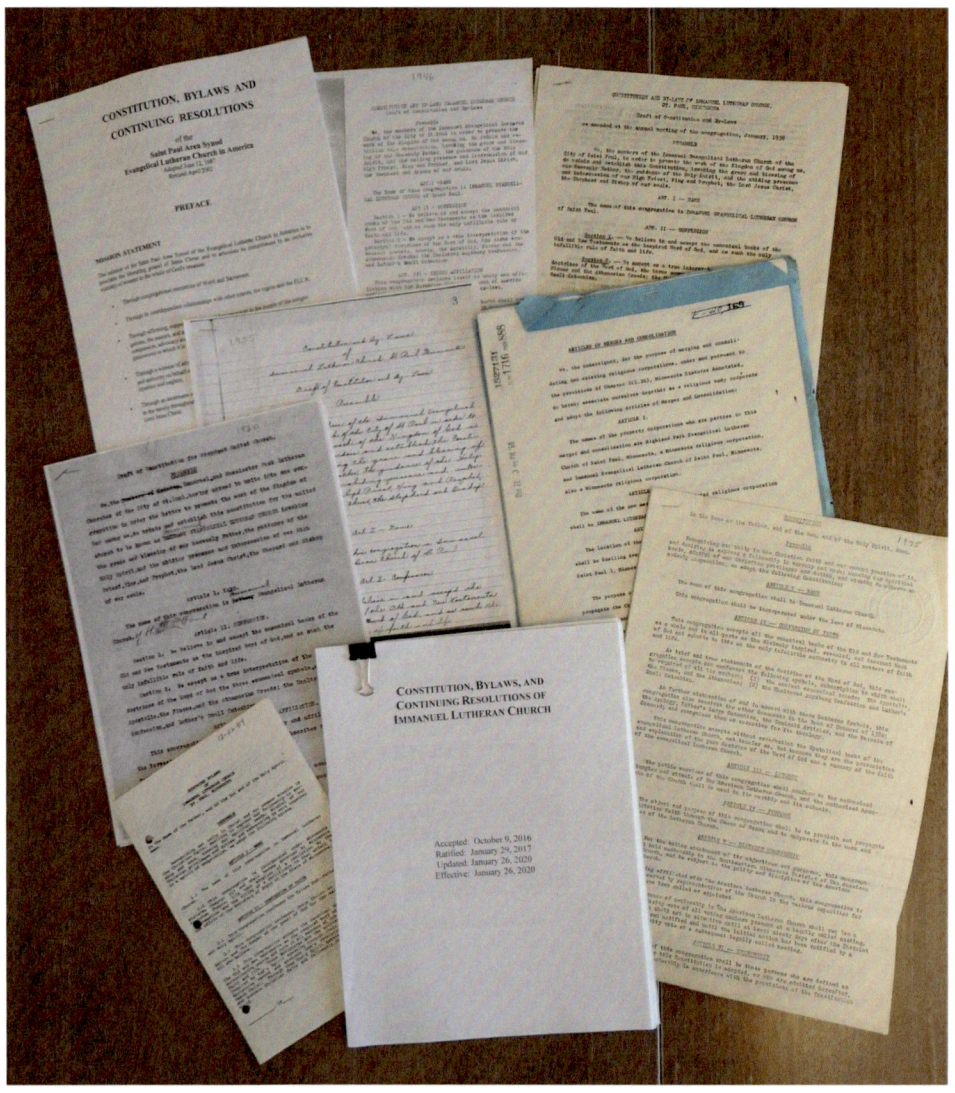

7-1. Collection of Immanuel Constitutions and By-Laws over the years (1921–2020)

The challenge of combining the two congregations (Immanuel and Macalester Park Lutheran) and their practices and culture in 1921 prompted the merging congregations to prepare a "Declaration of Conditions of Union."

One can assume that this Declaration aimed to resolve areas of contention. Following are some of the conditions:
- That chanting by the minister shall be discarded, the rubrics of the liturgy usually chanted by the minister shall be read by him.
- That in the case clerical vestments shall be used, the modified Oxford type of pulpit gown shall be employed.
- That as a rule the shorter form of the liturgy shall be employed.
- That the right of women to vote in the congregational meetings on an equality with men be recognized.

A draft constitution was prepared in 1921 following Immanuel's 1921 merger with Macalester Park Lutheran Church; no final, approved version has been found. The draft constitution specified that the officers were a president, vice president, secretary, financial secretary and treasurer, a five-member Board of Elders, a seven-member Board of Trustees, a three-member auditing committee, a Sunday School superintendent, one or more assistant superintendents, and an organist. To represent the merged congregations, two Elders came from Macalester Park and three from Immanuel; three Trustees came from Macalester Park and four from Immanuel. The church Council consisted of the pastor (no longer the Council president, but ex officio chair of the Council), the president (serving as vice-chairman of the Council), vice president, secretary (serving as secretary of the Council), financial secretary, treasurer, and the Boards of Elders and Trustees. The Elders were responsible for discipline and any member who did not attend worship for a period of three months or failed to contribute to the support of the church for one year was to "be summarily dropped from the church roll." However, those experiencing poverty or other sufficient causes that made contributing impossible were exempt.

The English and Norwegian languages shall be used in the public services as the congregation may from time to time decide, provided that at all times, as long as demand therefore exists, adequate provision shall be made for those members who because of their inability to understand the English language require services conducted in the Norwegian language. —Draft 1921 Constitution, Article IX. Language

In 1932, Pastor Bennie Duckstad served as president of the congregation. Immanuel had a Board of Elders, a Board of Deacons, a Board of Trustees, and a Music Committee.

> ❧ *"Members who will not submit to the discipline administered by the Board of Elders shall be brought before a business meeting of the church. If found guilty of misconduct or false doctrine, such members may be either temporarily or permanently suspended from membership in the church by a two-thirds vote of those present and voting. Should excluded members repent and ask forgiveness for wrongs committed, they shall be readmitted to full membership by vote of the congregation upon recommendation of the Board of Elders." —1936 Constitution and By-Laws*

By the 1946 constitution, the Board of Elders had increased to seven members and the pastor no longer served as president. The constitution expanded the officers to consist of the president, vice president, secretary, financial secretary, assistant financial secretary, and treasurer, plus a Sunday School superintendent and one or more assistant Sunday School superintendents. This constitution references a Board of Parish Education, composed of four members with the pastor, Sunday School superintendent, assistant Sunday School superintendent, and one representative from the Board of Deacons (as ex officio members). The pastor served as chairman of the Board of Deacons. Deacons ushered on Sundays when there was Communion. The Board of Deacons provided leadership of the church's ministry for serving the spiritual and physical needs of members and people beyond the church. Notes from 1946 indicate that the Board of Deacons was responsible for membership, worship and music, hospitality and visitation, and supervising the choir director and the parish worker. Two deacons assisted the minister on Communion Sundays (once a month). An amusing note from a February 28, 1950, meeting reports that the Deacons decided to crack down on the type of music played at church events.

The constitution was revised for phrasing and punctuation in 1958. The annual meeting was moved from the 2nd Monday in January to the 4th Monday to give the auditing committee and treasurer more time to prepare. In 1958, Immanuel had a Council consisting of seven elected officers (president, vice president, secretary, treasurer, financial secretary, assistant financial secretary, and assistant treasurer), three special officers, eight trustees, and 13 general members. The committees were the Committee of Church Property, Finance Committee, Committee on Worship and Music, Committee on Education and Literature, Committee on Membership and Stewardship, and Committee for Group Activities.

1960 saw significant changes resulting from the merger with Highland Park Lutheran Church. An official "Articles of Merger and Consolidation" was issued. No constitution from 1960 has been located, but it appears that the Board of Deacons was eliminated and their duties were assumed by the new church Council at the time of the merger. Immanuel's 1961 constitution allowed women to serve in positions of leadership. By 1964, the church Council was comprised of at least 36 members.

The 1975 constitution and by-laws increased the Board of Trustees to eight. The superintendent of the Sunday School was elected by the church Council. The superintendent, the president of the Brotherhood of Immanuel (men's group), and the president of the Immanuel Lutheran Church Women were members of the church Council, and the pastor was an ex-officio member. The president of the church Council, after consulting with the pastor, was charged with appointing committees on church property, finance, worship and music, education and literature, membership and evangelism, group activities, and other committees as needed. The duties of each standing committee were detailed. The Board of Deacons is not mentioned in the 1975 document, so it may have been eliminated in 1975 or in an earlier document.

The 1989 "Restated By-Laws" were written following the merger of the American Lutheran Church and the Lutheran Church in America to form the Evangelical Lutheran Church in America in 1988. Immanuel had been part of the American Lutheran Church. The document noted that the congregation invited members of all other Christian congregations to participate in Holy Communion. The president of the congregation appointed a three-person auditing committee. These by-laws offer the first mention of the Legislative Awareness and Social Action Committee as a program committee. Also identified are a Nominating Committee, Personnel Committee, and a Scholarship Committee. At this time, the church Council was comprised of 40 people:

President
Vice president
Secretary
Treasurer
Assistant treasurer
Financial secretary
Assistant financial secretary
Immediate past president
Superintendent of the Sunday School
Representative elected by the ushers
Representative elected by the men's organization
Representative elected by the women's organization
Representative elected by the alter guild
Representative elected by the Hi-League

26 additional members elected directly to the program committees by the congregation

The by-laws were revised in 2000 and the number of committees and the composition of the Council was changed significantly reducing the size of the Council to 13 individuals (president, vice president, secretary, treasurer, past president, and chairs of the eight program committees). This is the first document to authorize electronic communication ("a means of communication through which the Council members may simultaneously hear each other") as a valid Council meeting. The program committees were: Church Property, Education and Literature, Group Activities, Legislative Awareness and Social Action, Membership and Evangelism, Stewardship and Finance, Worship and Music, and Youth Ministry. Each program committee was composed of a chair and at least three other committee members, elected by the congregation. The chair of the youth ministry committee was the president of the Hi-League. Program committee chairs could appoint additional members. In addition to program committees, five congregational committees were identified: Executive, Nominating, Personnel, Scholarship, and Mutual Ministry Committees. This is the first document to address conflicts of interest and to include an indemnification clause.

The by-laws were revised again in 2006. The Council was increased to 16 members: president, vice president (president-elect), secretary, treasurer, past president, representatives of each of the eight program members, and (new in this revision) three at-large Council members elected by the congregation. Members of the program committees continued to be elected by the congregation. Committee chairs could appoint additional members, but they needed to be ratified by the Council. The program committees remained the same and the congregational committees were reduced to four (Executive Committee, Nominating Committee, Personnel Committee, and Mutual Ministry Committee) eliminating the Scholarship Committee. By this point, the Immanuel Foundation was awarding scholarships to students attending church-affiliated schools.

The 2012 by-laws revisions (approved at the January 2013 annual meeting) made the following changes:
Renamed the annual financial audit to the annual financial review.
Approved e-mail for official meeting notices.
Renamed the Legislative Awareness and Social Action Committee to the Social Action Committee.
Clarified committee representation on church Council, i.e., a committee's chair and representative on church Council may, but need not, be the same person.
Limited committee chairs to two consecutive terms.

7-2. Immanuel Council (2007)

> Allowed the Mutual Ministry Committee to be optional.
> Created a Communications Committee.
> Made other smaller changes for clarity and consistency.

In early 2015, the Saint Paul Area Synod informed Immanuel that the church had been operating with by-laws, but no approved constitution since the time the Evangelical Lutheran Church in America (ELCA) was formed in 1988. The Synod provided a model constitution, which a committee (Immanuel members Kelley Wells, Zach Marsh, Doug Wangensteen and Pastor Cindy Bullock) used to write a document that included the previously adopted by-laws. This document, "Constitution, By-Laws, and Continuing Resolutions," went through multiple reviews at the Synod and within Immanuel, and was presented to the Executive Committee on June 7, 2016, and to the Council on June 21, 2016. It was approved at a special congregational meeting October 9, 2016, with two minor amendments. A second required vote was taken at the annual meeting January 29, 2017, and the new document received unanimous approval.

As set out in the 2017 "Constitution, By-Laws, and Continuing Resolutions," the Council consisted of 16 individuals: president, vice president (president-elect), secretary, treasurer, past president, representatives of the eight program committees, and three at-large Council members. The program committees were Church Property, Education, Stewardship, Social Action, Membership and Evangelism, Finance, Worship and Music, and Youth Ministry. Congregational committees consisted of the Executive Committee, Nominating Committee, Personnel Committee, Mutual Ministry Committee (if one were appointed), and a Communications Committee. The pastor appointed the last four of these.

In 2018, two committees—Education and Literature, and Youth—merged to form the Children, Youth, and Family (CYF) Team, a single group overseeing children and youth programming from birth to graduation.

In January 2020, an updated version of the 2017 "Constitution, Bylaws, and Continuing Resolutions of Immanuel Lutheran Church" was approved at the annual meeting. The officers of the congregation are the president, vice president, past president, secretary, treasurer, assistant treasurer, financial secretary, and assistant financial secretary—all elected by the congregation. The Council is comprised of voting members of the congregation and consists of the president, vice president (president-elect), past president, secretary, treasurer, and three at-large Council members who are elected by the congregation at the annual meeting of the church. The pastor(s) shall attend the meetings of the Council without vote. The Council has general oversight of the life and activities of the congregation and, in particular, its worship life. The Council also is responsible for the business and charitable affairs, and property matters of the congregation. See Appendix L for Immanuel's 2022 Council, officers, and program team chairs.

The Congregation continues to have both congregational and program committees. The congregational committees are: Executive Committee, Nominating Committee, Personnel Committee, Mutual Ministry Committee, and Communications Committee. The latter three are appointed by the president. The congregational committees are largely responsible for church governance and operational issues.

For the present, Immanuel generally uses the term "program team" instead of "program committee" to distinguish between program and congregational committees. The program teams are: Church Property, Education, Stewardship, Social Action, Membership and Evangelism, Finance, Worship and Music, and Youth Ministry. The pastor appoints the chairs of the program teams. Program teams should have at least three members. The program committees largely deal with the ministry of the church. At the time of this writing, the Education and Youth Ministries Teams are subsumed under the Children, Youth, and Family Team.

Policies

Immanuel has approved special policies over the years, such as a "Donations & Memorials Policy" (approved by the Council in, 2001). Of particular note is the "Immanuel Lutheran Church Child Abuse Intervention and Prevention Policy" (approved by the Council in 1999; revised in 2012) and two policies approved in 2003: requirements for background checks for volunteers working with Immanuel's children and youth, and driver history checks for those who provide transportation.

Additional policies include:
- "Personnel Policies and Procedures Handbook" (approved by the Executive Committee, Jan. 9, 2018)
- "Background Check Policy and Procedures for Work with Children and Youth" (approved by the Council, 2003)
- "Financial Policies and Procedures" (revised April 16, 2021)
- "Budgeting" [and procedures for the general fund budget] (approved October 2020)

Current Program Teams and Congregational Committees and Their Responsibilities

Program Teams

Church Property

This team provides for the care and protection of all property of the congregation and for additions or alterations. It obtains and reviews bids for building additions or alterations, making recommendations to the Council when required. It is not responsible for long range planning for property needs and improvements, although members of the Property Team often have significant roles in major building projects.

Stewardship

This team is charged with developing and implementing plans to increase the congregation's financial and human resources both annually and for the long term, including coordinating with capital campaigns and other special appeals. It exercises oversight over the total fundraising activities of the congregation. Prior to 2006, the committee name was "Stewardship and Finance Committee." The name change was made to:

Promote a vital sense of stewardship and social life of the congregation.

Develop and implement plans to increase the congregation's financial and human resources.

Oversee fundraising activities of the congregation.

Study the need for new activities and organizations and take steps to make them happen.

The Stewardship Team organizes and coordinates the annual stewardship campaign. The group has provided stewardship education through adult forums and special programs, and works closely with other teams to do so. In 2000, the (then) Stewardship and Finance Committee implemented the "Simply Giving" program of electronic deposit, to facilitate easier giving by members and to create a more predictable pattern of giving over the year.

Social Action

This team informs the congregation and encourages involvement in service and justice opportunities. It provides forums and discussions about current social justice issues so that congregational members may make faith-informed decisions about their actions. The Social Action Team makes recommendations to the Council concerning benevolence partners and allocations.

The Social Action Team, formerly known as the Legislative Awareness and Social Action (LASA) Committee, has a long history of caring about and for the community, especially those who are homeless, hungry, or in poverty, by addressing their immediate needs. Immanuel members' gifts of time and money have often responded to these needs.

Many benevolence and service initiatives described in earlier sections of this book have been under the aegis of LASA and now the Social Action Team. Annual reports from LASA stress the Committee's role as a facilitator for volunteer opportunities. These include the Dorothy Day program, blood drives, metro Paint-A-Thon, the Giving Tree Christmas gifts, the parish nurse ministry, Crop Walk to fight hunger, "Undie" Sunday, soap drive, flood relief for Fargo, kitchen kits for shelters around the metro area, school supply collection, and more. In 1992, LASA took on a special project to tutor the children of the Cao family, one of the Vietnamese refugee families sponsored by Immanuel. Several Immanuel members took turns going each week to the family's home to help with schoolwork. Former pastor Joy Bussert (2002–2009) was an important catalyst for LASA and the Immanuel congregation to engage deeply with issues of social justice.

Social Action has hosted many learning opportunities to better understand pressing social concerns, locally and abroad. These are listed in Appendix I. In recent years, the Social Action Team has added energy to learning about racism and engaging in legislative advocacy and action, seeking to bring about long-term change. For example, Social Action has been involved with the Joint Church Antiracism Team (JCART), supporting learning and advocacy events especially related to Native American history and the role of the Lutheran Church, coordinating JCART events with those at Immanuel, and reporting on activities to the Council.

In 2017 and 2018, Immanuel pursued an initiative to make Immanuel a Dementia Friendly congregation. A committee was established and several goals were accomplished including: providing Dementia Friends training for Immanuel congregation members, establishing a resource center on the kiosk in the Gathering Space with information on identifying the signs of dementia and help in writing a dementia health directive, making three "memory bags" for the Immanuel library with activities and resources for persons with dementia and their caregivers, providing adult forum training on "Care for the Caregiver" and "Dementia Care in Sweden" using pet therapy, conducting an in-pew survey to identify needs in the congregation, and purchasing books for caregivers for the Immanuel library. Immanuel participated in the Dementia Friendly Faith Communities group that met regularly at Lyngblomsten and Saint Paul Neighborhood ACT (SPN ACT) on Alzheimer's. A coffee hour served brain healthy foods (blueberries, nuts, etc.) and provided handouts on Alzheimer's. The use of nametags for people to use during worship was initiated in 2017 as an aid for those with Alzheimer's and all who struggle to remember names.

In 2000, the Social Action Team set a specific goal to become more active in legislative awareness because an analysis at that time revealed that Immanuel's actions were heavily focused on direct services. Fulfilling this goal was carried out at Immanuel by hosting speakers and elected officials, offering learning sessions, writing postcards to legislators, and joining efforts with community advocacy and justice organizations including Metropolitan Interfaith Council on Affordable Housing (MICAH) and Joint Religious Legislative Coalition (JRLC).

The goal of increased legislative awareness also set off a trajectory of learning around the social concerns of the community including racism, the environment, healthcare, ending poverty, and more. In 2012, two controversial Minnesota state constitutional amendments were on the November ballot. LASA leadership learned a facilitation technique called "Respectful Conversations" to guide the congregation through several difficult topics including the Marriage Amendment (2012), Voter ID Amendment (2012), Gun Violence (2013), and The Political Divide (2016).

7-3. Gerry Erickson receiving a nametag; Sara Dreke Eyre in background (2017)

The group's focus continued to evolve based on a growing understanding of racism and the need to address it. An Immanuel group attended a "Journey to Justice: Facing White Privilege and Racism in Our Church" workshop in Minneapolis. The Team felt compelled to attend this after events, namely the July 2016 shooting death of Philando Castile and community reaction, in the community heightened the need to engage. The Social Action Team invited Immanuel members on a personal journey of learning and grappling with racism and white privilege.

This educational focus on race and racism and understanding how faith calls Christians to be involved in the political arena where social justice issues are debated sparked a new activism in 2015 for some members. Immanuel's association with advocacy organizations grew to include ISAIAH and Lutheran Advocacy MN. Individuals attended learning sessions on a wide variety of topics including homelessness and poverty, rallied at the Minnesota Capitol, met with elected officials, turned out voters, wrote to their Minnesota legislators, and wrote letters to the editor.

7-4. Respectful Conversation (2012)

In 2020 and 2021, in the midst of the COVID pandemic and the ensuing precautions to reduce the spread of the virus through stay-at-home orders, social distancing, wearing masks, and washing hands, the church and teams were determined to continue Immanuel's ministries while being apart. As invited by the Council, the Social Action Team set and fulfilled its goals of fundraising to benefit benevolence partners, continuing mercy work (direct service), and encouraging critical thinking and the application of Christian values and teachings in the voters' analysis, and learning about the history of race and racism. The murder of George Floyd in Minneapolis in 2020 and the local and worldwide reaction called Immanuel members to gather as a community to deal with difficult and challenging topics.

Membership and Evangelism

This team encourages the congregation in a continuing program of personal evangelism among the unchurched. It seeks to integrate new members into the life and activities of the congregation and to revitalize the indifferent and inactive members of the congregation. It introduces church literature and books for family devotion, and encourages concern and promotes relief for shut-ins and the needy in the congregation.

7-5. *Map of Immanuel members' homes (1945)*

In the early days of Immanuel, visitors were asked to complete a card found in the pews with their name and contact information and to indicate if they were interested in joining Immanuel—the pastor then would visit them. Communion cards were also in the pews so that a record of those taking Holy Communion could be kept and the information sent back to the home church of visitors.

A survey of homes in the area surrounding Immanuel was conducted in 1945 during Pastor Conrad Mervin Thompson's time at Immanuel. Follow-up was done with 500 "unchurched" families, and Immanuel's membership grew tremendously through this effort. This evangelism campaign was used as a model throughout the synod.

For many years, Membership and Evangelism delivered a dozen cookies to Immanuel visitors, famously made by Immanuel member Mabel Pappenfus. The group has organized orientations for new members and handled placing advertisements in local newspapers. A special gift bag was given to visiting Macalester students in the fall.

7-6. Mabel Pappenfus, famous for her cookies, pies, and fruit soup (2011)

7-7. Kim Thomspon and Lauren Seka (2013)

7-8. Sunday Coffee Hour provided by the Property Committee—Stephanie Alstead, Don Kyser, Ron Struss, and Lee English (2008)

In recent years, this group has sponsored an annual chili cook-off in January as part of the Wednesday night suppers. Sometimes called "Soup Suppers," these meals were originally held on Wednesday evenings in Lent and served only soup, but in May 2000 were expanded to be held September through May. The freewill offering collected at the suppers is donated to Keystone Community Services, formerly Merriam Park Food Shelf. Immanuel member Kim Thompson has organized the meals and shared information at the Wednesday suppers for several years.

During Lent (usually February through March), the group coordinates Lenten Fish Fry outings. Other activities have been progressive dinners, ballroom dance classes in 2009, an annual Easter breakfast, attending Saints and Twins baseball games, coordinating the preparation of church member photo directories, and preparing a luncheon for the annual meeting in January. Oversight of the Sunday coffee hour has been the responsibility of Membership and Evangelism as has been the annual spaghetti dinner and silent auction (in partnership with the Youth Committee). Many of these activities have been paused during the COVID pandemic.

Finance

This team prepares the annual budget of the congregation in consultation with the other teams and presents the proposed budget to the Council and the congregation for approval. It oversees the financial affairs of the congregation, the prompt payment of bills, the proper investment of the congregation's funds, and the creation and maintenance of financial policies and internal controls. The Finance Team procures all insurance covering the property and operations of the congregation, subject to the approval of the executive committee. The Parish Administrator (now the Church Administrator) serves as a non-voting member of the Finance Team.

Worship and Music

This team reviews and makes recommendations regarding the worship services of the congregation. It supervises the altar guild, ushers, and voice and handbell choirs, and advises the Council in the employment of organists and music directors. Funds from the Worship and Music budget are used to purchase music, musical instruments, robes, and hymnals.

This group recommended offering Communion at all services, which began in 2006. In 2010, Worship and Music implemented "Hanging of the Greens" to decorate the sanctuary for the Christmas season. This Team arranges for the seasonal sanctuary decorations and organizes a deep clean of the sanctuary before each Easter Sunday.

Children, Youth & Family

This team has oversight for the instructional programs of the congregation, including Sunday School, Vacation Bible School, Confirmation classes, Adult Forum, the nursery, and the library. It oversees the youth ministry including high school student trips to the Evangelical Lutheran Church of America National Youth Gathering, adventure trips, and mission/service trips. The group works closely with the Director of Children and Family Ministry and Director of Youth and Family Ministry to address educational programming for all ages.

Congregational Committees

Executive

The Executive Committee is composed of the president (who is its chair), vice president, secretary, treasurer, and past president. The pastor is an advisory member of the Executive Committee. The Executive Committee ensures that all policies, programs, and decisions of the Council and congregation are carried out. It is empowered to make decisions between Council meetings, subject to the control and direction of the Council at its next meeting.

Nominating

The Nominating Committee is chaired by the past president, who, after consulting with the president, vice president, and pastor, recommends the names of at least three members of the congregation to serve on that committee. The members of the Nominating Committee so selected are appointed by the president and ratified by the Council. The pastor serves as an advisory member of the Nominating Committee. The Nominating Committee nominates at least one candidate for each office to be filled at the annual meeting of the congregation and secures the consent of each candidate to serve if elected.

Personnel

The president appoints the Personnel Committee. All appointments to the personnel committee are reviewed and ratified by the Council. The Personnel Committee is responsible for developing, implementing, and thereafter overseeing the maintenance of job descriptions, personnel files, and a performance appraisal process for every paid staff member, including the pastoral staff; an organizational chart including all paid positions and reflecting the direct and indirect lines of reporting; and policies and procedures to facilitate communications between the pastoral staff and other paid staff. In addition, the Personnel Committee works with the pastoral staff as needed to develop and maintain their ability to manage staff. The Personnel Committee makes certain that all staff members are properly recognized for their work, and handles staff issues as part of the staff grievance procedure. The Personnel Committee advises and makes recommendations to the Council regarding employee benefit policies for staff.

Mutual Ministry

The Mutual Ministry Committee is now optional. It consists of five members. Members are nominated by current members of the committee and formally appointed by the Council in December of each year (or at other times when necessary to fill unexpired terms). The Mutual Ministry Committee aims to improve communication and build relationships within and between pastoral staff and the congregation when issues are raised by pastoral staff or members of the congregation. The Mutual Ministry Committee has no authority to set church policy or any other powers that supersede those of the Council.

Other Committees

The president, with Council approval, may establish one or more other committees (including a Call Committee) having the authority of the Council in the management of the business of the church to the extent determined by the Council. One example is the temporary Building Reopening Team, appointed in response to the COVID pandemic. Composed of Deb Ahlquist, Dale Fierke, Harvey Jaeger, Carl Johnson, Maria Reed, and Pastor Cindy Bullock, this group developed a multistage plan to guide building use and gradual reopening. As the situation evolved, the Team continued to revise the plan, which addressed such topics as building access, wearing of masks, social distancing, and how various building spaces should be accessed and used.

Past Committees

Scholarship Committees

At one time, Immanuel had the Lutheran Education Aid Fund (LEAF) Committee (later the Scholarship Committee) that provided scholarships to the youth of the congregation and encouraged them to attend church colleges and the seminary. For example, in 1959, funding was provided to Stanley West (Luther Seminary), Lorna Aalbue (St. Olaf College), Richard Jorgensen (Gustavus Adolphus College), and Karen Peterson (Seattle Lutheran Bible Institute). In the 1990s, the Council president appointed a Scholarship Committee each year to award scholarships to Immanuel members attending Lutheran colleges and seminaries. The Immanuel Foundation now distributes these scholarships.

Group Activities Committee

For several years, Immanuel had a Group Activities Committee, charged with coordinating and promoting intergenerational activities for increased fellowship and interaction for all members. Over the years, this committee was responsible for the church directory, annual congregational picnics, "Fat Tuesday" (Mardi Gras) socials, Wednesday suppers and the chili cook-off, high school graduation coffee hours in May, trips to Saint Paul Saints and Twins baseball games, coordinating Sunday coffee hours, and keeping the church pantry stocked with paper products, coffee, etc. Group Activities coordinated progressive dinners, ballroom dancing classes, summer beer crawls that visit microbreweries, and Lenten fish fry outings.

Group Activities was responsible for annual church picnics, which were often held in the fall. Church picnics have been a regular feature at Immanuel for more than a century. A panoramic photo was taken at a church picnic June 21, 1925. Immanuel member Shirley Bethke remembered one picnic to which members were asked to wear Biblical costumes. It rained on the disciples when they were reenacting the Last Supper. The donkey hired to add extra reality to some of the scenes got sick—all resulting in a memorable picnic. In 1976, the church picnic had a patriotic theme to celebrate the bicentennial. Guests wore vintage costumes and dressed in red, white, and blue. The 1994 picnic was held on the church grounds and 275 people attended. Music was performed by "Four Score," a male a cappella group. Children played games and ran relays. A dunk tank soaked the pastors and congregational members. The day ended with a softball game at Macalester College.

Governance and Organizational Structure

Group Activities also coordinated numerous potluck meals after Sunday services and congregational events, including annual meetings, welcome luncheons for new pastors, and farewell luncheons for departing staff members. The contributed food was always delicious, especially the desserts.

7-9. Potluck dinner (1980)

7-10. Easter breakfast (2013)

In the mid-1990s, the Group Activities Committee coordinated Active Christians Together Socially (ACTS). Approximately 40 sets of couples or singles formed groups who got together socially once a month.

In February 2002, Group Activities helped plan and serve a potluck dinner for Garrison Keillor's Wobegon Weekend. Out-of-town fans were promised a "real church basement potluck supper." Immanuel members Ray and Karen Lefto coordinated the evening. Immanuel women cooked "hotdish" casseroles and Jell-O salads (recipes for both provided by radio show staff) and the meal was served cafeteria-style in the basement. Some members complained that none of the recipes had been served at Immanuel in decades, but went with along with the radio show's directive—all for the nice fee that the Prairie Home Companion program paid the church for the evening. Keillor led a sing-along in the sanctuary. He generously allowed the collection of a freewill offering when told the proceeds would go to Immanuel's youth.

The Membership and Evangelism Team has assumed many of the activities and responsibilities previously under the purview of the Group Activities Committee.

7-11. Immanuel Church picnic (June 21, 1925)

Epilogue

Immanuel Lutheran Church has been fortunate to have had dedicated pastors and staff who have been our leaders and inspiration for more than 150 years. Throughout the history of Immanuel, the church has relied on the contributions of lay leaders (council members, committee and team chairs, deacons, trustees, Sunday School and Vacation Bible School teachers, and many, many others), the support of women's and men's groups, inspiration provide by many talented musicians, and the energy and dedication of the youth. Together we support each other and grow in faith. The Immanuel community is looking forward to new ministries yet to be discovered that will define Immanuel's direction during the next 150 years.

> "If we were flexible enough to be able to make this year happen (2020), whatever happens in the future we should be able to work around and incorporate because that is what we've done over the years—over the nearly 150 years that the congregation has been around. Hopefully, we can still be relevant and meaningful and still help people out. We want to be a part of it as long as we possibly can into the future."
> —Stephanie and David Alstead

> "I don't know where I would be without Immanuel. I always had people around supporting me. You have to work to have that kind of community."
> —Zach Danielson

> "Immanuel has been able to disconnect from the past and move into the future. . . . Immanuel is now confident in itself and able to move into the community."
> —Sue Klevan

"Our lives, days, and weeks have a rhythm and Immanuel is an important part of that rhythm."
—David Stark

"I hope we keep looking to the future instead of wishing for things that we had in the past. I hope that we become more diverse and include people from the neighborhood and that we make sure that they feel free to speak out."
—Phyllis Bentley

E-1. Immanuel Lutheran Church welcomes everyone—Roger Forman and Ingrid Mundt (2007)

Appendixes

Appendix A

Pastors of Immanuel, Macalester, and Highland Park Lutheran Churches

The visiting pastors, lay preachers, and seminarians who met with the early members of Immanuel were Haugeans. They followed the teachings of the Norwegian revivalist lay preacher Hans Nielsen Hauge (1771–1824), who led a pietistic, grass-roots movement. He was, in many ways, reacting to the state Church of Norway, which was seen as formal, lethargic, and dominated by the educated, privileged, upper classes. Hauge emphasized the priesthood of all believers, a personal religious experience, and vigorous lay leadership while adhering to Lutheran doctrine and catechetical instruction. He avoided what he considered "high" church liturgy and felt traditional vestments were pretentious and unnecessary. Hauge traveled around Norway, preaching as he crisscrossed the country. During Hauge's life, itinerant preaching, and religious gatherings held without the supervision of an ordained pastor in Norway were illegal. Hauge was arrested and imprisoned numerous times. He had a profound impact on religious practices in both Norway and the United States.

Elling Eielsen (1804–1883: see biography below) was a lay preacher and evangelist in the Haugean Lutheran reform movement in America who emigrated to the U.S. in 1839. Eielsen is considered the chief transplanter of the Haugean movement from Norway to America. He never attended a seminary, but was ordained in 1843 at the wish of his followers. He was not interested in organizing, but his followers established the *Evangelisk-lutherske kirke i Amerika* (Evangelical Lutheran Church in America), which was known as the Eielsen Synod, at the Jefferson Prairie Settlement, Wisconsin, in 1846. The synod was "low church," de-emphasizing formal worship and stressing personal faith in the Haugean tradition. Eielsen was a frequent visiting pastor to the Immanuel congregation in the early days.

The Eielsen Synod was rife with dissension, due in part to Eielsen's obstinacy, rigor, and orthodoxy. One consequence of the dissension was the creation of the *Hauges norsk lutherske Synode i Amerika* (Hauge Norwegian Lutheran Synod in America, or briefly, the Hauge Synod), which split from the Eielsen Synod in 1876. This new group founded the Red Wing Seminary as the Hauge Synod education center in Red Wing, Minnesota, in 1879; it closed in 1917. Thirteen of Immanuel's early pastors graduated from the Red Wing Seminary and five of Immanuel's pastors served as either professors or presidents of the Seminary and others had additional leadership positions in there. Both the Eielsen Synod and the Hauge Synod were opposed to drinking alcohol, dancing, gambling, and slavery.

In 1917, the Hauge Synod merged into the Norwegian Lutheran Church of America. That group was later renamed the Evangelical Lutheran Church in 1946 and then merged into the American Lutheran Church (ALC) in 1960. In a subsequent merger, the ALC became the Evangelical Lutheran Church in America (ELCA), of which Immanuel is now a member.

Much of the early history of church work among Norwegian Americans was part of what were called the "home missions" through which established churches sent out pastors, lay preachers, and student preachers to establish congregations, and visit, preach, and serve Communion to them. Many of Immanuel's early visiting pastors, lay preachers, and student preachers were part of the Hauge Synod's "Home Mission, South Dakota, and Minnesota" outreach initiative. Many of the early pastors and lay preachers visited Immanuel's early congregation several times, offering the liturgy (*Altergang*) and Holy Communion (*Nadvarsgang*). Several carried the title *Emissær* (emisor or emissary), a professional title used for lay preachers within the mission organizations in the Church of Norway. Normally an emissary had no theological education other than a full- or half-year course in Bible school. Almost without exception, the emissaries were recruited from the people, that is, from a social stratum of farmers, fishermen, and artisans. It was common for an emissary to work as a preacher during the winter and perform his other work in the summer. The emissaries traveled from place to place and held meetings in homes and small gathering places. Depending on the response, an emissary might stay in one place in revival for many weeks. Emissaries provided pastoral care at the meetings and spoke for repentance.

Many of Immanuel's pastors graduated from what is now Luther Seminary, originally called Luther Theological Seminary. Luther Theological Seminary was formed in 1917 when the Red Wing Seminary (Hauge Synod), Luther Seminary (operated by the Norwegian Synod in St. Paul), and the United Church Seminary (operated by the United Norwegian Lutheran Church in St. Paul) merged in conjunction with the merger of the three Norwegian Lutheran Church bodies. The name of Luther Theological Seminary was changed to Luther Seminary July 1, 1994. Three of Immanuel's pastors have been professors at Luther Seminary.

Note: The authors have used church records, county historical society records, personal contact with some individuals, and the sources that are listed at the book's bibliography to compile the biographies and provide as much information as possible. Any omissions and errors are inadvertent. Photos, detailed biographies, and supporting documents are available in the Immanuel Lutheran Church archives.

1871

Osten (Østen) Hanson (Holtan)
Visiting Pastor (also in 1881, 1884)
July 8, 1836 (Norway)–Aug. 4, 1898
Immigrated 1851. Farmer (1851–1861). Ordained in 1861. Married Marie Sophie Gulbransen, then Anne Haaven (Hoven). Pastor at Aspelsund, Minnesota (1861–1898). Hauge Synod president (1875–1876, 1887–1893). He was the founder of the Red Wing Seminary and also founder of the mission society that established the Norwegian Lutheran Church Mission in China. He was president of the board of regents of the Red Wing Seminary for several years. His sons **Martin Gustav Hanson** (see below—1884) and **Hans Adolph Hanson** (see below—1884) also were Immanuel pastors. "He came from Telemarken and God met him here and persuaded him to become his child. He was president of the Hauge Synod for many years, so he needs no further testimony." (comment from O.H. Oace, quoted in Gjerde and Ljostveit's *The Hauge Movement in America* (see Bibliography). Note: O. (Ole) H. Oace is listed as Immanuel president in 1917 and 1919.

1872

Hans Erikson Sether
Visiting Pastor (also in 1873, 1874, 1875, 1876, 1878, 1881, 1883)
Sept. 24, 1836 (Norway)–Dec. 13, 1892
Immigrated in 1867. Lay preacher. Ordained 1868. Married Kjersti Akelsen. Served congregations in Minnesota. "He was converted through **Ole Johanneson Kasa** (see below). His worldly father was very angry at this, and told Hans to make his choice between Christ and the farm. Young Hans answered: 'If the Sether farm stood on pillars of gold (*guldstolper*) I would not want it, if I had to give up Christ.' So he came to America in 1867. The Haugeans ordained him. He was a humble brother. We praise God for him." (comment from O.H. Oace)

Ole (Olaus) Johannesen Kasa
Visiting Pastor (also in 1875, 1878, 1883)
Nov. 4, 1821 (Norway)–Sept. 7, 1904
Soldier in Denmark (Schleswig war, 1848). Lay preacher in Norway and Sweden. Immigrated 1868. Ordained 1869 by **Elling Eielsen** (see below) in the Eielsen Synod and in 1876 in the Hauge Synod. Married Karen Hansen Rustad. Served congregations in Minnesota. Kasa never learned English and thought it

was a sin for Norwegians to learn to speak English (as reported by his great-great grandson.) Kasa was expelled from the synod because he believed that the Communion ritual, which—at that time—combined Communion with absolution (forgiveness of sins) was not consistent with the words of Jesus. He was persecuted because he believed that absolution and Communion should be separated in the liturgy. He continued to preach, although some churches were closed to him. The changes Kasa proposed were made to the liturgy after his death. His son **Johan Olsen [Olson] Kasa** (See Appendix B) entered the ministry and stated that the family had a good relationship with the Native Americans around their homestead in Otter Tail County, Minnesota.

Ole Andersen Bergh
Visiting Pastor (also in 1873, 1877)
Feb. 1, 1819 (Norway)–Nov. 28, 1907
Immigrated in 1860. Teacher, song leader (Klokker) and lay preacher (1839–1868). In 1845, Bergh's fervent testimony on repentance resulted in the conversion of **Ole Johanneson Kasa** (see above), who later emigrated to America. Ordained in 1868 by Hauge-Eielsen "people." Married first Sidsil Kasa, the sister of **Ole Johannesen Kasa**, then Anne G. Røgholt. He made his home in Kasson, Minnesota, and served congregations in Kasson, Faribault, and Webster, Minnesota, from 1868 to 1886, travelling widely and often going to Saint Paul. He was called "Old Bergh."

Elling Eielsen (Sunve)
Visiting Pastor (also in 1875, 1876)
Sept. 19, 1804 (Norway)–Jan. 10, 1883
Sunve was the name of the farm where he was born. Lay preacher in Norway, Sweden, and Denmark (1832–1838, jailed in Denmark for lay preaching in 1837). Immigrated in 1839. Ordained 1843 by Rev. F.A. Hofman, a German Lutheran pastor, becoming the first ordained Norwegian Lutheran minister in the United States. Married Sigrid Nilsen Tufte. Travelled as a home missionary, going to Illinois, Wisconsin, Minnesota, South Dakota, and Texas—always on foot. His followers organized the Evangelical Lutheran Church in America (Eielsen Synod) in 1846, and Eielsen served as its first president 1846–1883. Helped to found Lisbon Seminary, Lisbon, Illinois; Eielsen Seminary, Cambridge, Wisconsin; Hauge College and Eielsen Seminary, Chicago, Illinois. In 1842, he was instrumental in the publication of *Sandhed til gudfrygtighed* :

udi en eenfoldig og efter mulighed kort, dog tilstrækkelig, forklaring over sal. Dr. Mort. Luthers liden catechismo : indeholdende alt det, som den, der vil blive salig, har behov at vide og gjøre . . . med tilføielse af den uforandrede Augsburgske confessions artikler (Truth to Godliness: A Simple and, if Possible, Brief, Though Sufficient, Explanation of Dr. Martin Luther's Catechism . . . with the Addition of the Articles of the Unchanged Augsburg Confession)— Erich Pontoppidan's "Explanation of Luther's Catechism" (which emphasized pietism and personal experiences) and the Augsburg Confession. This book was the first Norwegian language book to be printed in the United States. To bring this about, he walked from Chicago to New York and back. He had already had Luther's Small Catechism translated and published in English *(Doctor Martin Luther's Small Catechism, with Plain Instruction for Children, and Sentences from the Word of God to Strengthen the Faith of the Meek)* in 1841. Note: Much of the preceding information is from M.O. Wee's book *Haugeanism;* see Bibliography. "He was a stern preacher of repentance, not so mild in his address, as his great predecessor, Hans Nielsen Hauge." (*Lutheran Almanac,* 1934)

1873

Torger Andrew (Andreas) Torgerson
Visiting Pastor (also 1881)
Jan. 26, 1838 (Norway)–Jan. 7, 1906
Immigrated in 1852. Attended Concordia College, St. Louis (1858–1861), Ft. Wayne Seminary (1861–1862), and Concordia Seminary, St. Louis (1862–1865). Ordained in 1863. Married Dina Anderson. Served churches in Iowa. Professor at Luther Seminary 1881–1882. His papers are at St. Olaf College in the Norwegian American Historical Association files. He wrote a history of his ministry.

1874

Christoffer (Christopher) O. Brohaugh
Visiting Pastor (also 1875, 1876, 1877, 1879, 1881, 1882, 1883)
June 2, 1841 (Norway)–July 2, 1908.
Immigrated in 1869. Ordained in 1873. Served as called pastor for both East and West Immanuel from 1893–1906. (See complete biography below.)

Ingvald Eisteinsen
Visiting Pastor (also 1881, 1882)
Sept. 25, 1843 (Norway)–June 27, 1901. Married Margit Olsen Stokke. Immigrated in 1872. Ordained 1874. Hauge Synod. President of Red Wing Seminary (1879–1981). Served congregations in Iowa, Minnesota, Illinois, and California.

1875
Lars Olson Rustad
Visiting Pastor (also 1876)
April 2, 1818 (Norway)–Jan.1, 1878
Immigrated in 1869. Ordained in 1870 in the Eielsen Synod. Farmer and lay preacher. Pastor at Norway Lake, Minnesota, and five other congregations in Minnesota from 1870–1878. Married Karen Husebye and then Marie Arak. Returned to Norway, where he died. Described as a "heart-stirring lay preacher and soul winner." (comment from O.H. Oace)

Tomas [Thomas] Olsen Eidem
Visiting Lay Preacher (also 1881, 1882, 1883)
Sept. 24, 1813 (Norway)–March 8, 1889
Married Randi Hovstand. Immigrated in 1866. He visited every Hauge congregation in Minnesota, but was never ordained. Described as a "singular man of God and powerful lay-evangelist." Also, "Eidem had an exceptionally good memory. Toward the end of his blessed career, when his eyesight was failing, he could read by heart, not only a few verses, but whole chapters without mistakes." (comment from O.H. Oace)

1876
Martin Gustav Hanson
Student Pastor (1876 to 1883)
July 11, 1859– Oct. 14, 1915
Served as Immanuel's first called pastor (1883–1892). See below—1884.

1877
Endre (Andrew) Johanessen
Visiting Pastor (also 1878)
Dec. 31, 1822 (Norway)–Jan. 17, 1887
Ordained in 1847. He was a teacher and lay preacher in Norway. Immigrated in 1866. Married Gunhild Marie Olsen. Served congregations in Illinois and Iowa. Left the Hauge synod to organize an Apostolic church.

Arne Ellendson Boyum
Visiting Pastor (also 1878)
April 7, 1833 (Norway)–Jul 29, 1913
Immigrated in 1853. Ordained by **Elling Eielsen** (see above—1872) in 1858. Founder and pastor of Arendal Lutheran Church in Minnesota 1858–1896. President of the Hauge synod 1876–1887. Married Anne Iverdatter Tupphellen. In his autobiography, he stated, "in 1871 the synod (Eielsen) had fourteen pastors, and in 1875, twenty-four pastors. I was then gradually relieved of the long journeys and could to a greater extent give my time to the churches that I served in Fillmore county. The lay people were very active, each in his own circuit to assemble for edification even if the pastor was not present."

1878–79
Pastors during these years had visited Immanuel in previous years and are described above.

1880–1883
Fredrick Herman Carlson
Half-time Pastor. Immanuel's first called pastor
May 24, 1834 (Sweden)–July 3, 1892
Immigrated in 1868. Ordained in the Eielsen Synod in 1869. While at Immanuel, also served a Lutheran congregation in Minneapolis 1880–1884, riding the train between St. Paul and Minneapolis. Married Margretha Catherine Berg. Served congregations in Iowa, Minnesota, and South Dakota. "He was a Swede and a Godly Christian pastor. He never kept on after it was time to quit. In his evening meetings there was full liberty to take part for other Christians." (comment by O.H. Oace) "The love of God flowed like a stream through his own heart. At Carlson's afternoon and evening services there were free testimonies and

prayers and singing after a short opening sermon. God's people were encouraged to use their talents. One of the strongest gifts Carlson possessed was to instruct the confirmands and reach their hearts." (from *The Hauge Movement in America*. n.p.: Hauge Inner Mission Federation, 1941).

Johannes (John) Larsen Kyllingstad
Seminary Student (at Immanuel 1882, 1883)
Aug. 14, 1829 (Norway)–Aug. 7, 1890
Married Anne Marthea Hansen. From 1863–1879, he served as a missionary in Zululand, South Africa, with his wife and children for the Norwegian Missionary Society. Traveling lay preacher in Norway (1880–1881). Immigrated 1881. Attended Red Wing Seminary (1881–1882). President and Theological Professor Red Wing Seminary (1881–82). Ordained 1888 in the Hauge synod. Emissary with Hauge Synod (1883–1888).

1881
Although Immanuel had a called pastor, it continued to host visiting preachers—Emissary Vold from Norway, Christoffer [Christopher] Olson Brohaugh (see below—1893), Emissary Christofferson, and others identified above.

Karl Christophersen Holter
Visiting Pastor and Emissary (also 1884)
Dec. 19, 1851 (Norway)–Nov. 7, 1923
Immigrated in 1862. Attended Augsburg Seminary (1875–1877). Ordained in 1880. Married Anna Marie Anderson. Served congregations in Minnesota, Illinois, and Iowa. He held leadership positions in the Hauge Synod for more than 20 years (secretary, vice president, mission treasurer). Publisher of *Ungdommens Ven (Young Friend)*, Familiens Magasin *(Family Magazine)*, and *North Star*. Founded K.C. Holter Publishing Company.

Gustav A. Christianson Gjerstad
Seminary Student
Sept. 3, 1856 (Norway)–June 1919
Immigrated in 1876. Attended Red Wing seminary (1879–1885). Ordained in 1885. Married Emma Urness. Served on the Norwegian Lutheran Church Mission in China Board. Granted a medical license (1899). Served congregations in North Dakota, Iowa, and Minnesota.

Anfin Olsen Utheim
Visiting Pastor (also 1882)
June 21, 1842 (Norway)–Aug. 18, 1913

In Norway, he traveled the country as a lay preacher and earned his living as a shoemaker. Immigrated 1870. In the U.S., he worked as a carpenter, farmer, and lay preacher. Ordained 1876 in the Hauge Synod. Married Marith Iversdatter Stølan and, after her death, Anne Olsdatter Trönnes. Founded and served the Lac qui Parle congregation in South Dakota from 1876 to 1907. Served congregations in South Dakota and Minnesota. He was president of the Hauge Synod in 1892–1896. A friend stated, "Utheim was a believing Pastor, conscientious in all his dealings, and evangelical in his preaching. He was a man of prayer. He had deep concern for his parishioners." Another friend stated, "Of the old pioneer pastors there are few who did more extensive and intensive missionary work than Rev. Utheim. Besides serving his own congregation, he reached out in all directions and called the Norwegian people together and organized them into permanent congregations, most of which are now large and prosperous and maintain their own activity both at home and abroad. He never failed to make use of lay talent when possible."

Lars (Louis/Lewis) Larson Nervig
Seminary Student.
April 10, 1853 (Norway)–April 24, 1927

Immigrated in 1872. Attended Red Wing Seminary (1879–1884). Ordained in 1884. Married Christine Kasa, daughter of **Ole Johannesen Kasa** (see above—1872). Served churches in South Dakota, Nebraska, Louisiana, Texas, and California, and organized eight congregations.

1882
Again, Immanuel continued to host visiting preachers, including Emissary Christofferson, Larson, and others named above.

Christian Christiansen Moe
Seminary Student and Visiting Pastor (also 1883, 1884)
Oct. 12, 1848 (Norway)–Jan. 31, 1910

Immigrated 1869. Engineer in coal mines in Iowa (1870–1875). Attended Augustana College in Illinois (1877), Augsburg Seminary (1878), then Red Wing Seminary 1879–1882. Ordained 1882. Married Marie Larsen Enger. Served congregations in Iowa and South Dakota.

Iver Christian Larson Hatlestad
Seminary Student (also 1883)
Born Feb. 2, 1853 (Norway)–Dec. 12 1909.
Immigrated 1881. Attended Augsburg Seminary (1881–1882) and Red Wing Seminary (1882–1884). Ordained 1884 in Hauge Synod. Married Louise S. Stangeland. Served congregations in Iowa and Minnesota.

Bersvend Anderson
Visiting Pastor (also 1883)
Dec. 7, 1821 (Norway)–June 14, 1917
Converted by Pastor **Ole Johannesen Kasa** (see above—1872). Lay preacher 1837–1876. Immigrated in 1876. Ordained by the Haugeans in 1878. First pastor of the Hauge Synod in the Red River Valley, then in Crookston and Canada. Married Marit Johansen. He lived to be 96 and was called "Old Bersvend." Anderson was a preacher and pastor for 80 years and trained and organized laymen in the ministry. He was an unusually prolific letter-writer, and wrote innumerable articles in religious papers, especially for the *Budbaereren (The Messenger)*, the newsletter of the Hauge Synod. He travelled by foot and horseback preaching to settlers in northern Minnesota and Canada. "Old Bersvend had an unusual personality. He was meek, tender, and cheerful with a vein of humor. He had good common sense and an unusual will-power. He was self-taught, self-made—above all, a God-taught and God-made man. He was careful in his life and his words. He was loving, humble, and genial. He was a gifted speaker, but spoke mostly in a mildly persuasive but interesting way. He had a word to fit every soul-condition. An official in Norway called him 'the layman's bishop.'" (Comment from O.H. Oace)

Johannes (Melom, Slaatland) Halvorsson
Visiting Pastor (also 1883)
Dec. 30, 1830 (Norway)–Nov. 11, 1892
Lay preacher and farmer in Norway. Immigrated 1870. Ordained 1872 in Eielsen/Hauge Synod. Married Marie Iverson Hytta. Served congregations in Minnesota. "He was an ordained laymen's pastor who had to live on a salary of $50 a year. So he had to put on his overalls and work for his living. Many of his church members were well-to-do. Halvorsen had many trials in his life, until God let his servant depart in peace." (Comment by O.H. Oace)

Emanuel Christopherson
Teacher and Emissary for *Lutherstiftelsen* (Luther Foundation), an organization for inner missions
June 23, 1849 (Norway)–March 23, 1909
Attended Christiania University, Norway (1868–1873). Immigrated in 1876. Ordained in 1876. Married Inger Nielsen. Served congregations in Wisconsin and Minnesota.

1883
Gunder Larson Graven
Visiting Pastor
Jan. 20, 1883 (Norway)–June 6, 1903
Shoemaker and lay preacher in Norway (1855–1870). Immigrated 1870. Ordained 1871 in Eielsen/Hauge Synod. Married Marit A. Olstad. Conducted revivals, founded churches in South Dakota, and served 12 congregations in eight counties in South Dakota 1892–1900. Founded Bethesda Orphan's Home in Beresford, South Dakota, in 1896. He was described as "a great soul-winner and a son of thunder." One young boy stated, "I can't go to sleep when he preaches."

Christian Christopherson Holter
Student Preacher
Apr. 11, 1854 (Norway)–Dec.20, 1922
Immigrated 1862 (with his brother, **Karl Christopherson Holter**; see above—1881) Attended Red Wing Seminary (1879–1883) Ordained 1883. Hauge Synod. Married Anna Anderson. Served congregations in South Dakota, Iowa, and Illinois. Editor of the *Lutheraneren (The Lutheran)* for two years. Editor of the Hauge Synod newsletter for 14 years.

Anders Olsen Oppegaard
Visiting Pastor
Dec. 31, 1841(Norway)–Sept. 19, 1919
Tailor and lay preacher (1859–1868). Immigrated in 1869. Ordained in 1878. Worked with Home Missions and China Mission. Founding member of Immanuel in 1871 along with his future wife, Maren Johanneson. After her death, he married Janna L. Ihle. Served congregations in Wisconsin and Minnesota. "He was a tailor from Norway. The Hauge Synod ordained him. He served sixteen congregations. Where he labored were found many Hauge Lutheran Bible Christians." (Comment from O.H. Oace)

1884
Elias Peter Hansen Harbo
Seminary Student
Feb . 6, 1856 (Norway)–April 10, 1927
Immigrated in 1880. Attended Augsburg Seminary (1881–1889). Ordained in 1889. Married Marthe Marie Larsen. Professor at Augsburg Seminary (1909–1927). Served congregations in Wisconsin and Minnesota. President of the Lutheran Free Church (1897–1899, 1901–1903, 1907–1909, 1918–1927).

Hans Adolph Hanson
Visiting Lay Preacher
May 10, 1863 (Minnesota)–Nov. 1940
Son of **Osten Hanson,** Immanuel's first visiting pastor (see above—1871). Attended Red Wing Seminary (1879–1882 and 1885–1888). Attended Curtis Business College in Minneapolis (1882–1884). Ordained 1888 in the Hauge Synod. Married Elizabet Christy. Served congregations in Wisconsin, Illinois, and Utah.

1884-1892
Martin Gustav Hanson
Pastor serving both East and West Immanuel. (1884–1892)
July 11, 1859 (Minnesota)–Oct. 14, 1915.
Son of **Osten Hansen,** Immanuel's first visiting pastor (see above—1871). Served as a student pastor for Immanuel (1876–1883). Attended Red Wing Seminary (1880–1884). Ordained at Immanuel June 1, 1884. Married Caroline Runice. Professor and president of Red Wing Seminary (1886–1887). Vice president of the Hauge Synod (1894-1899), president (1899–1905, 1910–1915). Worked with the China Mission Commission. Representative for the Hauge Synod in Norway (1914). Knight of St. Olaf (1912). Served congregations in Minnesota.

1893-1906
Christoffer [Christopher] Olson Brohaugh
Pastor.
June 2, 1841 (Norway)-July 2, 1908. Immigrated in 1869. Ordained in 1873. After serving as a visiting pastor at Immanuel for several years, he was called as Immanuel's pastor in 1893. Spent 1/3 of his time at East Immanuel and 2/3 at West Immanuel. In February

1901, he terminated his services to East Immanuel to devote his entire time to West Immanuel, making him Immanuel's first full-time pastor. Married Julia Nelson. Vice President of Hauge Synod. Served on the Board of China Missions. Served congregations in Minnesota and Illinois. Prolific author and editor.

1907-1909
Iver Anker Johanson
Pastor serving both West and East Immanuel.
April 10, 1874 (Norway)–Dec. 20, 1942. Was a sailor in Norway. Immigrated in 1892. Attended Red Wing Seminary (1893–1896) and Augsburg Seminary (1899). Ordained in 1899. Hauge Synod, Free Church. Married Charlotte Sophie Strandness. Served congregations in North Dakota, Norway, Wisconsin, and Minnesota. Mayor of Spicer, Minnesota (1913–1915). Visited Norway 1900–1902, 1914, and 1924–1925. In 1911, he received an award from Norway for his work in securing funds for a life boat for a coastal town in northern Norway. Through the organization, *Nordlandslaget*, he raised $5,000 in 1914 to be sent to Norway to support tuberculosis treatment, poor fishermen, and scholarships there.

1909–1913
Simon Christian Simonson-Norwich
(name on grave is Simonson)
Pastor serving both West and East Immanuel
March 27, 1877 (Nebraska)–Dec. 10, 1957.
Attended Red Wing Seminary (1884–1901) and Chicago Lutheran Seminary (1903–1906). Ordained in 1901. Married Kanutte Vaage. Served West Immanuel and East Immanuel. Served churches in North Dakota, Illinois, Iowa, and Minnesota.

1913–1917
Rasmus Severin Chelmen
Pastor
Oct. 20, 1884 (Iowa)–July 24, 1969
Attended Red Wing Seminary (1905–1913). Ordained in 1913. Married Mable Amanda Wigen. Served a joint call to Immanuel (1913–1917) and Solar Lutheran Church near Webster, Minnesota (1913–1921). Also served a congregation in Dawson, Minnesota (1921–1950).

1917–1921
Dr. Gustav Marius Bruce
Interim Pastor
Feb. 11, 1879 (Norway)–Oct. 12, 1963
Immigrated in 1884. Married Jensine Tomine Louise Augusta Julia Rold (Minnie) Jensen. Attended Red Wing Seminary (1902–1905). Ordained in 1906. Graduated from the University of South Dakota (BA, 1907). Professor at Red Wing Seminary (1911–1917). When the synod passed a resolution forbidding theological professors serving as regular pastors, Pastor Bruce was forced to resign his call as Immanuel's pastor. He and his wife continued as Immanuel members. Awarded Doctor of Philosophy, Hartford Seminary Foundation (1927) and Doctor of Divinity, Lutheran Theological Seminary, Chicago (1928). Vice president Luther Theological Seminary, St. Paul (1944–1949). Interim pastor who assisted with the merger of Immanuel and Macalester Park Lutheran churches in 1921. Served congregations in South Dakota, Illinois, and Minnesota. Wrote about the China Mission. Prolific author. Many of his papers are in the Immanuel Church file in the Luther Seminary archives. His son, **Seth Clarence Eastvold,** became a pastor. See Appendix B.

1921
Carl Johan Eastvold (born Østvold)
Pastor
March 19, 1863 (Norway)–July 23, 1929
Immigrated in 1880. Attended Red Wing Seminary (1885–1891) and Chicago Lutheran Seminary (1896–1897). Ordained in 1891. Married Ellen Sophia Nelson. President of the Hauge Synod (1904–1910, and 1917, when it merged into the Norwegian Lutheran Church of America). President of Jewell Lutheran College, Jewell, Iowa (1911–1912). President of the Board of China Mission (1912–1917). President of the Southern Minnesota District Norwegian Lutheran Church of America beginning in 1927. Laid the cornerstone for the basement of Immanuel Evangelical Lutheran Church at Goodrich and Snelling Avenues in 1921. Served congregations in Iowa, Minnesota, and South Dakota. His son, **Seth Clarence Eastvold,** became a pastor. See Appendix B.

1921–1924
John Sevrin Sunde
Pastor
Jan. 31, 1889 (Minnesota)–Oct. 6, 1953

Graduated from St. Olaf College (1912) and Luther Theological Seminary (1919–1920). Ordained in 1915. Married Aalga Johnette Skare. Served as interim pastor for Macalester Park Lutheran Church from January to May, 1920. Conducted services in the chapel at Goodrich and Snelling as the first called pastor of the newly merged congregation. Served congregations in North Dakota and Minnesota. His son, **Orville Jeremy Sunde,** became a pastor; see Appendix B.

1924–1945
Bennie Loyel Duckstad
Pastor
March 9, 1895 (Minnesota)–April 25, 1977

Graduated from Concordia College, Moorhead, Minnesota (1920) and Luther Theological Seminary (1924). Ordained in 1924. Married Lila Johanna Thoe. Left Immanuel to serve as U.S. Army chaplain in World War II. Second longest serving Immanuel pastor—for 21 years. He dropped Norwegian services in 1930 because he did not speak the language well. Served congregations in Minnesota. Continued as an interim pastor and as visitation pastor after retirement until his death.

1945
Henry Edmund Rasmussen, Sr.
Interim Pastor
May 13, 1867 (Illinois)–March 15, 1958

Attended Capital University, Columbus, Ohio (1882–1890). Ordained 1890. Married Lucy Ann Gray. Served congregations in Minnesota, Wisconsin, South Dakota, and Iowa. Editor of *Christian Youth,* 1891–1893. His son, **Henry Edmund Rasmussen, Jr.,** became a pastor. See Appendix B.

1945–1949
Conrad (Connie) Mervin Thompson
Pastor
April 2, 1917 (Wisconsin)–July 18, 2001

Graduated from St. Olaf College (1939) and Luther Theological Seminary (1945). Ordained in 1945. Married Swanhild Tverberg, who was born in Madagascar to Rev. Sven Tverberg and Elise Holland Tverberg, missionaries. Pastor Thompson instituted many changes to Immanuel that were significantly different from the Hauge tradition. Some people objected that he wore a white surplice and "chanted" the liturgy. He started a Young Peoples group that led to several marriages. During his tenure, the first professional assistant to the pastor was hired—Hilma Lundby, who was the youth director, parish visitor, and office secretary. Two worship services were conducted each Sunday. Between 800 and 1,000 people worshipped at the Macalester College gymnasium one Easter Sunday. A community-wide survey of the unreached population was conducted and a map with pins was constructed. A Board of Education was formed. The Altar Society was formed and, for the first time, people other than the pastor prepared the altar. He introduced stoles worn by the pastor. After serving Immanuel for two years, his services were broadcast on the radio. He was against alcohol. Pastor Thompson said, "the door of heaven and eternity is closed to both social drinkers and the drunkard." Served as an U.S. Air Force chaplain (Iceland, 1956). Served congregations in Minnesota and South Dakota. In 1953 at the age of 33, he was called to be the director of evangelism of the Evangelical Lutheran Church and the American Lutheran Church, serving in that capacity for 20 years. In 1970, Rev. Thompson also became the speaker and the director of the Lutheran Vespers (1971–1982), a radio program reaching millions of people in its weekly broadcasts on scores of stations in the United States. In 1956 Trinity Seminary, now part of Wartburg Theological Seminary in Iowa, awarded Conrad an honorary doctorate degree, and in 1982, St Olaf College awarded him the Distinguished Alumni Award in recognition of his service to the church, community and college. Many descendants entered the ministry. See Appendix B.

1949–1956
Ruben K. Mostrom
Pastor
April 20, 1909 (Wisconsin)–March 11, 1995.
Graduated from St. Olaf College (1930) and from Luther Theological Seminary (1933). Ordained in 1933. Married Inez Engebretson.  Immanuel replaced his Model A Ford for Christmas. Many Macalester Lutheran students attended Immanuel during Mostrom's tenure. He served congregations in Montana, Iowa, Minnesota, and Wisconsin. Retired in 1974. One of the first ten men inducted into the St. Olaf Athletic Hall of Fame—he was a four-time letterman in basketball, played semi-professional basketball in the Twin Cities, and was a St. Olaf College Regent at the college in Northfield. When recalling his time at Immanuel, he remembered, "I was the same old-fashioned gospel preacher and Inez worked hard as the church grew. Young couples were the majority and the old timers were the pillars." One time, after Pastor Mostrom admired the beauty of a large church on Summit Ave., the pastor there said, "I would greatly trade some of my flying buttresses for your strong pillars."

Appendix A

1957
Stanley Gordon West
Student Interim Pastor
April 13, 1932 (Wisconsin)–Jan. 21, 2015
His parents were Immanuel members Carleton and Lurine West. Attended Central High School, Macalester College, and University of Minnesota. Graduated from Luther Theological Seminary. Ordained in 1959. Married Shirley Mae Vinz;. Worked as a janitor, youth advisor, and assistant to the pastor at East Immanuel in 1955. Served as Immanuel's secretary in 1956. Served congregations in Minnesota, Illinois, and Montana. Director of Christikon Youth Camp in Montana for seven years. He shared his faith with youth through his gifted story-telling. Author of mysteries and a trilogy about Central High School. His first book, *Amos*, was made into a movie in 1985.

1957–1964
Dr. Einar Roald Carlson
Senior Pastor
March 9, 1925 (Madagascar)–March 13, 2015
His parents were missionaries in Madagascar. Attended Saint Paul Central High School. Graduated from St. Olaf College (1948), after a break to serve in the U.S. Navy during World War II. Graduated from Luther Theological Seminary (1951), Biblical Seminary in Manhattan (1951), and Princeton Theological Seminary (MTh, 1953), and New York University (PhD, 1969). Ordained in 1953. Married Marjorie Jean Mueller. The first Immanuel parishioners he met, other than the call committee, were the Immanuel youth group at the biannual Lutheran Youth convention in Missoula, Montana. He decided that Immanuel would be a great place to serve. Pastor of Immanuel during the 1960 merger with Highland Park Lutheran Church and the construction of the Education wing. Served congregations in New York, Wisconsin, and Minnesota. Three daughters entered the ministry or served Lutheran colleges. See Appendix B.

1960–1964
John Adrian Pfeiffer
Associate Pastor
Nov. 17, 1905 (Ohio)–Aug. 23, 1997
Graduated from Capital University, Columbus, Ohio (1927) and Evangelical Lutheran Theological Seminary (at that time part

of Capital University) (1930). Ordained in 1930. Married Miram Catherine. Was radio broadcaster for the Washington D.C. Council of Churches for ten years. Pastor at Highland Park Lutheran Church (1958–1960) and became the Immanuel's associate pastor as a result of the merger with Highland Park Lutheran. Named by Minnesota Governor Anderson to represent Saint Paul in the regional Project Action Conference. Served congregations in Maryland, California, Washington, Michigan, Wisconsin, and Minnesota. He was a church relations field representative for Carthage College, Kenosha, Wisconsin (1973–1982).

Luther Owen Tolo
Seminary Intern, Youth Pastor
Jan 5, 1938 (Minnesota)–
Graduated from Luther Theological Seminary (1962). Ordained at Immanuel Jun 10, 1962. Married Kay Luber. Served congregations in Minnesota and California.

1962–1963
William (Bill) Robert White
Seminary Intern, Youth Pastor
June 28, 1939 (Colorado)–

Graduated from the University of Wisconsin-Eau Claire, and Luther Theological Seminary (1965). Ordained 1965. Married to Sally Lee. Taught a high school Bible class and directed the youth programs at Immanuel while attending Luther Theological Seminary. Served Hollandale-Trinity Lutheran Church, Blanchardville, Wisconsin (1965–1968); then as assistant to the Bishop of the Michigan District (ELCA; 1968–1976); started a mission church in Mt. Pleasant, Michigan (1976–1991), and served as Senior Pastor of Bethel Lutheran Church in Madison, Wisconsin, (1991–2010). Retired in 2011 after serving 46 years as a pastor. At Bethel, he was the lead speaker on the TV program "Worship at Bethel," viewed by 30,000 people weekly over a six-station network. In retirement, he spends time as a writer, speaker, and the director of "Partners for Puerto Rico," a program that matches churches in the United States with churches in Puerto Rico. Author of numerous books, both fiction and nonfiction.

Appendix A

1964–1992
Elder Kenneth Bentley
Pastor
Oct. 5, 1927 (Iowa)–May 26, 2014

Graduated from Luther College (1949) and Luther Theological Seminary (1952). Ordained in 1952. Married Esther Tisthammer. Immanuel's longest serving pastor—for 28 years. Served as a chaplain in the U.S. Navy; retired from the Naval Reserve as a Navy Captain (1988). Served congregations in Iowa and Minnesota. Performed many one-man plays written by Immanuel member Elvina Loftness. He served on numerous boards and was active in the Synod. Pastor Bentley was passionate about caring for the poor and needy, and proud to make Immanuel barrier-free with the installation of an elevator. He was a founder of Southeast Asian Ministry and Meals on Wheels. He liked to use Charlie Brown humor and alliteration in his sermons, such as, "Wake up, watch out, wait for." He was pleased with the changes during his time at Immanuel allowing the ordination of women and the wearing of a white robe and stole, not a black cassock and white surplice. Retired from Immanuel in 1992—honored with a retirement reception at Macalester' Cochran Lounge July 9, 1992. Served as a visitation pastor with other congregations after retirement.

1964–1965
Raymond Charles Boyens
Seminary Intern. Youth Pastor
April 15, 1937 (Illinois)–Dec. 1, 2001

Graduated from Wartburg College, Iowa (1960) and Luther Theological Seminary (1967). Ordained in 1967. Married Judy Ellen Drew, then Janet Warwick. Served congregations in Iowa and Wisconsin.

1965–1972
Melvin Pernell Kaatrud
Visitation Pastor
Dec. 27, 1895 (Wisconsin)–April 12, 1972.

Ordained in 1921. Married Pearl Rosine Gaarder. Served as an U.S. Army chaplain during World War II (1942–1946). Served congregations in Illinois and Minnesota. Retired 1961. He served at Immanuel's first visitation pastor after retirement.

1966–1967
Rolfe Sven Johnstad
Seminary Intern. Youth Pastor
Aug. 6, 1935 (Wisconsin)–
Served four years in the U.S. Air Force (airborne radio operator). Graduated from Waldorf College, Iowa (AA, 1960), Luther College, Iowa (1962), and Luther Theological Seminary (MDiv, 1967). Ordained in 1967. Married Margaret Swenson. Served as the Youth and Music Director at Salem Lutheran Church, Glendale, California, after college graduation and before going to Luther Theological Seminary. Served as the youth pastor at Immanuel during his last year at the Seminary. Served congregations in California, Iowa, and Minnesota. Served as Development Director for Bethany Life Communities in Story City, Iowa, (1999–2004). Retired in 2004. After retirement, served as the music director and supply pastor at Christ the Servant Lutheran Church, Henderson, Nevada, (2004–2019). Serving as Visitation Minister at Our Savior's Lutheran Church, Sioux Falls, South Dakota, at the time of this writing.

1966–1970
James E. Tangen
Assistant Pastor
Feb. 4, 1936 (Minnesota)–July 17, 2001
Served in the U.S. Air Force 1954–1958. Graduated from Concordia College (1962) and Luther Theological Seminary (1966). Ordained in 1966. Married Connie Solberg. In 1966, Immanuel voted to call an ordained pastor as the assistant pastor instead of having a seminary intern. Pastor Tangen was Immanuel's first assistant pastor—he started July 1, 1966. Served congregations in Minnesota and Wisconsin.

1970–1977
Sylvan Edward Hengesteg
Assistant Pastor
Oct. 16, 1941 (Minnesota)–
Graduated from Luther College (1963) and Luther Theological Seminary (1970). Ordained in 1970. Married Junelle Hale. At Immanuel (his first call after ordination), he served as the youth minister, held confirmation camps at Heard's Acres in Park Rapids, and traveled with the youth to the national Lutheran youth gatherings in Houston and New Orleans. There was no parsonage for his family,

APPENDIX A

so they bought a house nearby. He said, "Immanuel felt Norwegian to me." Served congregations in Minnesota and as chaplain at Methodist Hospital Mayo Clinic, Rochester, Minnesota, for 25 years.

1972–1980
Paulus William Pilgrim, Sr.
Visitation Pastor
Nov. 4, 1908 (Minnesota)–Aug. 25, 1980
Graduated from Luther Theological Seminary (1932). Ordained in 1932. Married Elsie Erna Bartz and, after her death, Marguerite Gallagher. Served congregations in Minnesota. Retired 1971. After retirement, he served as an interim pastor and then Immanuel's visitation pastor.

1975–1976
William Jaye Beck
Seminary Intern
Sept. 21, 1947 (North Dakota)–Feb. 5, 2003
Graduated from the University of Washington (1969). Served as an officer in the U.S. Navy for four years. Graduated from Luther Theological Seminary (1977). Worked at Immanuel for four years including his year as an intern in 1975–1976. Ordained at Immanuel in 1977 by Pastor Hengesteg. Married to Mary Ann Small. Served Elim Lutheran Church, Hockinson, Washington, (1989–1999). Pastor for 25 years. Left ministry to work for Hewlett-Packard.

1977–1993
John Torris Lohre
Assistant Pastor
Sept, 10, 1945 (Illinois)–
Graduated from St. Olaf College (1967) and Luther Theological Seminary (1971). Ordained in 1972. Married Mary Alice Nasby. Concentrated on youth ministry at Immanuel, traveling with students to national youth conventions and mission trips in newly purchased bus. Helped with the restructuring of the Saint Paul Area Synod of the Evangelical Church in America. In 1989–1990, served as president of the board of the Saint Paul Area Council of Churches. Served congregations in Minnesota. Assisted with Immanuel's 150th anniversary service Oct. 10, 2021. Currently drives a special education bus and works as a supply pastor in congregations around Lake City, Minnesota.

1979–1980
Leif Ingvar Monson
Outreach Pastor
Nov. 5, 1924 (Minnesota)–Sept. 28, 1985
Served in the U.S. Navy (1942–1946). Graduated from Luther College (1950) and Luther Theological Seminary (1953). Ordained in 1953. Married Darlene Jean Blackman. Served congregations in Iowa and Minnesota. Part of one of the first drive-in worship services in Iowa.

1980–1999
Ralph Wilbur Glenn
Visitation Pastor
Dec. 14, 1914 (North Dakota)–Nov. 14, 1999
Son of Lutheran pastor, H.J. Glenn. Attended Augustana College and graduated from St. Olaf College (1936) and Luther Theological Seminary (1940). Ordained June 16, 1940. Married to Phyllis Utter. Served as a U.S. Army chaplain with the 90th Infantry Combat Division, which landed in Normandy on D-Day and fought in the Battle of the Bulge. Served congregations in California, New York, Iowa, Minnesota, and Montana. After retirement, served as Immanuel's visitation pastor for 19 years and loved to flavor his visits, talks, and reports with humorous stories.

1992–1993
Milo Leroy Engelstad
Interim Pastor
July 27, 1921 (North Dakota)–Jan. 9, 2018
Graduated from Concordia College, Moorhead, Minnesota (1942) and Luther Theological Seminary (1945). Ordained in 1945. Married Ruth Roem. Served churches in North Dakota, Michigan, and Minnesota. His final position was as visitation pastor at St. Luke's in Bloomington, where he served for more than six years. Served two terms as president of the Southeast Minnesota Synod of the American Lutheran Church (now ELCA). Served as a crisis intervention counselor with the Bloomington Police. Retired 1986.

Appendix A

1993–2000
Lawrence (Larry) Don Rehlander
Senior Pastor
Aug. 7, 1944 (Iowa)–
Graduated from Wartburg College (1966) and from Wartburg Theological Seminary, Iowa (1970). Ordained in 1970. Married Ellen Brue. Served as U.S. Navy and Marine Corps Reserve chaplain (1967–1977). Served congregations in Iowa, California, South Dakota, Montana, and Minnesota. During Pastor Rehlander's time at Immanuel, he started the Care Team, added a parish nurse position (the first in the Twin Cities), revised the Sunday School curriculum to match confirmation expectations, and held Goofy Olympics. Currently retired and living in Lake Elmo, Minnesota.

1993–1994
Philip A. Walen
Seminary student, Pastoral Assistant
Feb, 12, 1948 (Minnesota)–Sept. 9, 2015
Graduated from Augsburg College, Minneapolis (1970) and Luther Theological Seminary (1994). Served as a conscientious objector (1970–1972). Ordained in 1994. Married Christine Duncan and then Tereresa J. Mamberg (Teri). Served more than six churches in the Evangelical Lutheran Church in America from 1994–2013 as pastor or interim pastor helping congregations in transition. He was a gifted musician. He provided weekly online messages as part of his ministry.

1995–1997
Susan Smith
Associate Pastor
Jan. 21, 1949 (Indiana)–
Graduated from Concordia College in Seward, Nebraska (1971) and Luther Northwestern Theological Seminary (1993). Ordained in 1994. Married Rev. Larry Smith, an ordained minister of the Evangelical Lutheran Church. She was Immanuel's first woman pastor. *With One Voice* hymnal was introduced while she was at Immanuel. Served congregations in New Jersey, New York, Nebraska, and Minnesota. Retired in 2014.

1997
Philip Gotsch
Interim Associate Pastor
Jan. 15, 1949 (Minnesota)–
Graduated from Dana College in Nebraska (BS, 1971) and Luther Theological Seminary (MDiv, 1975) Ordained in 1975. Married Janice Hartsook. Served congregations, including Como Park Lutheran Church, St. Paul, Minnesota. Retired.

2000
Dr. Dana Nissen
Interim Senior Pastor
Feb. 9, 1953 (Minnesota)–
Graduated from University of Minnesota (BA, 1979), Luther Theological Seminary (MDiv, 1983), Lutheran School of Theology at Chicago (1991), and Graduate Theological Foundation (PhD, 2009). Graduate Certificate, Biomedical Ethics and Healthcare Policy, Loyola University Chicago (2014). Ordained in 1984. Married to Rev. Dr. Kwanza Yu, who became the first woman of color ordained in the American Lutheran Church in 1983. Served congregations in Texas, Illinois, and Minnesota. Assisted with Immanuel's 150th anniversary service Oct. 10, 2021. At the time of this writing, is an adjunct faculty member at Concordia University (St. Paul), Augsburg University, and University of St. Catherine.

1999–2009
Dr. John Charles Marboe
Associate Pastor, then Senior Pastor
May 1, 1962 (Minnesota)–
Graduated from Luther Seminary (1998). Ordained in 1998. Married Andrea McDonald. Started as Associate Pastor Jan. 1, 1999, called to be Senior Pastor June 18, 2000. Changed to three-quarter time appointment in 2005 while attending Pacifica Graduate Institute (MA, 2005–2007; PhD, 2007–2011). During his time at Immanuel, the Building Bridges remodeling project added space for gathering, learning, and outreach to the community. He enjoyed working as a part-time garbage man from 2011 to 2018. Serves as pastor at Zion Lutheran Church, St. Paul, and teaches as an adjunct professor at the University of Minnesota in the Sociology Department at the time of this writing.

2000
David A. Quarberg
Interim Senior Pastor
March 31, 1931 (Wisconsin)–

Graduated from St. Olaf College (1953) and Luther Theological Seminary (1960). Ordained 1961. Married Genevieve Marie Kelly. Served three years in the U.S. Navy between college and seminary. Served congregations in California, Indiana, Illinois, and Minnesota—last call as senior pastor at Grace Lutheran Church, Apple Valley (1984–1997). Known as "Pastor Q."

2002–2009
Dr. Joy Marie Bussert
Associate Pastor
December 20, 1951 (Nebraska)–

Graduated from Augustana College, Rock Island, Illinois (1974) and Yale Divinity School (MDiv, 1977). Ordained in 1978. Awarded PhD from Union Theology Seminary (2002). Associate Executive Director of the Minnesota Council of Churches (1981–1985). Served as parish pastor in Minnesota, staff for Council of Churches, interim pastor, and faculty at Luther Theological Seminary. Work focused on justice, mercy, peace, and the elimination of violence against women. Fourth generation pastor. Retired.

2009–2011
Dr. Marcus D. Pera
Interim Pastor
March 12, 1938 (North Dakota)–

Graduated from Concordia College, Ft. Wayne, Indiana (1960) and Concordia Seminary, Saint Louis, Missouri (1972); earned a Master of Divinity and Masters in Sacred Theology from Concordia. Received a Doctor of Ministry at Wartburg Theological Seminary, Dubuque (2002). Ordained 1964. Married to Nancy Jeanne. First called to serve a congregation in Illinois. Served as campus pastor at Southern Illinois University, University of Arizona, and University of Cincinnati, and was the Mid Country ELCA Director for Campus Ministry for 21 years. Part of the Pastoral Care Team at Hope Lutheran Church, The Villages, Florida, at the time of this writing.

2011–
Cynthia (Cindy) Happel Bullock
Pastor
Jan. 16, 1960 (Maryland)–
Graduated from The College of William and Mary in Williamsburg, Virginia (BS, 1981) and Lutheran Theological Southern Seminary, Columbia, South Carolina (MDiv, 1986). Married Brian Bullock. Served on the Candidacy Committee with the Saint Paul Synod of the ELCA and as a First Call Mentor for over 15 years. Served congregations in Richmond, Virginia, Richardson, Texas, and West St. Paul.

2017
Samuel John Wolff
Summer Sabbatical Interim Pastor
July 16 1946 (Nebraska)–
Graduated from Pacific Theological Seminary, Berkeley, California (1972). Ordained in 1976. Masters of Theology in Islamic Studies from Luther Theological Seminary. Married Christine (Cindy) Walker. Served as a parish pastor in Los Angeles and as a missionary in Nairobi, Kenya, and Dar es Salaam, Tanzania, for 21 years. Served in Frankfurt, Germany, as a pastor of an international congregation, and in Ministry in Christian/Muslim Relations in East Africa, Europe, and the U.S. Served in interim ministry at Easter Lutheran, Eagan; Saint Paul Reformation, Saint Paul; and Memorial Lutheran, Afton (all in Minnesota). Teaches in the areas of cross culture ministry and Christian-Muslim relations.

APPENDIX A

Macalester Park Lutheran Church—Norwegian Lutheran Church of America Synod(merged with Immanuel Lutheran Church in 1921)

1918–1919
Daniel H. Halverson
Pastor
April 24, 1887 (Norway)–Aug. 1, 1972
Immigrated in 1906. Attended Red Wing Seminary (1910–1916), University of Minnesota (1912–1915), and. Luther Theological Seminary (1917–1918). Was a journalist (1912–1915). Ordained 1918. Married Christine M. Kasberg. Served churches in Minnesota.

1919–1920
Dr. Gustav Marius Bruce
Interim Pastor
See above: 1917–1921.

1920
John Sunde
Interim Pastor (January–May 1920)
See above: 1921.

Dr. Joseph Walter Johnshoy
Pastor (May–August 1920)
Jan. 21, 1891 (Minnesota)–Sept. 19, 1947
Graduated from Luther College (1911). Attended Luther Theological Seminary (1911–1914) and Oslo University (1914–1915). Ordained in 1915. Married Helga Larsen. Taught philosophy and classical languages at Concordia College, Moorhead, Minnesota ((1925–1947). Served congregations in California, Minnesota, Wisconsin, and North Dakota. Author of several religious books. Four sons entered the ministry: **Arthur Herman Johnshoy, Edward Walter Johnshoy, Norman Casper Johnshoy,** and **Ralph Johnshoy.** See Appendix B.

Martinus Casper Johnshoy
Pastor
June 29, 1886 (Minnesota)–Dec. 9, 1944
Brother to **Joseph Walter Johnshoy** (above). Attended Luther College (1905–1906), Northwestern Conservatory of Music

(1909), University of Wisconsin (1912), and Luther Theological Seminary (1914–1915, 1917–1919, 1920–1922). Married Olava Wollan Troen. Studied Hebrew and Sacred Music at Luther Theological Seminary (1921–1922). Ordained in 1919. Composer, orchestrator, editor, translator, teacher, and pastor in Wisconsin and Minnesota. Posthumously granted U.S. Patent 2,397,740 for "Communion Wafer Tray."

Highland Park Lutheran Church
(merged with Immanuel Lutheran Church in 1960)

1927–1936
Eugene Herman Julius Pfeiffer
Pastor
Nov. 14, 1897 (Minnesota)–Dec. 25, 1987
Graduated from Luther College, St. Paul (1918) and Luther Theological Seminary (1921). Ordained in 1921. Married Renata Bertha Schlick. Served in the U.S. Navy during World War I. Served congregations in Minnesota, Michigan, Illinois, and Wisconsin. Retired 1969.

1935–1936
Arthur R. Wachholz
Pastor
March 5, 1897 (Wisconsin)–Oct. 23, 1987
Graduated from Luther College, Decorah, Iowa (1923) and Luther Theological Seminary (1926). Served in the U.S. Navy during World War I. Ordained in 1926. Married Minnie Benson. Served churches in Minnesota, Iowa, and Colorado. Father of **Rev. Luther Gerhard Wachholz.** See Appendix B.

1936–1943
[George] Ivan Menchhofer
Pastor
Oct. 10, 1911 (Ohio)–Oct. 14, 2000
Graduated from Capital University (1933) and Trinity Seminary (1936). Ordained in 1936. Married Bonnie L. Teal and, after her death, Norah Edwards. Served congregations in Ohio after leaving Highland Park Lutheran Church.

Appendix A

1943–1948
Dr. Edwin Julius Cornils
Pastor
Oct. 27, 1913 (Minnesota)–April 19, 1997
Graduated from Wartburg College (1940) and Wartburg Theological Seminary (1943). Ordained in 1943. Married Dorothy Lucille Woerth. Served congregations in St. Paul, Minnesota, and Berlin, Wisconsin; was a staff member in the Department of Stewardship and Finance of the American Lutheran Church (ALC) in Columbus, Ohio; Western Regional director of stewardship and executive vice president of the South Pacific District of the ALC. He was awarded an honorary doctorate of divinity by California Lutheran University. Father of **Rev. Stephen Cornils.** See Appendix B.

1949–1953
Elmer Herman Doerring
Pastor
June 13, 1899 (Iowa)–April 1984
Graduated from Wartburg College (1922) and Wartburg Theological Seminary (1926). Ordained in 1926. Married Elsa Clara Bredow. Left to be pastor at Lutheran Church of Our Savior, San Bernardino, CA. Served congregations in South Dakota, Iowa, Minnesota and California. Retired 1964.

1953–1958
Paul Frederick Metzger
Pastor
April 11, 1918 (Ohio)–April 25, 1986
Attended Capital University for one year, then served five years in the U.S. Army during World War II. He married Marie Behle. Attended Wartburg College (1845–1847), University of Dubuque, Iowa (1947–1948), and graduated from Wartburg Theological Seminary in Iowa (1950) Ordained in 1950. Served congregations in Wisconsin, Minnesota, and Iowa.

1958–1960
John Adrian Pfeiffer
Pastor
Nov. 17, 1905 (Ohio)–Aug. 23, 1997
Ordained in 1930. See above: 1960.

Appendix B

Sons and Daughters of Immanuel, Macalester Park, and Highland Park Lutheran Churches Who Became Pastors, Missionaries, and Served the Church in Leadership Positions

The following information is as accurate and complete as possible.

Harold Edgar Aalbue
Jan. 12, 1916–Dec. 4, 1976.
Son of Immanuel members Solfest and Clara Aalbue. Graduated from Saint Olaf College (1937) and Luther Theological Seminary (BTh, 1941) and ordained at Immanuel on June 8, 1941. Married Betty Janice Rusinko. Served congregations in Oregon and Washington. His son **Joseph Paul Aalbue** (1944–) became a Lutheran pastor (see below).

Joseph Paul Aalbue
Sept. 19, 1908–Aug. 24, 1939.
Son of Immanuel members Solfest and Clara Aalbue. Married Iola Marie Brenne. Attended Concordia Junior College, University of Minnesota, and graduated from Luther Theological Seminary in 1935. Ordained at Immanuel June 9, 1935. Principal of American School at Kikungshan, a school established for the children of Lutheran Missionaries in China. Died in the Matilda Hospital, Hong Kong, of appendicitis and subsequent peritonitis. Buried at Hong Kong Cemetery, Happy Valley, Hong Kong. Iola (Mrs. Joseph Paul Aalbue) spent four years in the Norwegian Lutheran Mission Field.

Joseph Paul Aalbue
June 2, 1944–
Born in Eugene, Oregon, to **Harold Edgar Aalbue** (see above). Grandson of Immanuel members Solfest Clara Aalbue. Named for his uncle (see above). Graduated from Pacific Lutheran College (1969) and Luther Theological Seminary (MDiv, 1970). Ordained in 1970. Served congregations in Texas, South Dakota, and Washington.

Lorna Marie Aalbue Anderson
Feb, 23, 1938–2021
Born in Hong Kong while her father **Joseph Paul Aalbue** (1908-1939; see above) was a missionary there. Granddaughter of Immanuel members Solfest

and Clara Aalbue. Graduated from Central High School, St. Paul. Received a BA from Saint Olaf College, Northfield, Minnesota. Moved to Denmark in 1967 where she was ordained in 1982. She served the Sundkirken parish in the outskirts of Copenhagen as a priest in the Danish Lutheran Church. Her passion was working with children, young people, refugees, and ministering to non-Danish-speaking Christians. Married Arne Anderson.

Lloyd C. Anderson
July 26, 1924–Dec. 10, 1962
Spent two years in the U.S. Navy (1946–1948). Graduated from Luther College (1950) and Luther Theological Seminary (1953). Married Lorraine Bergland. Member of Immanuel while at Luther Theological Seminary. Served congregations in Minnesota and Iowa.

Dewey Brevik
Oct. 16, 1920–Feb. 1968
Served as an assistant chaplain with the U.S. Army 1943–1945. Graduated from St. Olaf College (1950) and Luther Theological Seminary (May 17, 1953). Ordained 1953. Member of Immanuel while attending the Seminary. Served as pastor of Trinity Lutheran Church (Linn Grove, Iowa), then as assistant director of admissions at St. Olaf College.

Janet Audrey Carlson
Feb. 11, 1957–
Daughter of former Immanuel pastor **Einar Roald Carlson** (see Appendix A: 1957). Graduated from St. Olaf College (1978). Attended Luther Seminary 1979–1980 and 1994–1996. Ordained 1996. Served congregations in Minnesota and California. Resigned from the ministry.

Kristine Louise Carlson
April 20, 1952–
Daughter of former Immanuel pastor **Einar Roald Carlson** (see Appendix A: 1957). Graduated from St. Olaf College (1974) and University of Minnesota (MA, 1978), and Luther Theological Seminary (MDiv, 1982). Ordained 1982. Married Morris Owen Wee. Served Christ Lutheran Church, Minneapolis, until retirement.

Dr. Paula Jean Carlson
June 6, 1954–
Daughter of former Immanuel pastor **Einar Roald Carlson** (see Appendix A:

1957). Graduate of St. Olaf College (1976) and Columbia University (M.A., M. Phil., PhD). Married Rev. Dr. Thomas Schattauer. Taught at several Universities and served as vice president at St. Olaf College. Tenth president of Luther College (2014–2019).

Merrill Almon Clark
July 7, 1930–Feb. 10, 2018
Son of Clayton Clive Clark Senior and Violet (nee Geckler) Clark, members of Highland Park Lutheran Church. Graduated from Wartburg College, Iowa, and Wartburg Seminary (1955), and was baptized, confirmed, and ordained (in 1955) at Highland Park Lutheran Church. Ordained in both the American Lutheran Church and the Missouri Synod Lutheran Church. Married Katherine (Katie) Mueller. Served as a missionary in Papua New Guinea for 12 years beginning in 1955.

Dr. Stephen J. Cornils
1944–
Son of former Highland Park Lutheran Church Pastor **Edwin Cornils** (see Appendix A: 1943). Graduated from Wartburg Theological Seminary, Iowa (MDiv, 1970). Ordained 1970. Awarded a DMin from Pacific Lutheran Theological Seminary, Berkeley, California, in 1981. Served congregations in Minnesota and currently on the Board of Directors of Wartburg Theological Seminary, Dubuque, Iowa.

Seth Clarence Eastvold
Dec. 19, 1895–Feb. 1963.
Son of former Immanuel Pastor **Carl Johan Eastvold** (see Appendix A: 1921). Graduated from St. Olaf College (1916) and Luther Theological Seminary (1920). Ordained 1920. Married Enge. Served several Lutheran parishes throughout the Midwest over 23 years. President of Pacific Lutheran College (1943–1962). First vice president of the Evangelical Lutheran Church (1948–1960). Wrote several books, including *Rev. C.J. Eastvold, D.D.—His Life and Work* (1930), a biography of his father.

Donald James Fisher
Oct. 3, 1928–May 7, 2008
Born in Winthrop, Minnesota, to Alphi and Gladys Fisher. Served in the U.S. Army for two years. Taught high school Bible class at Immanuel in 1958–1959 while attending Luther Theological Seminary, from which he graduated (1961). Ordained at Immanuel May 28, 1961. Served congregations in

California and New Mexico. He was the nephew of Immanuel member Mrs. Jack Ehlers.

Ernest (Ernie) O. Gilberts
Aug. 20, 1919–April 8, 2008
Lt. Col, in the U.S. Army Air Corps in World War II and in the U.S, Air Force in Korea. Attended Luther Theological Seminary 1958–1961. Ordained 1961. Member of Immanuel while attending Luther Theological Seminary. Married Agnes Bonkrude. Served congregations in Wisconsin.

Hans Adolph Hanson
May 10, 1863 (Minnesota)–Nov. 13, 1940
Son of **Osten Hanson,** who was Immanuel's first pastor in 1871(see Appendix A: 1871). Attended Red Wing Seminary (1879–1882 and 1885–1888). Attended Curtis Business College in Minneapolis 1882–1884. Served Immanuel as a visiting lay preacher in 1884. Ordained 1888 in the Hauge Synod. Married Elizabeth Christy. Served congregations in Wisconsin, Illinois, and Utah.

Karen Ethel Holmberg-Smith
Feb. 21, 1960–
Daughter of Immanuel members Hart and Shirley Holmberg. Participated in "Rejoice" musical at Immanuel. Attended Highland Park Senior High School, graduated from Gustavus Adolphus College (BA, 1982) and Luther Theological Seminary (MDiv, 1987). Ordained in 1987. She baptized longtime Immanuel member Vernon (Bud) Jorgenson's grandson.

Julius Martin Hovland
Nov. 28, 1916–July 18, 1982
Son of Immanuel members Cornelius and Ann (nee Amundson) Hovland. Attended Luther Theological Seminary and was ordained at Immanuel June 6, 1943. Married Gladys Magdalene Johnshoy (Oct. 17, 1942), who was the daughter of **Dr. Joseph Walter Johnshoy,** a pastor of Macalester Park Lutheran Church (see Appendix A: 1920).

Arthur (Art) Herman Johnshoy
Aug. 22, 1921–April 1, 2010
Son of former Macalester Park Lutheran pastor **Dr. Joseph Walter Johnshoy** (see Appendix A: 1920). Graduate from Concordia College (1943) and Luther Theological Seminary (1945). Ordained Sept. 30, 1945 at Trinity

Lutheran Church in Moorhead, Minnesota. Married Velma Dyrstad. Served congregations in Minnesota and South Dakota. Retired in 1984. Father of current Immanuel member Jan Johnshoy.

Edward Walter Johnshoy
Oct. 16, 1917–April 28, 1996
Son of former Macalester Park Lutheran pastor **Dr. Joseph Walter Johnshoy** (See Appendix A: 1920). Married Naomi J. Larson. Graduated from Concordia College (1939) and Luther Theological Seminary (1947). Ordained 1947. Served in the U.S. Army during World War II. Served congregations in North Dakota, Washington, and Minnesota.

Norman Casper Johnshoy
March 1, 1923–Aug. 26, 1995
Son of former Macalester Park Lutheran Church pastor **Dr. Joseph Walter Johnshoy** (See Appendix A: 1920). Attended Concordia College (Moorhead, Minnesota) and graduated from Luther Theological Seminary (1948). Ordained 1948. Married Norma Leone Lindem, Mary Ann Lindem, and Lois Margaret Nielsen. Served as a U.S. Army chaplain, stationed in Turkey, Germany, and Alaska. Served congregations in California.

Paul Gehordt Johnshoy
July 22, 1921–Nov. 2, 2002
Son of former Macalester Park Lutheran Church pastor **Martinus Casper Johnshoy** (see Appendix A: 1920). Attended Concordia College, Moorhead for three years until 1942, then served 52 months in the U.S. Army Air Corps, including one year in Italy. Married Esther May Marquette. Graduated from University of Minnesota (BA 1948). Graduated from Luther Theological Seminary (BTh 1951). Ordained 1951. Served congregations in Minnesota and South Dakota.

Ralph Ernest Johnshoy
May 20, 1925–
Son of former Macalester Park Lutheran pastor **Dr. Joseph Walter Johnshoy** (see Appendix A: 1920). Graduated from Concordia College, Moorhead, Minnesota (1949) and Luther Theological Seminary (1953). Ordained June 1953. Married LaVonne Johnson. Served in U.S. Navy as Seaman 2nd Class during World War II (1945–1947). Served congregations in North Dakota, Wisconsin, and South Dakota. Father of current Immanuel member Marlene Johnshoy.

Marlan Monroe Johnson
Dec. 17, 1935–
Member of Immanuel. Attended Central High school and Hamline University (BA, 1957). Was a private in the U.S. Army for six months. Graduated from Luther Theological Seminary (1962). Ordained in 1962. Married Sharon Ursula Higgins. Served congregations in Iowa and Minnesota. Gave many presentations on the life and work of Dietrich Bonhoeffer.

Dr. Mark Jolivette
July 6, 1951–
Son of **Norbert L Jolivette** (see below). Member of Immanuel. Graduated from Luther Seminary and ordained in 1977. Married Sharon Lee McClure. Served as a Captain in the U.S. Navy Reserves for 30 years and rose to Head Chaplain for the entire Navy Reserve. Served congregations in Wisconsin.

Norbert Lee Jolivette
Dec. 20, 1923–Feb. 24, 1993
Served in the U.S. Navy 1943–1946. Graduated from St. Olaf College (1950) and Luther Theological Seminary (1953). Ordained 1953. Member of Immanuel while attending Luther Theological Seminary. Served congregations in North Dakota and Iowa. Served as Dean of the Des Moines Conference of the American Lutheran Church. Two sons became pastors: **Mark Jolivette** and **Thomas Jolivette**.

Thomas Jolivette
July 17, 1954–
Son of **Norbert L. Jolivette** (above.) Graduated from Augustana College (1976) and Luther Theological Seminary (1980). Ordained in 1980. Began as a parish minister serving both Samuel Lutheran Church and Holmes Lutheran Church in Eagle Grove, Iowa. Worked at Waldorf University in development (1983–1994), and at Luther Seminary as major gifts consultant (1994–1999). President of Waldorf College (1999–2004). Returned to Luther Seminary in 2004 as "Philanthropic Advisor" (2004–2010), then as Vice President for Seminary Relations (2010–2014). Executive at Kairos and Associates (2015–).

Johan Olsen [Olson] Kasa
June 8, 1859 (Norway)–March 20, 1948
Son of **Ole Johannesen Kasa**, Immanuel visiting pastor (see Appendix A: 1872). Immigrated in 1868. Attended Red Wing Seminary (1880–1886).

Graduated from Red Wing Seminary July 17, 1887. Ordained 1887 in the Hauge Synod. Married Anna Bergerson. Served a congregation in Wallingford, Iowa, and other congregations for seven years while working an 80-acre farm. Member of the Iowa Legislature (1891). Left the ministry and had several businesses.

Dr. Arthur Mitchell Knudsen
Sept. 1, 1906–July 1984
Born in Brooklyn, New York, to Andreas and Maren Knudsen. Attended Luther Theological Seminary (1936). Married Grace Petersen. He and his wife were Immanuel members. Immanuel added a blue cross to the church's "Service Flag" in recognition of his military service during World War II. Served as Secretary of Division of English Missions, Board of American Missions, Lutheran Church in America.

Julius Henry Erdman Kolberg
Sept. 18, 1897–Aug. 27, 1979
Graduated from Saint Paul Lutheran College (1927) and Luther Theological Seminary (1930). Ordained in 1930. Married Hilda Hageman. Charter member of Highland Park Lutheran Church. Served congregations in Minnesota, Iowa, Wisconsin, and Canada. Father of Pastor **Rudolph Kolberg** (see below).

Rudolph Kolberg
April 11, 1931–
Son of Pastor **Julius Kolberg** (see above). Graduated from Wartburg College (BA, 1953) and Wartburg Seminary (BD, 1957). Ordained 1957. Married Dorothy Hueter. Served congregations in Illinois.

Dr. Marc Kolden
Jan. 15, 1940–July 15, 2017
Graduated from Harvard (1962), Luther Theological Seminary (1966), and received his MA (1969) and PhD (1976) from the University of Chicago. Married Sally L. Bakke. Member of Immanuel while attending Luther Theological Seminary. Ordained 1978 at Immanuel. Served as Associate Pastor of Our Redeemer's Lutheran Church, Helena, Montana. Joined the Luther Theological Seminary faculty in 1981, assuming the position of academic dean in 1996. Rejoined Immanuel when he assumed the faculty position at Luther Theological Seminary. He often preached at Immanuel and spoke at the Adult Forum. Author of numerous books and articles.

Dr. Kathryn Mary Lohre
March 22, 1977–

Daughter of former Immanuel Associate Pastor **John Lohre** (see Appendix A: 1977). Graduated from St. Olaf College (1999). Received MDiv. from Harvard University and a Doctor of Divinity (*honoris causa*) from the Graduate Theological Foundation in recognition of her contributions to women's interfaith issues and pluralism. From 2011–2013, served as president of the National Council of Churches USA, the first Lutheran and youngest woman to serve in that office. At the time of this writing, serves as Assistant to the Presiding Bishop of the Evangelical Lutheran Church in America and Executive Director of Ecumenical and Inter-Religious Relations & Theological Discernment.

Edwin Herbert Maas
Dec. 17, 1927 (Wisconsin)–Oct. 20, 1994

Attended University of Wisconsin in Business Administration (1951). Graduated from Luther Theological Seminary (1957). Ordained in 1957. Married Bernice May Amundson. Both are buried at Fort Snelling National Cemetery. Served as an U.S. Army chaplain (1957–1977). While in the Army, he served in Oklahoma, Germany, New Mexico, Vietnam, Indiana, Korea, and Illinois. After retiring from the Army, he served as pastor at St. John's Lutheran Church, Howard Lake, Minnesota (1976–1984). After this calling, they moved to St. Paul and joined Immanuel. Rev. Maas served as a chaplain at the Minnesota Veterans Administration hospital until his death.

James Francis (Frank) Mossman
Aug. 13, 1931–Jan. 13, 2010

Born in Watertown, South Dakota to Louis and Ella Mossman. Served in the U.S. Army 1950 to 1952. Married Norma Kautz. Graduated from Luther College (1953) and Luther Theological Seminary (1957). Member of Immanuel. His mother, Mrs. Swan Person Glemaker (her second marriage), was a longtime member of Immanuel. Ordained at Immanuel on June 23, 1957. Served congregations in Minnesota, California, and New Mexico.

Paul Arthur Otto
Feb. 10, 1929–March 18, 2006

Graduated from Waldorf College, Luther College, and Luther Theological Seminary (1961). Served in the U.S. Marines during the Korean War. Attended Immanuel while at Luther Theological Seminary. Ordained in 1961. First served four congregations in South Dakota, flying to the outlaying parishes by plane; also served congregations in Wisconsin.

Henry Edmund Rasmussen, Jr.
Sept. 3, 1905–Nov. 8, 1974
Son of former Immanuel Interim Pastor **Henry Edmund Rasmussen, Sr.** (see Appendix A: 1945). Graduated from Luther Theological Seminary and ordained 1945. Married Jemima Helena Osheim. Served congregations in Iowa, South Dakota, Minnesota, and North Dakota.

Liane Elizabeth Sundin Rock
March 8, 1928–
Daughter of Immanuel member Sherman Sundin. Lived in Saint Paul during World War II. Graduated from Minnehaha Academy in 1946. Graduated from Macalester College (1950) majoring in Religion. Graduated from Luther Theological Seminary (1983). Ordained 1983. Served at Saint John's Lutheran Church in Zimmerman, Minnesota.

Kermit Roisen
Oct. 18, 1925–April 8, 2012
Served in the U.S. Navy during World War II. Graduated from St. Olaf College (1950) and Luther Theological Seminary (1953). Married Marian Ruth Miller. Attended Immanuel while at Luther Theological Seminary. Ordained 1948. Served as a missionary in Madagascar 1953–1968. Served congregations in Nebraska and Iowa.

Phillip Robert Ruud
Nov. 2, 1955–
Son of Immanuel members Robert and Elizabeth Ruud. Baptized and confirmed at Immanuel. Graduated from St. Olaf College (1977) and Luther Theological Seminary (MDiv, 1981). Ordained at Immanuel in 1981. He received a call to serve at the First Lutheran Church at Blooming Prairie, Minnesota. He served as pastor at First English Lutheran Church, Cannon Falls, Minnesota, for 30 years, retiring in January 2022. He wrote, "I am so thankful for my faith, which was rooted in me growing up at Immanuel." Married Therese. His son, **Charles R. Ruud,** is an ordained Lutheran pastor.

Charles (Charlie) Robert Ruud
Oct, 4, 1981–
Son of **Phillip Robert Ruud** (see above). Graduated from St. Olaf College (2004) and Luther Seminary (2008). Ordained 2008. Married Rebecca (Becky) Jo Peterson. Was a professional baseball player for the St. Paul Saints and a star

pitcher (2005–2009). Served congregations in Minnesota. At this time of this writing is Associate Pastor at Mount Olivet Lutheran Church, Minneapolis, Minnesota.

Lloyd Harris Smith
Dec. 6, 1918–Jan. 20, 2014
Attended Immanuel while at Luther Theological Seminary. Graduated from Luther Theological Seminary in 1953. Ordained 1953. Married Margaret Wagnild. Brother of Immanuel member Robert Smith and son of Manley and Sarah (Lerfald) Smith. Served as a missionary to the Sudan and Cameroon.

Orville Jeremy Sunde
June 17, 1927–June 17, 2017
Son of former Pastor **John Sevrin Sunde** (see Appendix A: 1921) and Aalga Sunde (nee Skare). Graduated from Concordia College, Moorhead (1948). Married H. Marjorie Tenold. Served in the U.S. Army (1953–1955), attained rank of Sergeant. Graduated from Luther Theological Seminary (1958). Ordained 1958. Served congregations in North and South Dakota and Minnesota.

Dr. Deanna Thompson
Dec. 2, 1966–
Granddaughter of former Immanuel Pastor **Conrad Mervin Thompson** (see Appendix A: 1945) and Swanhild Tverberg Thompson. Daughter of **Dr. Mervin Thompson** (see below). Graduated from St. Olaf College (1989). Married Neal N. Peterson. Graduated from Yale University Divinity School (1992, Masters of Art and Religion/Religious Studies). Attended Vanderbilt University and awarded PhD, Theology/Theological Studies (1998). Religion Professor at Hamline University, 1995–2018, Chair of Hamline Religion Department, 2003–2008, and 2018–2019. Director of the Lutheran Center for Faith, Values, and Community, and Martin Marty Regents Chair in Religion and the Academy, St. Olaf College, 2019–present. Former member of Immanuel Lutheran Church. Author of several books.

Karis Thompson
Jan. 20, 1980–
Granddaughter of former Immanuel Pastor **Conrad Mervin Thompson** (see Appendix A: 1945) and Swanhild Tverberg Thompson; daughter of **Nathan Thompson** (see below). Graduated from Luther Seminary (2006, MA in

Congregational Mission and Leadership). Married Matthew Trefz. She has worked to cultivate a 21st century faith community in the Fargo-Moorhead area and worked with Redeemer Lutheran Church in Minneapolis.

Dr. Mervin Everett Thompson
June 18, 1941–
Son of former Immanuel Pastor **Conrad Mervin Thompson** (see Appendix A: 1945) and Swanhild Tverberg Thompson. Grandson of Rev. Sven Tverberg and Elise Holland. Graduated from Concordia College (1963) and Luther Theological Seminary (1967). Ordained 1967. Married Jacqueline Kay Morstad. Served congregations in Minnesota and Iowa. Teaching Pastor and Professor, Lutheran Church of Hope, West Des Moines, Iowa, 2003 to present. Prolific author of articles and books.

Mark Conrad Thompson
Nov. 23, 1945–
Son of former Immanuel Pastor **Conrad Mervin Thompson** (see Appendix A: 1945) and Swanhild Tverberg Thompson. Grandson of Rev. Sven Tverberg and Elise Holland. Graduated from the University of Michigan (1967, BA Ed), Luther Theological Seminary (1969), School of Theology at Claremont, California (1972, Dr. of Religion), Hamline University (MA ESL). Ordained 1973. Served congregations in Minnesota. ESL teacher at Saturn and Como Park Elementary Schools, St. Paul, 1993–2010. Named one of 2006 "American Stars of Teaching" by the U.S. Department of Education for his work with Hmong English Language Learner students.

Nathan J. Thompson
Jan. 15, 1951–
Son of former Immanuel Pastor **Conrad Mervin Thompson** (see Appendix A: 1945) and Swanhild Tverberg Thompson. Grandson of Rev. Sven Tverberg and Elise Holland. Graduated from Concordia College, Moorhead, Minnesota (1973) and Luther Theological Seminary (MDiv, 1977). Ordained 1977. Married Kim J. Morris. Served congregations in Minnesota.

Zachary (Zach) Thompson
Feb. 15, 1978–
Grandson of former Immanuel Pastor **Conrad Mervin Thompson** (see Appendix: 1945) and Swanhild Tverberg Thompson. Son of **Rev. Nathan Thompson** (see above). Graduated from Concordia College (2000) and Luther Seminary

(2004, MDiv, Youth and Family Certificate). Ordained 2004. Married Alexi Larae Olson. Served congregations in Minnesota. Senior Pastor, Calvary Lutheran Church, Golden Valley and Minnetonka, Minnesota, 2018–present.

Luther Gerhard Wachholz
July 2, 1929–March 21, 2019
Son of **Arthur R. Wachholz,** former pastor of Highland Park Lutheran Church. Graduated from Wartburg College, Iowa (1951) and Wartburg Seminary, Iowa (1955). Ordained 1955. Served congregations in Oklahoma, Iowa, and Nebraska. Married Geraldine Van Dyke. Left the ministry in 1975 on the advice of physicians.

Stanley Gordon West
April 13, 1932–Jan 21, 2015
Son of Immanuel members Carleton and Lurine West. Ordained 1959. Served Immanuel as a student Interim Pastor (see Appendix A: 1957).

Carl Johan (John) Martin Westphal
July 19, 1861(Denmark)–June 17, 1936
Immigrated 1874. Attended Red Wing Seminary, 1885–1890. Ordained in 1890. Married Elisabeth Karoline [Caroline] Larsen [Larson] (Dec. 20, 1867–April 23, 1914), daughter of Immanuel founding members Bergethe [Bergitte] Kristine Olsen [Olesdatter] Larsen (1837–1896) and Hans Bergh [Berg] Larsen (1842–1925). Served congregations in Minnesota, Wisconsin, Canada, Montana, and North Dakota. His son, **Obed William Westphal** (see below), became a pastor.

Obed William Westphal
Feb 12, 1906–June 17, 1994
Ordained 1943. Served congregations in Minnesota and Iowa. Married Esther Louise Nelson. He was the grandson of Immanuel founding members, Bergethe [Bergitte] Kristine Olsen [Olesdatter] Larsen (1837–1896) and Hans Bergh [Berg] Larsen (1842–1925), and the son of **Carl Johan (John) Martin Westphal** (see above) and Elisabeth Karoline (Caroline) Larsen Westphal.

Appendix C

Church Secretaries, Parish Administrators, Church Administrator

Note: Church records for names, dates, and length of employment are sometimes incomplete. In the late 1990s, the part-time secretaries overlapped.

1945–1948	Hilma Lundby was employed in multiple roles (youth director, office secretary, and parish visitor). She was the first professional assistant to be hired for the pastor.
1948–1956	Audrey Lawrence, Secretary
1956	Stanley Gordon West, Secretary (temporary, following Audrey Lawrence's resignation)
1956–1957	Janice Johnson, Secretary
1958–1959	LaVine Skog, Secretary
1959	Laurice Trapp, Secretary
1959–1963	Ardelle Hendrickson, Secretary
1964	Fern Rasmussen, Secretary
1965–1966	Mrs. Stan (Barbara) Molstad, Secretary
1966–1967	Alice Borg, Secretary
1968	Patsy Weiderholt, Secretary
1969	Bernice Sawyer, Secretary
1971	Linda Hoxtell, Secretary
1975	Barbara Molstad, Secretary
1982	Patti Linman, Secretary
1983	Janice Myrmoe, Secretary
1983–1999	Jane Lilleodden, Secretary, and Jane Kropp, Part-time Secretary
1996–1999	David Ottoson, Part-time Secretary
1999–2004	Stacey Klein, Parish Administrator
2004–2019	Russ Carlson, Parish Administrator
2019–	Deanna Hesse, Church Administrator

Appendix D

Immanuel Members for 25 Years or More

Note: Members are listed with their spouses or partners.

Deb Ahlquist & Steve Mundt
Dorothy Andersen
Mark & Sandy Anderson
Marlys Anderson
Daniel & Gay Bartholic
Gordon Bauer
Phyllis Bentley
Shirley Bethke*
Lee Bjerke
David & Kathleen Brudevold
Mark Brudevold
David & Susan Christenson
Barbara Columbus
Amy & Richard Currier
Thomas & Micheale Currier
Jody Dahl
Doug & Ann Derr
Lewis & Dorothy Dohman
Lori Dohman
Peter & Kay Draine
Ashley Dubay
Jimmy & Marilyn Dubay
Lori & Joseph Dufresne
Russell & Bonnie Edhlund
Dennis & Hafizan Engebretson
Linda Engelken
Geraldine Erickson
Dale Fierke & Doris Karlisch
Ruth Flom
Craig & Elsie Fohrenkamm
Sara Fohrenkamm
Roger Forman*
Cynthia & Ronald Gohl

June Grounds
James & Darlene Hagquist
David Hedlund & Jean Sazevich
Curtis & JoAnn Hogenson
June Husom*
Harvey & Elaine Jaeger
Peggy Johnson & Lee English
Vernon Jorgensen*
Joseph & Jacqueline Kelly
Harriet Kidder
David & Sue Klevan
Daniel & Kristin Klinger
Ina Kubesh
Donald Kyser & Tari Johnson
Scott Kyser
Kirsten & Timothy LaPean
Roger & Mary Larson
Julie & Jeff Levine
Paul & Tara Mattessich
Raymond & Helen Mikkelson
Sue Mitchell
Joan Mundahl
Laron & Susan Mundahl
Pearl Odland
John & Karen Osen
Raymond & Terri Peterson
Judie Prayfrock
Kathleen Raiter
Nancy Reidell
Kathy Robey & Thomas Cline
Ross & Patrica Robey
Todd & Leah Robey
Jerald Sandahl

Dick Sarafolean
Henry Seka & Diane Laker-Seka
John & Gloria Skalbeck
David & Alice Stark
Richard Stelter
Ruth Strand
Richard Sundberg
John & Linda Tantzen
Mark & Kimberly Thompson
Mary Gwen Thompson
Richard & Caroline Thompson
Valerie Thompson
Daniel Thorson

Janet Thorson
Kristine Thorson
Loanne Thrane
Patricia Tiller
Mike & Rhonda Tjaden
Mike & Jane Tripple
Andrew Urness
Wayne Veum
Doug & Peg Wangensteen
Phyllis Wert
Mary Wolf
James & Lynnette Zika

*Members with the longest Immanuel membership.

Appendix E

**Sunday School Superintendents, Secretaries, and Treasurers;
Directors of Christian Education; and Director of Children and Family Ministry**

Sunday School superintendents were volunteer members of Immanuel until the position of Director of Christian Education became a paid position in 1994. Information about the early years is incomplete.

Superintendents and Directors of Christian Education
- 1915–1945 Solfest J. Aalbue, Superintendent
- 1921 also Hans G. Grove, Miss Christensen, V. Gunderson—at the time of the merger with Macalester Park Lutheran
- 1925–? Hans G. Grove, Superintendent
- …
- 1945–1955 Stanley A. Uggen, Superintendent
- 1955–1964 Kenneth A. Berg, Superintendent; Rachel Husom was the Assistant Sunday School Superintendent
- 1960 Ben Trap joined with Kenneth Berg to serve as superintendents when the Sunday School increased to 372 students after the merger with Highland Park.
- 1964–1973 Rachel Husom, Superintendent
- 1973–1975 Marilyn Seams, Superintendent
- 1975–1993 Marilyn Goldberg, Superintendent
- 1994–2000 Judie Prayfrock, Director of Christian Education
- 2000–2017 Deb Ahlquist, Director of Christian Education
- 2017– Emily King, Director of Children and Family Ministry

Secretaries and Treasurers of the Sunday School
- 1933–1945 Carl Gustafson
- 1945–1946 Ruth Hauger
- 1946–1947 Maxine Leonardson
- 1948–1950 R.W. Helgeson
- 1950–1953 Robert F. Lambert
- 1953–1955 John L. Larson
- 1955–1956 Donald Drake & Vernon Jorgensen
- 1956–1996 June Husom

Appendix F

Choir Directors, Ministers of Worship and Music, and Directors of Worship and Music

Note: Church records for director names, dates of service, and the names of the choirs directed are sometimes incomplete.

1917	David Anderson, Choir Director.
1918–1919	Roy Harrisville, Choir Director.
1925	D.R. Anderson, Choir Director.
1932	Harry E. George, Choir Director.
1934	Mr. A.O. Christensen directed the Children's Choir and the Junior Choir.
1935	Harry E. George directed the Senior Choir.
1937–ca.1940	Robert Chandler of Hamline University directed the Senior Choir.
1940s	Helen Tweet directed a Women's Choir.
1941	Mr. Weibel, Choir Director.
1942	Harry George, Choir Director.
1945	Juleen Mattern, Choir Director.
?–1946	Mr. Gronberg, Choir Director.
1946–1951	Herman Madland, Choir Director.
1947–1949	Mrs. Clifford Peterson directed the Senior Choir.
1951–?	Winifred Greene Aalberg directed the Senior Choir; she was a wife of a Luther Theological Seminary student.
1953	Harold Jacobson directed the Senior Choir.
1953	Esther Anderson (Mrs. Morgan Anderson) was Children's Choir director for many years.
1956	Dr. R. Fuglestad, Choir Director.
1957–ca 1960	Mrs. Allen Ashley directed the Cherub, Junior, and Senior Choirs.
1959–1961	Mrs. Elroy Nerness, Choir Director.
1961	Mrs. Harold Williamson (Melba) directed the Senior and Junior Choirs, and Mrs. Allen Ashley directed the Cherub Choir.
1962	Mrs. Harold Williamson (Melba) directed the Senior and Junior Choirs, and Mrs. Grant Judd directed the Cherub Choir.

1963	Mrs. Thomas Lee (Joan) directed the Junior Choir for the first half of the year. In September, Grant Judd took over Senior Choir, Mrs. Grant Judd directed the Junior Choir, and Sharon Meredith took over the Cherub Choir.
1966	James Hauge directed the Senior Choir.
1967	Melba Williamson directed the Treble Choir.
1969–1970	Pastor Dennis Larson directed the Senior Choir. Nancy and Marilyn Cross directed the Youth Choir.
1971	David Ketterting, Choir Director.
1974–1975	Dick Clark directed the Adult Choir; Marilyn Nielsen directed the Children's Choir/s.
1975–1977	Connie Youngdahl directed the Adult Choir; Marilyn Nielsen directed the Children's Choir/s.
1978–1980	Norm Heitz directed the Adult Choir; Mary Bakke directed the Children's Choir/s. Shirley Evans directed the High School Choir.
1980–1981	Cary John Franklin directed the Adult Choir and Handbell Choir; Mary Bakke directed the Children's Choir/s.
1981–1982	Rob Reid directed the Adult Choir and High School Choir.
1981–1985	Karen Gladen directed the Children's Choir/s.
1982–1983	William (Bill) Smith, Choir Director.
1984–1993	David Stark directed Adult Choir, Afternoon Handbells, Evening Handbells.
1985–1994	Janet Cruse directed the Children's Choir and, starting in 1986, Children's Handbells. At one point, she had both a Children's and a Junior High Handbell Choir.
1994–1999	Sara Birkeland directed Adult Choir, Children's Choir, and Handbell Choirs.
1999–2000	Rick Paulsen, Minister of Worship and Music, also directed Handbells.
2000–2005	Andrew Birling, Choir Director. Also directed Handbells; became the organist 2004–2005.
2005–2006	David Stark, Interim Choir Director.
2006–2011	Rebekah Schulz, Director of Music and Worship, directed the choirs and Handbells. She became ¾ time Minister of Music in 2010.
2011–2012	David Stark. Interim Choir Director.
2012–	Chris Cherwien, Director of Worship and Music (full-time position): directs the Adult (Cantorei), Youth (Middle C.), Children's (Choristers), and Adult Handbell (Jubilate Ringers) Choirs.

Appendix G

Organists

Note: Church records for names, dates, and length of employment are sometimes incomplete.

1916–1917 Mabel Martinson
1917–1919 Joseph Johnson
1920 Lillie Olson
1921 Joseph Johnson, Alice Knudsen (at the time of the merger is Macalester Park Lutheran)
1925–1966 Chelsie Heiden Jorgensen played the organ for many years, with some breaks for health issues. In 1929, Lucille Selvog was the organist. Thelma Bilden was the organist for some years in the 1930s. Mrs. Arthur Gordon also assisted Chelsie Jorgensen for many years.
1967–1978 Harold Jacobson. Ethel Woostohoff and Sharon Meredith also are listed as organists in 1969.
1978–1998 Dr. Larry Wilson
1998 Victoria Smith (interim)
1999–2004 Ann Braaten
2004–2005 Andrew Birling (hired as choir director, then expanded responsibilities to add organ)
Rob Reed
2005–2007 Ivanna Sabanosova (also directed a children's choir)
2007–2011 Megan Baumann Engel (also directed a children's choir in 2010)
2011 Marilyn Lueth (interim)
2012–2013 Donald Livingston
2013–2014 Dr. Larry Wilson (interim)
2014–2021 Julie Lindorff
2021 Kathy Handford Lund (interim)
Aug. 2021– Peter Aldrich

Appendix H

Youth Directors, Youth Ministers, and Directors of Youth and Family Ministry

Note: Names and dates of service are as accurate as could be determined from the sources available.

- 1945–1948 Hilma Lundby was hired as the first director of youth, church secretary, and held other duties
- 1949 Wendell Frerichs, Luther Theological Seminary student. He assisted with the work with young people and lived in the parish house.
- Oct.–Dec. 1959 Carl Guthals served as youth director for a time in 1959 while he was at Luther Theological Seminary.
- Dec. 1959–1962 Luther Tolo, Luther Theological Seminary student (first to officially be given the title of "Youth Director"); he was initially a volunteer, then was paid $150/month.
- 1962–1963 Bill White, seminary student and intern
- 1963–1965 Raymond Boyens, seminary student and intern.
- 1965–1966 Rolfe Johnstad, seminary student and intern
- 1966–1970 In 1966, Immanuel voted to call an ordained pastor as the assistant pastor instead of having a seminary intern primarily ministering to the youth. Pastor James E. Tangen was Immanuel's first assistant pastor—he started July 1, 1966; his focus was the youth.
- 1970–1977 Pastor Sylvan Edward Hengesteg followed Pastor Tangen as Immanuel's assistant pastor and also focused on the youth. William Beck worked part time with youth beginning in November 1976.
- 1977–1993 Pastor John Lohre followed Pastor Hengesteg as assistant pastor and, again, his primary ministry was to the youth. Subsequent assistants were called "Associate Pastor" and did not have a specific focus on youth.
- 1995–1997 Dana Magi, seminary student, Youth Minister
- 1997–2000 Matthew Martin, seminary student, Youth Minister
- 2000–2001 Jill Dykema, Youth Minister

2001–2007 Jenna Sethi, Youth Minister; switched to full-time in 2002 with funding support from the Immanuel Foundation. She also was charged to work with area college students and young adults.
2007–2009 Allison (Allie) Tunseth, Interim Youth Director. She was Jenna Sethi's sister; the position reverted to part-time.
2009–2011 Matthew Tingler, seminary student, was hired as the confirmation teacher.
2010–2012 Katie Burkardt, Youth Coordinator
2012–2015 Robin Wayne, Director of Youth and Family Ministry
2015–2022 Michelle Stillwell, Director of Youth and Family Ministry

Appendix I

Learning and Advocacy Activities Sponsored by the Social Action Team, 1997–2021

In the spirit of Micah 6:8: "What does the LORD require of you? To act justly and to love mercy and to walk humbly with your God," we acknowledged how little we knew about the issues and lived experiences of the marginalized in our society, and sought out forums, lectures, books, and movies to discuss and learn.

- 1997: Forum on Child Abuse Prevention Awareness. Immanuel Council voted to become Covenant Church, meaning that Immanuel pledged to take proactive steps to teach staff and volunteers how to deal with child abuse as a responder and preventer.
- 1999: Forums on Healthy and Effective Parenting—part of Child Abuse Prevention; Wonderfully Made: Preparing Children to Learn and Succeed; and Domestic Violence.
- 2001: Candidate Forums; forum on Racism, the Christian, and the Environment.
- 2002: Candidate Forums.
- 2003: Forums on Conflict in Iraq; Youth Homelessness; Domestic Violence; Healthcare Legislation.
- 2004: Adult forums on Tanzania; Minnesota Civil Rights Movement; Affordable Housing; Joint Religious Legislative Coalition Update; St. Paul Area Chamber of Commerce Update; Models of Moral Deliberation; Concerns of Aging;, Project Home; Life & Ministry of Dietrich Bonhoeffer.
- 2004/2005: Co-hosted with Adult Education a discussion of the ELCA Social Statement on Sexuality, including same gender unions, ordination of gay and lesbian persons, and pastoral responses to families .
- 2005: Adult forums on Living in a Time of Terrorism; Engaging Congregations in Violence Prevention; Climate Change and its Implications; A Heart for Kids in the Heart of the City; Common Hope; and Ending Poverty: A 20/20 Vision.
- 2006: Adult forum on Affordable Housing by MICAH (Metropolitan Interfaith Council on Affordable Housing).
- 2007–2008: Study on International Peace and Ending Poverty (along with Synod initiative).

2013: Forums: Three-part Synod Forum organized by Immanuel Lutheran church members on The New Jim Crow: Mass Incarceration in the Age of Colorblindness; ILC forum for comments on the ELCA Social Statement on Mass Incarceration

2014: Attended the Martin Luther King, Jr. breakfast and workshops sponsored by the Saint Paul Area Synod Anti-Racism Task Force based on the resource "One Body, Many Members: A Journey for Christians across Race, Class and Culture"; held respectful conversations on hospitality and ministry; attended an ISAIAH-sponsored convention "Binding the Covenant" (attendance sponsored by an Immanuel Foundation Bright Ideas grant).

2015: Book Study on Jim Wallis' *On God's Side: What Religion Forgets and Politics Hasn't Learned about Serving the Common Good.*

2015: Webcast—ELCA Bishop Elizabeth Eaton on Confronting Racism.

2015: Prayer Vigil—joined the Minnesota Council of Churches' year-long prayer vigil for the victims of the Emmanuel African Methodist Episcopal (AME) Church shooting in Charleston, South Carolina.

2015: ISAIAH Press Conference on Juvenile Justice Reform.

2015: Candidate Forum: St Paul City Council and School Board.

2016: Respectful Conversations on the political divide using *Healing the Heart of Democracy,* by Parker Palmer; discussed *Waking Up White, and Finding Myself in the Story of Race,* by Debbie Irving. Attended a joint conference with the Minneapolis Synod called "Journey Toward Justice: White Privilege and Race in Our Church." Read *A Good Time for the Truth: Race in Minnesota,* 16 essays edited by Sun Yung Shin.

2016: Advocacy—prayer vigil for Philando Castile; standing with Black Lives Matter demonstrators; supporting water protectors at Standing Rock.

2016: Advocacy—worked with ISAIAH on campaign to encourage Saint Paul City Council to support earned sick and safe time for hourly workers. Also lobbied for raising the minimum wage, paid family leave, and universal Pre-K.

2017: Advocacy—worked with Minnesota Legislature on universal Pre-K, increasing minimum wage, and gun control.

2017: Education and Exploration: Immigration and Sanctuary; education continued through the Journey to Justice group; shared a Ramadan meal with our Muslim neighbors; toured sacred sites with Native American leaders; watched the documentary *The 13th,* by Ava DuVernay, about the change to the Constitution after the end of the Civil War. Sponsored a three-part series on Islam and the Muslim faith.

2018: Forum—along with Mount Zion and Gloria Dei, sponsored a Community Conversation on Poverty in Minnesota.

2018: Advocacy—participated with ISAIAH with input from 22 other advocacy organizations to develop a faith agenda to focus legislative actions calling for a multiracial democracy that honors every person's dignity and a caring economy that allows everyone to thrive. Attended caucuses and candidate forums through ISAIAH. Phone banked to get out the vote, which passed $15 minimum wage in Saint Paul.

2019: Speaker Forum hosted by Saint Paul Area Synod Churches: *Waking Up White* by Debbie Irving; presented "Leveling the Playing Field: Interrupting Patterns of Power and Privilege," an interactive workshop involving mapping power, patterns, and interventions.

2019: Book Discussion: *Evicted: Poverty and Profit in the American City,* by Matthew Desmond, a St. Paul Public Library Read Brave book

2019: Advocacy through ISAIAH: Passed residential coordinated trash collection in St Paul; St Paul School Board candidate research visits; advocated issues from the Faith Agenda.

2020: Zoom workshops: response to George Floyd murder; monthly "Talking About Race" discussions and JCART (Joint Church Anti-Racism Team) events with Pilgrim Lutheran, Macalester Plymouth United, and Hamline United Methodist Churches.

2020: Advocacy through ISAIAH: attended caucuses and meeting with legislators to advocate the Faith Agenda, specifically drivers' licenses for immigrants, paid family and medical leave, 100 percent clean energy; affordable, quality, accessible childcare; and more.

2021: Book Discussion: *Dear White Peacemaker: Dismantling Racism with Grit and Grace,* by Osheta Moore and Jen Hatmaker.

2021: Advocacy through ISAIAH, which led to passing rent stabilization in St Paul; continued advocacy for items on the Faith Agenda at the state level.

Appendix J

The "First Era" of Troop 90 began in 1934 and was sponsored by the Immanuel Lutheran Men's Club.

Herbert Page	1934–1935
T.B. Knudson	1936–1937
Goodwin Kolstad	1938
Robert McMillan	1939
H.A. Daum	1940–1942
A.T. Jorgenson	1943–1944
A.M. Kurzeck	1944–1945
Roland Wilsey	1946

In the fall of 1946, Troop 90 had 12 Scouts registered, but Immanuel did not re-charter the Troop. The reason given was "No boys or leadership."

The "Second Era" of Troop 90 began in 1952 and was sponsored by Immanuel Lutheran Church.

Robert Pope	1952	Bob Grieman	1986–1987
Don Hisdahl	1953–1954	Bob Kirk	1988–1989
John McDonald	1955–1957	Richard Haus	1990–1991
Ernest Anderson	1958	Russ Edhlund	1991–1995
Jack LaVold	1959	David Miller	1996–1998
Walter Hensel	1960	Mike Fischer	1998–2000
Donald Curtis	1961–63	Tim Swanson	2001–2008
Dave Knudson	1964–1967, 1969, 1971	Paul Kaardahl	2009–2011
		Kevin Kuta	2012–2013
Jerry Sandahl	1968	Matt Arnett	2014–2015
Merle Erickson	1970–1977	Blair Johnson	2015–2016
Bob Schilling	1978–1981	Eric Amann	2017–2019
Frank Severin	1982	Patrick Kelly	2020–present
Jan Karlstrand	1983–1985		

Appendix K

Immanuel Lutheran Church Presidents

Note: In the early years, the pastor was the church president. As is the case with much of Immanuel's early history, several gaps exist—therefore the list of presidents is incomplete.

1917	Ole H. Oace (born in Norway 1848)		
1918	Hans G. Grove (born in Norway 1860)		
1919	Ole H. Oace		
1921	Pastor Gustav Marius Bruce (at the time of the merger with Macalester Park Lutheran)		

. . . .

1927–1929 Hans G. Grove

. . . .

1935 Martin M. Wangensteen (born in Norway 1884; grandfather of Dr. Douglas Wangensteen, president in 1988, 2014)

. . . .

1940–1942	Solfest J. Aalbue	1967	Walter Harris
1943–1944	P. Rasmussen	1968	Al Forman
1945	A.E. Gordon	1969	Walter Albrecht
1946	R. Nyhus	1970	Dr. James Olin
1947	H.A. Arne	1971	Robert Kroll
1948	Joseph M. Jorgensen	1972	John Falck
1949–1950	Jack C. Ehlers	1973	Norman Schwendeman
1951–1952	Spring	1974	Harold Holmgren
1953	Everett Needels	1975	Al Martin
1954	Dr. M.H. Thornton	1976	Hart Holmberg
1955–1956	James Forchtner	1977	John Kropp
1957	Stanley Uggen	1978	Roger Lilleodden
1958	Sylvan L. Lyksett	1979	Frank Mabley
1959–1960	Marvin Merrick	1980	Nancy Granrud
1961	Harry Brooks	1981	Ray Mikkelson
1962	Harold Jacobson	1982	James Hagquist
1963	Dr. Hillard Thornton	1983	Margitt Skobba
1964	Leland Lafon	1984	Richard Sundberg
1965	Arthur Gordon	1985	Mark Jacobson
1966	Robert Granrud	1986	Robert Bauman

1987	Ray Peterson	2005	Greg Knopff
1988	Dr. Douglas Wangensteen	2006	Tara Mattessich
1989	Deanna Anderson	2007	Scott Norquist
1990	John Otteson	2008	Sue Klevan
1991	Roger Needels	2009	Marlin Osthus
1992	Kenneth Berg	2010	Mark Thompson
1993	Donald Gerhardt	2011	Stephanie Alstead
1994	Ralph Thrane	2012	Ron Struss
1995	June Husom	2013	Lee Bjerke
1996	Larry Cruse	2014	Dr. Douglas Wangensteen
1997	Dan Mueller	2015	Kelley Wells
1998	Mike Tripple	2016	Chase Hippen
1999	Darrell Frohrib	2017	Ann Derr
2000	Douglas Derr	2018	Joe Dufresne
2001	Peggy Johnson	2019	Kelley Wells
2002	Loanne Thrane	2020	Paul Mattessich
2003	Paul Mattessich	2021	Deb Ahlquist
2004	Russ Edhlund	2022	Jeff Schmidt

Appendix L

2022 Immanuel Lutheran Church Council, Officers, and Program Team Chairs

Leadership Team
Jeff Schmidt, Council President
Deb Ahlquist, Past President
Rhonda Tjaden, Vice President/President Elect
Martha Hansen, Secretary
Mark Thompson, Treasurer
Nick Consoer, Member at Large
Karen Osen, Member at Large
John Toso, Member at Large

Officers
Jackie Hippen, Assistant Treasurer
Ross Robey, Financial Secretary
David Alstead, Assistant Financial Secretary

Program Team Chairs
David Alstead, Worship & Music
Gay Bartholic, Stewardship
Mary Gwen Thompson, Children, Youth, & Family
Harvey Jaeger, Property
David Hansen, Membership
Christine Danielson, Social Action

Bibliography

Buegler, Todd. "The History of the Youth Gathering," *The ELC Network: Children, Youth, & Family Ministry* (July 5, 2018). https://elcaymnet.blog/2018/07/05/the-history-of-the-youth-gathering.

Elling Eielsen Sundve, 1804–1883: foredrag haldne på Eielsen seminaret på Voss 3, 5, August 1979. Voss Preteverk: Voss Norway, 1980.

Evangelical Lutheran Church. *Biographical Directory of Clergy*. Augsburg: Minneapolis, 1988.

Evangelical Lutheran Church in America. "Evangelical Lutheran Worship: History." https://download.elca.org/ELCA%20Resource%20Repository/History_of_ELW.pdf?_ga=2.219949465.1663561879.1634847137-1786994145.1633379628.

"Historical Look at Women's Participation Rates in the Labor Force." *Free by 50* (Oct. 31, 2010). http://www.freeby50.com/2010/10/historical-look-at-womens-participation.html. [Sources cited in the article include the Bureau of Labor Statistics, and others.]

Gjerde, Severin S., and Peder Ljostveit. *The Hauge Movement in America*. n.p.: Hauge Inner Mission Federation, 1941. Luther Seminary Library. Also: www.haugeinnermission.com/site/default.asp?sec_id=180000138. Note: Most of the quotations about early pastors are from this book.

Jensen John M, Carl E Linder, and Gerald Giving, compilers. *A Biographical Directory of Pastors of the American Lutheran Church*. Augsburg: Minneapolis, 1962.

Kelly, John. "Starting in the '70s, Married Women's First Names Were Including in *Post* References," *Washington Post*, Nov. 23, 2019.

Lovoll, Odd S., ed. *The Promise of America: A History of the Norwegian American People*, rev. University of Minnesota Press: Minneapolis, 1999.

Luther College, Decorah, IA. "Luther College Archives." www.luther.edu/archives.

Luther Seminary Archives, St. Paul, MN. The Archives hold the archive of Luther Seminary and its precursors, Augsburg Seminary, the Hauge Synod School, Red Wing Seminary, and Northwestern Lutheran Theological Seminary; and the archives of ELCA Region 3, along with records of many of the precursor church bodies of the synod. Records in the ELCA Region 3 collection date from 1843 and cover church communities in North Dakota, South Dakota, and Minnesota, with additional material from Wisconsin and Iowa

Macalester College Digital Archives, *The Mac Weekly*. http://edu.arcasearch.com/usmnmac.

Mickelson, Arnold R. Mickelon, editor; Robert C. Wiederaenders, associate editor. *A Biographical Directory of Clergymen of the American Lutheran Church*. Augsburg: Minneapolis, 1972.

Norlie, O.M., et al. *Norsk Luterherske Prester I Amerika 1843-1915*. Augsburg: Minneapolis, 1915.

Norlie, O.M. *Norsk luterske Prester I Amerika 1843-1913, samlet af Pastor O.M Norlie med Hjaelp af Pastor K. Seehus,* etc. Augsburg: Minneapolis, 1914.

Norlie, O.M. *Norsk luterske Prester I Amerika 1843–1915, samlet af Pastor O.M Norlie med Hjaelp af Pastor K. Seehus,* etc. Augsburg: Minneapolis, 1915.

Peterson, John, Olaf Lysnes, and Gerald Giving, compilers. *A Biographic Directory of Pastors of the Evangelical Lutheran Church*. Augsburg: Minneapolis, 1952.

Tjornehoj, Susan. "Of Reindeer, Hunger, and Hope: The Story of Brevig Mission and Shishmaref Lutheran Churches." *MetroLutheran* (Feb. 22, 2011), https://metrolutheran.org/2011/02/5376.

Wee, M.O. *Haugeanism: A Brief Sketch of the Movement and Some of Its Chief Exponents.* Self-published: St. Paul, 1919.

Who's Who among Pastors in all the Norwegian Lutheran Synods of American 1843–1927. 3rd ed. Augsburg: Minneapolis, 1928. https://archives.augsburg.edu.

Zane, Matthew. "What Percentage of the Workforce Is Female?" *Zippia* (March 1, 2022). www.zippia.com/advice/what-percentage-of-the-workforce-is-female/#:~:text=46.6%25%20of%20the%20workforce%20is,force%20participation%20rate%20of%2067.9%25. [based on U.S. Bureau of Labor Statistics, released Feb. 28, 2022].